Scenography Expanded

Performance + Design is a series of monographs and essay collections that explore understandings of performance design and scenography, examining the potential of the visual, spatial, material and environmental to shape performative encounters and to offer sites for imaginative exchange. This series will cover design both for and as performance in a variety of contexts including theatre, art installations, museum displays, mega-events, site-specific and community-based performance, street theatre, design of public space, festivals, protests and state-sanctioned spectacle.

Performance + Design takes as its starting point the growth of scenography and the expansion from theatre or stage design to a wider notion of scenography as a spatial practice. As such, it recognises the recent accompanying interest from a number of converging scholarly disciplines (theatre, performance, art, architecture, design) and examines 21st-century practices of performance design in the context of debates about postdramatic theatre, aesthetic representation, visual and material culture, spectatorship, participation and co-authorship.

SERIES EDITORS

Stephen Di Benedetto

Joslin McKinney

Scott Palmer

The History and Theory of Environmental Scenography: Second Revised Edition

Arnold Aronson

978-1-4742-8396-0

The Model as Performance: Staging Space in Theatre and Architecture

Thea Brejzek and Lawrence Wallen

978-1-4742-7138-7

Scenography Expanded

An Introduction to
Contemporary Performance Design

EDITED BY
JOSLIN MCKINNEY AND SCOTT PALMER

Bloomsbury Methuen Drama
An imprint of Bloomsbury Publishing Plc

BLOOMSBURY
LONDON · OXFORD · NEW YORK · NEW DELHI · SYDNEY

Bloomsbury Methuen Drama
An imprint of Bloomsbury Publishing Plc
Imprint formerly known as Methuen Drama

50 Bedford Square
London
WC1B 3DP
UK

1385 Broadway
New York
NY 10018
USA

www.bloomsbury.com

BLOOMSBURY, METHUEN DRAMA and the Diana logo are trademarks of Bloomsbury Publishing Plc

First published 2017
Reprinted 2017

British Library Cataloguing-in-Publication Data
A catalogue record for this book is available from the British Library.

ISBN:	HB:	978-1-474-24438-1
	PB:	978-1-474-24439-8
	ePDF:	978-1-474-24441-1
	eBook:	978-1-474-24440-4

Library of Congress Cataloging-in-Publication Data
Names: McKinney, Joslin editor. | Palmer, Scott, 1958- editor.
Title: Scenography expanded : an introduction to contemporary performance design /
edited by Joslin McKinney & Scott Palmer. Description: London ; New York :
Bloomsbury Methuen Drama, 2017. | Includes bibliographical references and index.
Identifiers: LCCN 2016048849| ISBN 9781474244398 (pbk.) | ISBN 9781474244381
(hardback) Subjects: LCSH: Theaters–Stage-setting and scenery. Classification: LCC
PN2091.S8 .S298 2017 | DDC 792.02/5–dc23 LC record available at https://lccn.loc.gov/2016048849

Series design by Burge Agency
Cover image: *Peace Camp* by Deborah Warner in collaboration with Fiona Shaw, July 2012. (© Chris Hill/Scenic Ireland)

Series: Performance and Design

Typeset by Integra Software Services Pvt. Ltd.
Printed and bound in Great Britain

Contents

List of Illustrations

Figures

Plates

Contributors

Arnold Aronson is Professor at Columbia University, New York, USA, and the author of several books including *Ming Cho Lee: A Life in Design* (2014); *Looking into the Abyss: Essays on Scenography* (2005) and *American Avant-Garde Theatre: A History* (2001). In 2007, he served as the General Commissioner of the Prague Quadrennial of Stage Design and Theatre Architecture. He is co-editor of *Theatre and Performance Design* journal and editor of the forthcoming Routledge *Companion to Scenography*.

Christopher Baugh is Emeritus Professor of Performance and Technology at the University of Leeds, UK. He has worked extensively as a scenographer and has written widely on the history, theory and practices of scenography including the monograph *Theatre, Performance and Technology: The Development and Transformation of Scenography* (2014).

Maaike Bleeker is Professor in Theatre Studies at Utrecht University in the Netherlands and President of Performance Studies international (PSi). Her book *Visuality in the Theatre. The Locus of Looking* (2008) appeared with Palgrave. She is currently completing a monograph about movement, media and corporeal literacy.

Thea Brejzek is Professor of Spatial Theory at the University of Technology Sydney, Australia. She researches constructions of performativity in spaces of social, cultural and political engagement, including urban and public space, exhibition and media space. She is currently co-writing the book *The Model as Performance: Staging Space in Theatre and Architecture*.

Ethel Brooks is Associate Professor of Women's and Gender Studies and Sociology at Rutgers University, USA. She is Tate-TrAIN Transnational Fellow at the University of the Arts, London, where she was the US-UK Fulbright Distinguished Chair (2011–2012). Brooks is the author of the award-winning *Unraveling the Garment Industry: Transnational Organizing and Women's Work* (2007).

Jane Collins is Professor of Theatre and Performance at Wimbledon College of Art, University of the Arts, London, UK. She is co-editor of *Theatre and Performance Design: A Reader in Scenography* (2010) and currently co-edits the Routledge journal *Theatre and Performance Design*.

Stephen Di Benedetto is Chairman of the Department of Theatre Arts, and Associate Professor of Theatre History at the University of Miami, USA. He is an associate editor of the journals *Scene* and *ASAP/Journal* and publications include *The Provocation of the Senses in Contemporary Theatre* (2010), *An Introduction to Theatre Design* (2012) and *Designer's Shakespeare* (2016).

Dorita Hannah is Professor of Interdisciplinary Architecture, Art and Design at the University of Tasmania, Australia, and Adjunct Professor of Stage and Space at Aalto University, Finland. Her creative work, teaching and research focus on creative arts intersections. Hannah co-edited *Performance Design* (2008) and is currently completing *Event-Space: Theatre Architecture and the Historical Avant-Garde* (2017).

Kathleen Irwin is Professor of Scenography and Associate Dean Graduate Studies and Research in Media, Art and Performance at the University of Regina, Canada. She is currently co-editing a collection of writing on contemporary indigenous performance in Canada to mark the 150th anniversary of contact in 2016–17.

Joslin McKinney is Associate Professor in Scenography at the University of Leeds, UK. She is the lead author of *The Cambridge Introduction to Scenography* (2009) and has published articles on the materiality and agency of scenography. She is currently writing a book on practices and concepts of 'construction' in the theatre.

Marcela Oteíza is Assistant Professor of Theatre at Wesleyan University, USA. Her body of work focuses on scenographic contemporary practices. She is currently working on a video documentary, *Santiago (en) Vivo*, about street and site-specific performances that occur during the Festival International Santiago a Mil, Chile.

Scott Palmer is Associate Professor in Scenography at the University of Leeds, UK, co-convenor of the International Federation of Theatre Research Scenography Working Group and an associate editor of the journal *Theatre and Performance Design*. His publications include *Light* (2013) and several articles on new ways of thinking about lighting as a creative performance practice.

David Shearing is a designer and academic based in the UK. His research and practice explores the nature of audience engagement with design materials and spaces. He is currently creating large-scale scenographic interventions in city spaces that disrupt everyday behaviours. He is currently a visiting lecturer at the University of Leeds. More details are available on his website www.davidshearing.com.

Nebojša Tabački is a freelance scenographer based in Berlin, Germany, working in theatre, film and TV industry. He is the author of *Kinetische Bühnen* (2014), a monograph about the visionary concepts of kinetic scenography and multifunctional theatre buildings of the 1960s and the 1970s as influenced by the modernist architectural heritage.

Melissa Trimingham is Senior Lecturer in Drama at the University of Kent, UK. Her current research interests centre around cognitive approaches to scenography. She has authored a monograph, *The Theatre of the Bauhaus: The Modern and Postmodern Stage of Oskar Schlemmer*, and several articles and chapters in books on scenography, costume, puppets and autism.

Foreword

Arnold Aronson

When I was in graduate school in the early 1970s, one of the text books for our theatre history class was Allardyce Nicoll's *The Development of the Theatre*, an essentially scenographic history of mostly European theatre. (That such beautifully produced and lavishly illustrated books on the subject could exist – and be affordable on a student budget – suggests how long ago this was.) I can still remember reading the section on the Baroque 'scenic spectacle' and being captivated by the more than fifty black and white images of designs by Torelli, Santurini, Juvarra, Jones, Piranesi and others – all previously unknown to me. But the ones that made the deepest impression were those by the members of the Bibiena family. And there was one in particular, identified simply as 'Theatrical Design by Giuseppe da Bibiena' of an elaborate palace interior. I stared at it, awestruck. It depicted sumptuously columned and arched arcades that seemed to stretch into divergent infinities, impossibly high chandeliers and wall sconces, and a soaring dome that dwarfed a table of banqueters downstage centre. At a time when the mainstream theatre I was seeing was still dominated by box sets of domestic interiors, while the increasingly ubiquitous black boxes trafficked in the minimalist and decidedly unglamorous décor of what Grotowski termed 'poor theatre', this vision of Baroque splendour was a stunning revelation. If one purpose of art – some would argue *the* purpose – is to create something we cannot experience in our quotidian existence, then here was an example of the power and potential of scenography to create previously unknown worlds. The Bibienas expanded ideas of what scenography could accomplish (and certainly expanded my understanding of design – probably contributing to my own future trajectory as a scholar).

As I will explain momentarily, the 'expanded scenography' of the Bibiena family and their contemporaries involved an attempt to defy the restrictions of the proscenium frame by exploiting the opportunities that such a frame made possible. But the term 'scenography' itself, in recent decades, has seemingly escaped the bonds of the stage altogether. Despite some ambiguity, at least in the English-speaking world, as to the meaning and use of the term, most people understand scenography as a reference to theatrical design (though its first definition in the *OED* refers to the technique of perspective representation in architecture). I define it as the sum total of the visual, spatial, and aural components of a performance. However, building upon its theatrical meanings and origin, scenography has been increasingly applied to any discipline or practice that employs visual or spatial organizing principles in order to convey information. A good example can be seen in a recent review of an exhibition in Geneva, Switzerland, of photographs by Dana Hoey, a contemporary American artist who creates large-scale photos of scenes that seem to be captured from life but are, in fact, carefully staged and often have implicit narratives with feminist themes. She would have seemingly little in common with Giuseppe Galli da Bibiena – working not only in a different time and place but in a medium that did not even exist then. Yet a review in *L'Oeil de la Photographie* twice refers to her 'scenography' to describe the poses and relationships of individuals, the clothing, props, décor, lighting and overall arrangement of elements within the frame (Gavard-Perret 2016). Hoey's use of such strategies in composing her photographs is not an unusual idea within the art world, but the use of the term 'scenography' to refer to her methodology is a fairly recent development. How did 'scenography' as a descriptor of stage settings come to be applied to the formal arrangement of a photographic image?

To understand that transformation, indeed, to understand the very premise of this book, one has to go back to art critic Rosalind Krauss's 1979 essay, 'Sculpture in the Expanded Field' (1979: 30–44), probably the first use of the adjective 'expanded' to describe the growth of an art form beyond its traditional limits and associations. More recently, scholar Alan Read intentionally echoed Krauss's phrase in the title of his book, *Theatre in the Expanded Field: Seven Approaches to Performance*, in which he, too, examines the shifting parameters of the discipline in which *theatre* has largely been subsumed by *performance*. Krauss, looking at a particular genre of artwork that had emerged in the 1960s and 1970s, notably earthworks and industrial constructions by artists such as Mary Miss, Richard Serra, Robert Morris and Robert Smithson, sought to examine why these works – most of which seemed to have little formally, structurally or contextually in common with their classical and traditional precedents – were designated as sculpture. This is not the place to rehearse her specific arguments, but any discussion of an expanded field has to recognize the importance of Krauss's contribution to such (re)thinking. Alan Read saw in her argument the importance and usefulness of historicity, the placing of apparently new forms within a historical continuum, 'an essentially evolutionary theory that is indeed essentialising as it secures essences in the place of dissonances and disturbances to the system' (Read 2013: xxv). Such an approach may allow us to view scenography in a similar fashion. By focusing on the organization of the visual field and spatiality – or perhaps more accurately, the perception of spatiality – we can see theatre scenography residing within a much larger framework of art, architecture and social practice.

Historically, design in the theatre had almost always referred to the visual field against which a performance occurred. Even as changes in staging and technology allowed performers to move more deeply into a scenic environment, they still tended to act against a background rather than within a space. Certain architectural stages such as those of ancient Greece, early modern England or the Noh theatre of Japan, for example, emphasized spatial relationships over décor but the performance remained within the identifiable framework of a stage.

But just as Krauss's sculptures no longer needed pedestals nor galleries, nor a singular relation to a spectator gaze, so too contemporary performance needs neither traditional stage nor standard relationships between performer and spectator. Very often, it is the visual-aural-spatial construct of such performance that shapes and determines the response of the spectators. The scenography moves not merely from background to foreground, but very often from accessory to content: scenography as the generative element of performance as well as its primary meaning.

The grandeur of the Bibiena design I encountered in Nicoll's book was a product of the *scena per angolo* – multi-point or angled perspective. This technique allowed the Bibienas and their contemporaries to create an image that implied a scenic scale no longer perceived as an extension of the auditorium but as having an independent existence. There was a desire to escape the physical boundaries of the stage and create an alternative world; the stage and the auditorium appeared to exist in two separate spheres in which scale and even the laws of physics and optics were different from each other. It was, quite literally, an expanded scenography, although it remained within the confines of the still relatively young proscenium stage. The proscenium arch, in fact, exemplifies the contradictory impulses of scenography. From the time of its emergence in the 17th century, partly as a practical solution to hiding the increasingly elaborate stage machinery, partly as a picture frame to enhance perspective illusionism, the theatre has alternately embraced the confines of the stage and attempted to reach beyond its bounds. The ancient Greek theatre with its open structure (some two millennia before the proscenium arch) implicitly incorporated everything within the visual landscape into the scenography, the Roman theatre, a few centuries later, blocked out that world with the high *scaenae frons* and the unified enclosing architecture of the theatre. The processional theatre of medieval Europe transformed entire cities into scenic landscapes while the Renaissance brought the theatre indoors and invented the proscenium. Richard Wagner invited the audience to project itself metaphorically across the mystic chasm onto the ideal world behind the double proscenium, but Wagner's disciples within the avant-garde sought ways to break down barriers and unify the stage and auditorium, spectator and performer, and to move out of the theatre altogether.

More recently, the introduction of video – particularly live video feed – and projection into the tangible world of the stage is leading to disruptions and dislocations in the time and space continuum of the stage, something I have called 'the dematerialization of the stage' (Aronson 2012: 86–95). But even this – the introduction of digital technologies onto the stage – still foregrounds a relationship to the traditional stage. The stage must exist if it is to *dematerialize*. But if, as Performance Studies and other disciplines have demonstrated, the notion of performance extends well beyond traditional notions of theatre and into a much broader range of human activity, then scenography becomes a means by which such performance is presented. The visual-aural-spatial field becomes both a site for the enactment of performance as well as a defining tool in creating such performance. Michel de Certeau famously described space as 'practiced place' (1984: 117), by which he meant the way in which an urban landscape becomes a city through human activity and behaviour. In a similar way, we may say that human activity, and the sites of human activity, become performance through the application of scenography – the process of transforming a landscape into a meaningful environment that guides performers and spectators alike through a visual and spatial field imbued with meaning.

Viewed in this way, scenography, of course, encompasses the traditional and historical forms of theatre as it always has, such as West End and Broadway musicals, fringe performances and operas; but it may also serve as a tool for understanding Carnival, theme parks, art installations, site-specific performance, ritual and festival performances, sporting events, architecture, processions and parades, political events and even urban streetscapes, to list but a few examples. But it goes even further. The visual, spatial and aural fields (and occasionally the olfactory and tactile components) serve to organize – through intentional creation or by the active foregrounding of perception – the relationship of spectators to an event, space or object. In this it bears some relation to Alain Badiou's 'event' (*l'événement*) (2013). Though Badiou here is primarily concerned with political systems, his notion of an event as that which exposes the hitherto unrepresented multiplicities that lie beneath the surface of a social order can be applied to theatre as well.

Scenography makes the underlying structures of representation visible, presenting the spectator with multiple (and sometimes contradictory) understandings that expand a literal text. Meaning is replaced by relationship.

This is most apparent in site-specific works in which scenography is not a newly created aesthetic product but a transformation of existing space and structures. Site-specific scenography foregrounds the spectators' interaction with the surrounding environment and their increased awareness of the emblematic signs inherent within the space. Even in the most innocuous entertainments that employ such strategies, the political dimension becomes inescapable. Similarly, scenography's ineluctable absorption and exploitation of new technologies – something that has typified theatrical production since the *mechane* of ancient Greece – often serves to transform modes of perception.

Expanded scenography sits well within what many fields and disciplines increasingly refer to as the posthuman. Ariane Lourie Harrison notes that 'Posthuman theory extends … beyond the body and into the built environment, imagining designed space itself as a prosthetic and producing new understandings of a "nature" that itself can no longer be conceived as an originary or neutral ground' (2013: 8). What better description of the power and agency of scenography? Scenography is no longer limited to decorative or metonymic functions but now sits at the centre of interactive networks. Expanded scenography is at once a tool, a system, a process and a generative organism for understanding the complex environment in which we live.

Acknowledgements

Joslin McKinney and Scott Palmer would like to acknowledge the work of the contributing authors and the work of wider international networks that have generated vibrant discussions about scenography over the recent past. In particular, the scenography working groups of the International Federation for Theatre Research (IFTR) and the Theatre and Performance Research Association (TaPRA) and the newly formed Performance Design working group for Performance Studies international (PSi) have been valuable fora for debate and the sharing of new ideas about scenography.

In this same period, the Prague Quadrennial of Performance Design and Space, under the leadership of Sodja Lotker, has been a source of inspiration and has further challenged thinking about what contemporary performance design is and the variety of forms it can take.

There are many individuals who have contributed to these networks and while we can't thank them all, we would like to make special mention of Rachel Hann, Minty Donald, Simon Banham and Arnold Aronson, who have all made particularly helpful and astute contributions that have, in one way or another, influenced the preparation of this volume.

Joslin and Scott would also like to thank colleagues and students in the School of Performance and Cultural Industries at the University of Leeds for their interest and support for this project. At Bloomsbury, we thank Mark Dudgeon for his advice and guidance in developing the *Performance + Design* series, of which this book is the inaugural volume.

Marcela Oteíza would like to thank Prof. Cláudia Tatinge Nascimento for her invaluable assistance. She would like to thank theatre directors Ignacio Achurra and Roger Bernat for their generous participation in her interviews.

Nebojša Tabački would like to thank Mauricio Moe DeFendi and Wanda Han Show Management for their help and Siemens AG and Wynn Las Vegas for permission to use production images. He would also like to thank Toma Tasovac, Matthias Kuder, Jasna Russo and Vanja Savić for their suggestions and Rosanne Adelman for her copy-editing advice.

Introducing 'Expanded' Scenography

Joslin McKinney and Scott Palmer

Scenography has long been associated with the design of settings for the performance of dramatic works on stage. However, the capacity for scenography to operate independently from a theatre text, as 'visual dramaturgy' (Lehmann 2006: 157) and as the central component of a performance, not merely as a backdrop to a play, is now widely in evidence.[1] And scenography, it seems, can happen anywhere, including 'our home, a restaurant, a cruise ship, a parking lot, a public square, a theatre venue, a parliamentary building and Everest' (Lotker and Gough 2013: 3). These developments reflect wider trends of hybrid practices in theatre, performance, art and architecture as well as a tendency towards the blurring of boundaries between performance and audience. But the rapid expansion of scenographic practice, especially since the millennium, has left little room for reflection on what its defining characteristics might be, and therefore what the particular contribution that scenography both within and beyond the theatre is making to contemporary performance. Rosalind Krauss suggested that in trying to accommodate heterogeneous new forms within the category of sculpture, 'that it is, itself, in danger of collapsing' (1979: 33), and the same concern might be raised now regarding the category of scenography.

While there is general agreement about the proliferation of contexts in which scenography might now be located, there has been little discussion to date about the underlying principles or strategies on which these expanded practices rest. Contemporary approaches seem to bear little relation to historical forms of scenography which aimed at the depiction of an illusory idealized world within a carefully controlled theatrical environment, although they might be considered to have affinities with scenographic experiments in modernist and postmodernist theatre, such as those explored by Edward Gordon Craig, Russian constructivists or visionaries such as Antonin Artaud. But at the same time, it is limiting to see this expanded field only in terms of historical forms of theatrical scenography; we need a new framework for this new field. A frame of theatrical performance centred on the needs of the text, or on those of the performer, is not sufficient to explain the diverse ways in which contemporary forms of scenography can operate or reflect the political, social, cultural or ecological impact that scenographic interventions can make through performance events. In this edited collection we have brought together a collection of essays that address ceremonial performance, mobile technologies and screen-based performance, site-specific and street performance, architectural scenography, performance architecture and experimental work at the intersection of art and theatre, commercial spectacle, applied theatre practice, activist performance and immersive installation and together these represent the forefront of current thinking about scenography and contemporary performance design. Our purpose within the book is to try to understand scenography not simply as a by-product of theatre but as a mode of encounter and exchange founded on spatial and material relations between bodies, objects and environments. In this introductory chapter, we have used a broadly non-representational approach (Thrift 2007)[2] in order to explore and propose overarching principles and concepts of 'expanded' scenography that emerge from a re-structuring of theatrical scenography and the newer configurations of design and performance that arise from it. As well as setting aside the usual, predominant concerns of text and performer, we have prioritized the perspective of the spectator rather than the intentions of the scenographer and as a consequence there is a focus on the spatial, multisensorial and material aspects of contemporary performance. This represents a re-focusing of the scenographic lens in order to illuminate the eventual, processual nature of much contemporary scenography and brings into sharper definition the characteristics of expanded scenography as a new field.

Rapid expansion

To place our concerns in some context it will be useful to set out some of the indicators of the expansion of scenography in the last fifteen years and some of the ways that this has impacted on terms and definitions.

A significant shift from traditional notions of scenography can be seen in The Prague Quadrennial of Space and Performance Design (PQ), the largest and pre-eminent international festival of contemporary theatre and performance design. Since its inception in 1967, it has provided an overview of trends and new developments in global scenography. Artists from all over the world participate in exhibiting designs for recent performances and celebrating the diversity of approaches to scenography as an interpretive, expressive and potentially transformative medium. Since the inauguration of PQ, its evolving forms of presentation and scope of practice serve to illustrate how scenography has outgrown its function as a technical and illustrative support to dramatic literature or 'the foundation of the final concrete shape of the drama' (Prague Quadrennial archive online). At PQ 2015 (18–28 June 2015), scenography was conceived as a 'reading and writing' of space with a responsibility not simply to the intentions of a playwright but also to its 'social function'; its capacity to provide 'a place of connection and difference' (Prague Quadrennial of Performance Design and Space 2015: 10–11). Whereas the 1967 event consisted exclusively of presentations of scale models of theatre set designs, displays of costumes and associated drawings, festivals since 1999 have been 'moving away from displaying artifacts' and towards actively creating them (Prihodova et al. 2016). Performative installations, immersive experiences and scenographic interventions in the streets of Prague now take place alongside static exhibits. Scenographic practice has expanded from an exclusive function as a craft-based practice serving the performance of a theatrical text to incorporate autonomous art practices that operate in contexts beyond theatre buildings and engage directly with social as well as the cultural dimensions of contemporary experience. As a result, the role of the scenographer is often now blurred with that of the artist and the activist. At the same time, the role of the spectator is likely to be co-constructive and often participatory as the experience of the audience becomes central. While the example of PQ demonstrates a clear affinity between these diverse forms, the difficulty of applying the category of scenography to them all has become apparent and the amendment of the name of the festival in 2011 from 'Scenography and Theatre Architecture' to 'Performance Design and Space' reflects that in some measure.

Meanwhile the expansion of a scholarly interest in scenography and the accompanying publications has been equally rapid. At the beginning of the millennium, Pamela Howard addressed the question *What is Scenography?* (2002) in the context of the work of professional theatre designers and the sense that the significance of their work and contribution to performance making was overlooked. As 'a holistic approach to making theatre from the visual perspective' (125), Howard's use of the term 'scenography' signified that designers could claim creative parity with directors and performers. Little more than a decade later, in a special issue of the *Performance Research* journal, 'On Scenography' (2013), the editors Sodja Lotker (the artistic director of PQ from 2008 to 2015) and Richard Gough declared that scenography has expanded to the point that it can be 'built by a scenographer, a collective of artists, an architect or nature itself' or 'found by an actor, a dancer or a spectator' (Lotker and Gough 2013: 3).

In between these two points several influential publications have addressed scenography by looking both backwards and re-assessing work from the past (Baugh 1994, 2013; Aronson 2005; McKinney and Butterworth 2009; Palmer 2013, 2015) and by analysing contemporary practice (Hannah and Harsløf 2008; Brejzek et al. 2009, 2011) with an insistence on the distinct contribution that scenography makes to the experience of performance and its capacity as an autonomous form. As part of this activity, terms such as 'extended' scenography (Brejzek et al. 2009), 'expanding scenography' (Brejzek 2011) and 'expanded scenography' (den Oudsten 2011; Lotker and Gough 2013) have more recently been applied to a very wide range of interdisciplinary and cultural contexts, but the significance of them, especially in relation to more traditional notions of scenography, has not been fully articulated. These authors suggest that theatrical concepts can be adapted to the broader context of expanded scenography, for example, *mise en scène* (Brejzek 2010: 112), narrativity (den Oudsten 2011) and dramaturgy (Lotker and Gough 2013) but again, the relationship of old and new forms of scenography has been very little discussed.

At this moment, we seem to be in the middle of a 'scenographic turn' which is 'reframing debates and changing established epistemologies in theatre and performance discourse and related cultural, historical, social and political fields' (Collins and Aronson 2015: 1). But if debates about the potential of the scenographic as a critical practice or as a way of thinking about performative encounter are to have purchase, we need to consider more carefully the concepts that underpin expanded scenographic practice as a field while avoiding the danger of the category of scenography expanding so far that it collapses altogether.

A starting point in this needs to be the relationship between what has been called 'classic' scenography and its expanded form (den Oudsten 2011). As Krauss suggested for expanded sculpture, it can't be explained simply in terms of an all-encompassing history of the form and construction of 'elaborate genealogical trees' (Krauss 1979: 44). Rather, expanded scenography (as with expanded sculpture) might be seen as the result of ruptures and re-structurations in scenography more generally that offer 'an expanded but finite set of related positions' that help to define it as a field (1979: 42).

Dorita Hannah and Olav Harsløf (2008) have suggested that 'performance design' is more suitable a term than 'scenography' to encompass a more extensive and autonomous practice that incorporates artists from across the fields of 'architecture, music, theatre, literature, linguistics, gastronomy, fashion, fine arts, film, media or choreography' (2008: 13). It is a deliberately loose term and has been influential in helping to establish new connections and affinities across a very broad range of practices. Yet within performance design, ideas about scenography are nonetheless foundational and persistent and at this juncture they offer a way to think about what diverse and expanded practices might have in common. We have therefore held on to scenography as a point of reference and as a means of focusing on key concepts that have emerged in part from new understanding about the potential of scenography a century or more ago. Expanded scenography does not represent a complete break with theatre practice, but it does represent a new way of thinking about the spatial, material and design-based aspects of performance. The recent growth in publications about scenography, past and present, have brought about a partial re-structuring and re-alignment such that we are able to see scenography as a discipline in its own right that has 'its own logic, its own distinctive rules' (Lotker and Gough 2013: 3). Yet what those rules are and the significance they may have for theatre and for arts practices more widely has yet to be debated. The identification of expanded scenography offers an opportunity to initiate that discussion.

In this introductory chapter, we ask what characteristics define 'expanded scenography' as a practice, how are they different from practices of scenography as previously understood? And how can these defining characteristics be applied in these new contexts? To begin, we adapt Krauss' method of 'logical structure' (1979: 44) to identify shifts and ruptures in historical scenography in order to gain a new perspective on contemporary understandings of scenography.

Re-structuring scenography

There are at least three points in the history of scenography that would seem to have laid the foundations for its expansion. They are perhaps not ruptures in the way that Krauss invokes, but they are at least shifts or re-structurings. The first is the shift, through the early part of the 20th century, from scenography being viewed mainly as a superficial and decorative element towards an understanding that it can also make 'significant statements about reality' (Brecht cited in Willett 1986: 70). The second is the rise of 'postdramatic' theatre (Lehmann 2006) and the re-configuring of traditional hierarchies of Western theatre where the literary had generally predominated and the third is the proliferation of new spatial forms for theatre and performance.

'Skenographia' can be traced through Aristotle's *Poetics* to the 4th century BCE (Small 2013: 111). From the Greek roots 'sken-', referring to the stage, and 'graph-', to processes of representation such as writing/drawing, it has been translated by contemporary scholars as 'stage painting' (Small 2013: 111) or 'scenic writing' (Aronson 2005: 7). Despite its attractions, it was considered by Aristotle to be simply spectacle and the least important aspect of serious drama.

So the origins of scenography have been intrinsically linked with the idea that theatrical presentation delights and dazzles at the same time as it disarms the critical faculties of the viewer. This widespread view, bolstered by the 'literary bias' at work in much theatre criticism and scholarship (at least in the English language), has been extremely influential and has helped establish a deep-seated anxiety over the direct appeal of the visual and its capacity to overturn 'the rational aspects of language' (see Kennedy 1993: 5–6). But theatre practitioners in the early part of the 20th century, such as Adolphe Appia, Edward Gordon Craig, Robert Edmond Jones, Caspar Neher and Oskar Schlemmer, questioned these assumptions about the superficiality of scenography and showed how scenographic gestures created by the orchestration of design elements in themselves could make affective, profound and potentially transformative visual statements. Through the composition of 'action, words, line, colour and rhythm', the stage space itself could become a 'self-sufficient art form independent from literature' (Fischer-Lichte 2008: 185). The work of modernist scenographers cleared the way for a new conception of scenography where it could be a construction in its own right with its own inherent logic or meaning and capable of a dialogue or even a confrontation with other elements of the theatre. Craig and Schlemmer, for example, both understood volumetric stage space as an active and vital component of performance. In combination with other materials, especially light, the predominantly illustrative capacity of paint and canvas that characterized earlier forms of scenography was challenged by new concepts of scenography as an event. Josef Svoboda, who pioneered scenographic techniques using the material qualities of light, thought of the scenographic stage as a 'psycho-plastic space' that would materialize at the moment of performance in the presence of an audience; 'true scenography is what happens when the curtain opens and can't be judged in any other way' (Svoboda in Burian 1971: 15). This concept of scenography is clearly much more than 'scene painting'. No longer associated only with the static visual image, scenography is multi-sensorial and dynamic, both responsive to and constitutive of dramatic action.

The capacity of scenography as an autonomous practice has been made more visible by what Hans-Thies Lehmann (2006) identified as 'postdramatic theatre'. Lehmann's survey of late 20th-century Western theatre points to the de-hierarchization of practice so that the scenography may be the prime focus of performance as much as the text or the performers. As well as highlighting scenography as a strategy of performance, companies such as Societas Raffaello Sanzio, the Wooster Group and La Fura dels Baus also shift the ways the work is experienced. The polysemic and open-ended nature of scenography allows, or even requires, that spectators take an active part in making sense of the performance. In Lehmann's view, spectators are enfolded in the process and manifestation of postdramatic performance and this leads to a 'more shared than communicated experience' (Lehmann 2006: 85).

Meanwhile, the interest of many theatre artists in working beyond the confines of the traditional theatre building has foregrounded the centrality of space and environment as intrinsic to the experience of performance. The origins of this shift can be traced back to the fertile interactions of performance and art that flourished in the 1960s and 1970s (Kaye 2000: 1–12) and with the means to escape 'theatrical disciplinary systems' and to create radical and resistant work (Birch and Tompkins 2012: 7). In site-specific work, and in work where the relationship of the audience to the performance is not already pre-determined, scenography is often focused on shaping the interface between the performance and the audience, and the organization or curation of space is therefore a central feature. Drawing on Richard Schechner's notions of 'Environmental Theater' (1973), Aronson developed the idea of 'environmental scenography' (1981) where the framing and positioning of the audience is seen to be a fundamental aspect of all performance that takes place outside theatre buildings, whether that be folk performance, ritual or avant-garde theatre, and one which governs the haptic, proxemic and essentially experiential dimension of performance. Furthermore, this re-structuring of the traditional relationships between performers and spectators brings about temporary communities through a 'fusion of the aesthetic and the social' that may lead to 'collective action' (Fischer-Lichte 2008: 55).

Although the potency of space as part of a scenographic toolkit was already evident in the work of theatre modernists, its potential effect became even more apparent through site-specific practice. Common to both postdramatic and site-specific forms of performance is the idea that space and scenographic elements can 'speak their own language' (see Heiner Goebbels cited in Lehmann 2006: 86). Cliff McLucas, designer and co-director of Brith Gof, saw that both the extant site (the 'host') and the temporary scenography that was brought to it (the 'ghost') were significant in the creation of meaning. The materiality, history and character of the host co-exist, not necessarily congruent with and potentially in tension or paradox with, the ghost of the scenography (Pearson 2010: 35–37).

Taken together, these shifts amount to a restructuring of the way scholars now think of scenography and provide the pre-conditions for an expanded form of scenography. Central to these pre-conditions is the role of the audience, or, more precisely, the spectator. Alongside the scenographic experiments with theatre form in the early and mid-20th century came a growing recognition of the active contribution of audiences to the theatre event. Vsevolod Meyerhold speaking in 1929 said:

> We produce every play on the assumption that it will be still unfinished when it appears on stage. We do this consciously because we realize that the crucial revision of a production is that which is made by the spectator. (Meyerhold cited in Bennett 1997: 7)

Meyerhold's scenographic experimentation included new approaches to visual representation, for example in *The Fairground Booth* (1906) and *The Magnanimous Cuckold* (1922), and different configurations of the stage. In the proposed design for the 'discussion play' *I Want a Child* (1926), for example, El Lissitsky's setting took over the whole of the theatre space removing all divisions between stage and auditorium to facilitate an environment in which the spectators would be free to interrupt. Strategies such as these that sought to question the relationship of the stage space and audience space were adopted by a wide range of practitioners in the avant-garde theatre of the 1920s and 1930s (e.g. Prampolini, Piscator, Artaud). The tradition was extended in the 1950s and 1960s through the work of Brecht, Grotowski, Kantor and given new impetus by experiments in art practice, that while rejecting theatre, embraced performance. Together, these strategies and induced more active relationships between the actors and the audience. These new approaches to the design of theatrical space challenged existing notions of both the role and form of theatre and helped to dismantle the kinds of viewing relationships that had been established through the 18th and 19th centuries by theatre architecture that disciplined the gaze of the audience towards a picture frame and the illuminated scene within in it.

A traditional approach to scenography as a creation of a complete representation of the world viewed within the frame of the proscenium is, in Tim Ingold's terms, a 'hylomorphic' model of art that sees inert matter (*hyle*) given form (*morphe*) and meaning by an artist (2012: 432). The role of the viewer in this case is to read backwards from the finished object 'to an initial intention in the mind of an agent' (Ingold 2010: 91). Ingold, however, sees making and experiencing art as a process of 'following materials'; an iterative exchange between materials and: artists and viewers alike. A similar shift has occurred in scenography where audiences have needed to become more active interpreters of the scene before them or around them. Theatre companies such as Toneelgroep, The Builder's Association and the Wooster Group that use video and screen technology to effect a 'multiplication and mobility of signs' (Kaye 2007: 209) have their lineage in the avant-garde theatre of Eisenstein and Piscator and the 'Theatre of Images' (Marranca 1996) that grew out of experimental art and theatre in the United States and Europe in the 1960s (Klich and Scheer 2012: 39). This kind of work consciously calls into question processes of seeing and perceiving (Aronson 2005: 94) and the subjective role of the spectator. Postdramatic forms with their layered, polysemic and visceral registers of address have accentuated the interpretive role further while site-specific performance and other experiments with the positioning and movement of spectators have also placed new emphasis on the effect of space as material element in the experience of the performance.

One marker of these new (or newly conceptualized) relationships is the proliferation of terms that have been recently coined to augment our habitual use of 'audience' or 'spectator'. The word audience is problematic for scenography not only because it refers to hearing and not seeing but because it suggests a homogeneity of reception that 'risks obscuring the multiple contingencies of subjective response, context, and environment' (Freshwater 2009: 5). Meanwhile, the word spectator, which emphasizes the individual and the scopic realm has been considered to designate a passive and compliant role. This view has been partially corrected by Jacques Rancière (2007) but new terms are also helpful, especially in pinning down the role of the audience in relation to the scenographic. Maaike Bleeker thinks of the spectator not as a passive observer but a 'seer' who combines what they think they see with subjective experience to augment and extend scenography; 'we always see more than is there … projections, fantasises, desires and fears' (2008: 18). Stephen Di Benedetto, meanwhile, uses the word 'attendant', in the sense of one who has a contributory role in a ceremony, to account for the way that spectators are fully engaged through mind and body simultaneously (2003: 102).

The perspective of the perceiving body is especially useful in developing expanded scenography as a distinctive field. Although contemporary practice has expanded beyond the stage, beyond theatre texts and bodies performing them and beyond the traditional demarcations of disciplinary training, it has held on 'for the most of human history' to the constant of 'the human observer' (Aronson 2008: 32). As we have pointed out above, in the context of expanded scenography, this observer is likely to be conceived in a less detached way than in former times. However, the acknowledgement of their fundamental role in the evental nature of meaning-making is a useful one as a core principle for expanded scenography as it provides a crucial point of connection with the principles of scenography as they emerge from the development of theatre scenography in the 20th century.

Scenography scholarship has tended to focus on the impact of the role and the person of the scenographer (e.g. Burian 1971; Holmberg 1996; Parker 1996; Doona 2002; Howard 2002; Rewa 2004) but the perspective of the spectator offers some helpful orientations on expanded scenography. In the first place it gives emphasis to the event of performance, as it unfolds in the presence of an observer or participant, rather than on static artefacts or on the intentions of the artist and therefore underlines the imaginative and creative role that spectators have in engaging or interpreting the work. It conceptualizes scenography as a performative act or 'encounter' (Hannah and Harsløf 2008: 15) rather than simply one of communication. Secondly the perspective of the spectator highlights the experiential and embodied nature of scenographic experience and the dynamic interaction of bodies, environments and materials that expanded scenography aims to generate. This shift of perspective is not intended to deny the role of the scenographer or the other craftspeople and technicians involved in the designing, making and operating of scenography (indeed several of the chapters in the book deal specifically with the roles of both scenographers and technicians). Neither is it intended to place the spectator in any kind of hierarchical relationship to the other human and non-human elements of scenographic performance. But it does reframe traditional views of scenography in order to gain a fresh view of the broader potential of performance design.

Principles and defining concepts of expanded scenography

Starting from this central principle of the spectator, we can re-consider the shifts in scenography during the 20th century and look at them anew for the purposes of defining and shaping reflection on expanded scenography. The considerations of space and site, the operation of the aesthetic in the context of performance and the capacity of design elements to contribute to meaning-making processes that have been identified above, can be lifted from an exclusively theatre-based context and applied to a wider range of performance practices. From the perspective of the spectator, we have identified three overlapping and inter-related concepts of the manifestation and experience of scenography in an expanded form that can assist with identifying the distinctive features and concerns of expanded scenography. The first of these is relationality and the way that scenography facilitates spaces of encounter; that may be in the form of encounters between spectators and performers in ways that are conventionally familiar, but it might also encompass encounters with other spectators, spaces, sites and objects. The second is affectivity and the operation of the aesthetic at the level of the individual. The final concept is materiality, by which we mean the properties and capacities of things, places, bodies and the ways they interact and impact on our experience and understanding of performance and of the world more generally.

Relationality

A significant amount of the work that is discussed in terms of expanded or extended scenography is concerned with the ways that scenography organizes spaces so that intersubjective or empathetic encounters and, potentially, some re-imagining of existing social structures might take place. In expanded scenography, urban space is often re-conceived through the way in which spectators or participants are enabled to see familiar environments in fresh ways. In Invisible Flock's *Bring the Happy* (2012, ongoing), individual's memories were collected and pinned to a map of their city using glass rods to indicate a 'happiness rating' and to create 'a new emotional geography'. These stories were then subsequently retold in a live performance and celebration of the place (Invisible Flock 2012). In Dries Verhoeven's *The Big Movement* created in 2006, a small custom-built 'cinema' complete with red plush seats and velvet curtains is installed in a city centre. Viewers are shown a live feed of the space directly outside and real life is projected as a sub-titled film where 'unsuspecting passers-by play the main roles' (Verhoeven 2006). In different ways both of these performances use scenographic strategies to position spectators in ways that are unfamiliar and open up the possibility of new insights about themselves, others and the spaces we all inhabit.

In this volume, Dorita Hannah discusses Rimini Protokoll's *Situation Rooms* (2011, ongoing) that uses hand-held devices in an immersive and interactive environment to allow audience members to assume the various positions of real people 'implicated in, and affected by' the international arms trade, to put themselves in the shoes of others, as it were. In this example, the encounters are carefully planned and orchestrated by the scenographer (Dominic Huber), but in other examples in this volume, the scenography is deliberately envisaged as more open-ended; bringing together performers, audiences and spaces so that 'bodies and environments collide' (Lotker and Gough 2013: 6) in more diverse ways. This can be seen for example in the street performance examples of Festival Internacional Teatro a Mil in Santiago de Chile that Marcela Oteíza analyses and the Romani interventions in city streets that form the focus of the chapter by Jane Collins and Ethel Brooks. What is common in these examples is that the 'positioning' and 'situating' functions of scenography (Anderson 2013: 109) are as important as the interpretive or expressive functions. Sigrid Merx has said that approaching scenography as a process of 'activating the shifting of positions' reveals the political nature of scenography. In expanded scenography the socially engaged focus of much of the work is demonstrated not simply by what can be seen but by 'a practice that determines, organizes and refigures who and what is there to be seen and heard' (2013: 54).

Bourriaud's theory of 'relational aesthetics' (2002) or 'judging artworks on the basis of the inter-human relations which they represent, produce or prompt' (2002: 112) is an obvious point of reference. Shifting focus from the artwork as autonomous to the artwork as a relational object where its operation is founded on a network of relationships 'between individuals and groups, between the artists and the world' and 'between the beholder and the world' (2002: 26) parallels the shifts that have occurred with a re-visioning of scenography and the emergence of expanded scenography. This is especially evident with regard to the processual and evental way that scenography works and the way that spectators are thereby implicated. Bourriaud's theory has sparked renewed consideration about the relationship in arts practices of the aesthetic to the social, but as Shannon Jackson points out, we should be wary of these polarizing debates that set autonomy against heteronomy or aesthetic innovation against social effects (see Jackson 2011: 43–74). In expanded scenography, the relational dimension is rarely instrumental or simply 'feelgood' in the way that critics of relational aesthetics such as Claire Bishop have characterized it (Bishop 2004). The relationality of expanded scenography often incorporates 'more complex social antagonisms' at varying scales (Jackson 2011: 59). For example, Theatre NO99's *Unified Estonia* (2010), that Kathleen Irwin discusses, used scenographic means to activate a 'hyper-populist' fictitious political party and expose 'the hidden mechanisms of populist politics' (NO99) through an event involving over 7,000 participants, and, in contrast, Melissa Trimingham's analysis of the *Imaging Autism* project casts scenography as a medium in which radically different understandings of the world can be brought face to face in intimate encounters. Even work that might be considered popular spectacle, and therefore, merely celebratory and devoid of deeper significance, might, through its scenographic qualities, stimulate new ways of seeing familiar locations. Royal de Luxe's 'giant spectaculars', for example, bring citizens into close proximity with their city and with each other through the arrival of giant visitors. Their incongruous and exotic presence has a visceral effect that, potentially, stimulates and unsettles quotidian experience (McKinney 2013). In Deborah Warner and Fiona Shaw's *Peace Camp* (2012), clusters of small illuminated tents installed in coastal locations lent a new perspective to the UK's coastal borders. These translucent structures, glowing with fluctuating light between dawn and dusk and accompanied by a soundscape of whispered love poems from all over the British Isles, were an evocative yet ambiguous presence, both comforting and strange (see cover image).

Relationality is not only concerned with intersubjective, human encounters but also with the way spectators might be positioned in relation to the natural and built environment. Companies such as NVA, for example, use scenographic interventions (such as large-scale, technically innovative and beautifully orchestrated light shows) to explore and re-define reciprocal relationships between people and spaces both urban and rural. There are potential overlaps here with the ways that architecture has been considered as an active 'spatial event', rather than a durable object (Hannah 2011: 55) and the 'dramaturgies' of architecture and public space (Turner 2010, 2015) but within that discipline, scenography can be considered as a distinct 'agency' that brings out the 'dramaturgy inherent within architecture' (von Arx 2016: 83). There is an inherent notion of performance and event in architecture, which as a time-based art-form is 'experienced with all of our senses as we progress through space' and therefore it is through scenographic strategies that the latent dramaturgical potential of the built environment is activated.

Affectivity

Despite the socially engaged nature that is characteristic of much (but not all) expanded scenography, it usually deals in affect rather than effect. The ways in which scenography engages the attention of spectators – through the organization and transformation of space, through the selection and manipulation of images and through the action of the scenographic materials themselves – are often indirect and oblique; an experience or a set of potentialities rather than a singular message. And it is not an exclusively scopic experience but something that appeals to the whole body of the spectator. Josephine Machon points to the synaesthetic nature of what she has termed 'visceral performance' (2009), in her analysis of the work of companies such as Punchdrunk, dreamthinkspeak and Shunt, much of which is deeply scenographic in nature. These experiences, characterized by being created in 'found', non-theatre buildings, are often designed around a requirement for the audience to navigate space, with and between other bodies and usually under low lighting. The recent popularity of such multi-sensory 'immersive' events might be traced to companies such as La Fura dels Baus and De La Guarda who's anarchic, celebratory *Villa Villa* (1998) impacted on audiences in major cities across the globe. This performance used an extraordinary combination of scenographic elements to constantly alter the audience's perspective. The first part of the performance was staged entirely above the audiences' heads and progressed with aerial performers in flying harnesses, bungee ropes, and an assault of the senses that included loud rhythmic drumming, glaring lighting, wind and rain. A programme note attempted to explain the importance of the visceral experience: 'The tide produced by the audience is a fundamental part of the emotional upheaval of this show, where everything is fragile, everything is changeable except our tempests' (1998). The bodily appeal of this kind of work evokes Antonin Artaud's vision of theatre as a material, physical language where colour, movement, gesture sound and light operate together in a dense network of non-verbal signs, 'a constant play of mirrors' or 'spatial poetry' (McKinney and Butterworth 2009: 33–34).

This is not to say that scenography is always an assault on the senses. Scenography often works gradually, over time, accumulating associations and meanings as a performance unfolds in a temporal as well as a spatial dimension. Verdensteatret's *The Telling Orchestra* (2004–2006) was an interconnected assembly of electronically and mechanically automated objects delicately assembled from discarded material, flotsam, rubbish; old wire, metal, driftwood, rusty nails, and bones that were further animated by projected light and a soundscape. There was no discernible narrative structure but gradually the performance of the objects accrued layers of strange and unsettling images that resonated well beyond the time-frame of the performance itself (McKinney 2013). This makes the precise effects of scenography hard to pin down and it is a reminder of the phenomenological nature of experience, or what Maurice Merleau-Ponty calls 'the thickness of the pre-objective present' (2002: 433) that scenographic experience has been aligned with (McKinney 2015). Scenography tends to generate understanding that is founded in sensual, emotional and aesthetic responses on the part of the viewer. Minty Donald, whose own scenographic performances have explored the relationship between humans and waterways, suggests that 'performance manifests in the sensorial, affective and more-than-cognitive' giving access to communicative registers 'which are frequently overlooked, or inaccessible, in linguistic modes' (Donald 2016: 3).

In this book, David Shearing's work immerses spectators in affective environments where scenographic materials condition and frame a 'mindful' experience for his participants. In performances such as *The Weather Machine*, space, light, sound, tactile experience and smell combine in a scenography of assembled 'distractions'. Shearing's aim is for spectators to dwell in this affective space, attuning themselves to the way the space and the things in it are working on their bodies as a way of re-connecting with ourselves as sensing bodies. For Trimingham, the rich sensory and affective environment created for the *Imagining Autism* project also proves to be a powerful means by which researchers can feel and have some insight into the experience of the autistic children they are working with.

By drawing attention to the affective and multi-sensorial nature of scenographic imagery, we do not mean to deny that socially and cultured informed readings of scenography are important too; clearly the inversion, juxtaposition and playful appropriation of familiar signs and tropes can be central to the way that expanded scenography works. In this book, they are especially evident in the resistant practices of Romani artists that are discussed by Jane Collins and Ethel Brooks. But even here, the employment of these various signs and strategies operate within the multi-layered spaces of the historical city and against the backdrop of notions of identity, difference and racism in ways that open up an affective destabilization rather than a clear-cut, didactic message for social change.

The shift away from direct communication that Lehmann detects in postdramatic theatre is also addressed by James Thompson when he considers affect, that is 'the bodily sensation that is sustained and provoked particularly by aesthetic experiences' as a 'precondition for critical engagement with the world' (Thompson 2009: 135). Thompson argues that affect (as manifested through intense feelings of joy or terror) is a step on the way to achieving effective social change, but recent scholarship in perception and cognition in the theatre (see Shaughnessy 2013a) suggests that bodily-based and affective responses to the aesthetics of performance might in themselves constitute a kind of understanding. It is becoming easier to appreciate how the composition of 'action, words, line, colour and rhythm' that Fischer-Lichte invokes (2008: 185) is a thing (or a network of things) in itself and not only a representation of something else. Maaike Bleeker's chapter shows in detail how paying attention to the aesthetic dimension of scenography in the case of Kris Verdonck's *End* (2008) is in itself a form of 'thinking through matter'. The kind of thinking or meaning-production that is induced here is not logocentric or rhetorical but what might be described as 'a meeting between material and sensation' (O'Sullivan 2005: 56).

Materiality

Hannah and Harsløf have pointed out that 'the dynamic role played by seemingly inanimate places and things' (2008: 11) has largely been excluded from the history of theatre and performance. But the agentic capacity of materials and structures in or as performance is coming to be recognized, especially as this is understood and harnessed by expanded scenography. Theories of new materialism which consider technological and natural materialities to be 'actors alongside and within us' (Bennett 2010: 47) have been influential in developing the idea of agentic capacity of materials in scenography (Donald 2014, 2016; McKinney 2015; Beer 2016). This goes beyond Veltrusky's concept of the 'action force' of stage objects that is observed when they become dynamically interchangeable with human performers (Veltrusky 1964: 88) and encompasses 'immersive and immutable phenomena' such as the wind and water that Minty Donald works with in her site-specific performances (Donald 2014: 130).

In more conventionally theatrical settings too, the immutability of materials has become a notable feature. Katrin Brack's designs are often centred on a single material; confetti, theatrical snow, fog, tinsel or balloons in abundance. These designs are not environments for performance as much as performers in their own right. Even though some of the designs have an interpretive element (e.g. the fog-filled stage of *Ivanov* (2006) reflects the characters' states of mind), this is superseded in performance by the way the materials respond to the physical capacities of the stage and the way that performers have to improvise with them. Fog is extremely sensitive to temperature and drafts within the building as well as prevailing atmospheric conditions. Although these materials can be controlled to an extent, they cannot be completely mastered (see McKinney and McKechnie 2016). Even the feats of engineering required to stage the aquatic spectacles that Nebojša Tabački describes in this volume cannot reduce water to a state of full compliance.

Scenography, in fact, derives much of its affect from the 'vitality of matter' (Bennett 2010) and our capacity to discern it. In making processes, the qualities of different materials and mediums emerge as distinct entities. Working on *The Telling Orchestra*, Verdensteatret found that, over time, the interplay of 'different media started to generate images and stories on their own – as if the construction itself was hinting to what it was capable of expressing' (McKinney 2013: 67) and this vitality is as important from the perspective of spectators as it is for scenographers. Ingold proposes that the 'textility' of making and viewing art should replace outmoded ideas of the artistic process where the genius artist gives form to otherwise inert matter and the viewer's role is to decipher the intended meaning. In expanded scenography, the spectator is often in direct contact with materials, immersed in them or otherwise touched by them. As Gernot Böhme points out, the powerful influence of atmosphere in theatre settings and beyond is derived from the way in which things, especially elements such as light and sound, can 'radiate outwards' and can be 'felt present in space' (Böhme 2013: 5–6). The relational nature of much expanded scenography underscores the potential of the material in performance; meanwhile, the affective register that emerges is in part a result of this new-found appreciation of materials and what they can do. Meanwhile, spectators, it should be acknowledged, are also materials. Their physical presence, energy, attention and response to the other elements of scenography become part of it in its expansion. This concept is foregrounded in Shearing's *The Weather Machine* where the presence of human bodies both influence and disrupt the scenographic environment but are integral to the designed experience.

Current discussions about the relationship between human and non-human (or 'more-than-human' as Donald has it) both in art and in the world more generally are influential in thinking about how scenography works and how spectators experience it. Bennett describes the relationship as an 'assemblage' or a 'material cluster of charged parts' (Bennett 2010: 24) while Karen Barad (taken up in this volume by both Bleeker and Irwin) sees 'intra-action' as an understanding that results from '*a direct material engagement with the world*'' (Barad 2007:49 original emphasis) that takes matter seriously 'as active participant in the world's becoming' (Bleeker in this volume). As Donald points out, 'an ability to discern the vitality of matter' (Bennett 2010: 119) is important as a scenographic process but it might also contribute to understanding in terms of cultural geography and ecology. Indeed, Tanja Beer has used these perspectives on materialism to argue for ecologically engaged practice in scenography (Beer 2016) and Donald suggests a heightened awareness of lively materials might be a way to resist dominant anthropocentric views of human/ environment relations (Donald 2014, 2016).

These propositions for concepts of expanded scenography emerge from the restructuring of theatre scenography through the early part of the 20th century and from postdramatic and site-specific performance practices that have exposed the further potential for scenography as a cultural form. They are largely interdependent and together they articulate what might be considered distinct about expanded scenography, in contrast to say 'expanded dramaturgy' (Turner 2010) or 'expanded theatre' (Read 2013). These concepts point towards new frames of reference with which expanded scenography might be both identified and further interrogated.

Organization of the book

All of the essays in this book, in one way or another, address relationality, affectivity or materiality and the attendant social, aesthetic and ethical considerations that accompany them. Therefore we have taken a rather more pragmatic approach to the organization of the chapters. This is intended to help the reader to navigate the range and breadth of contemporary work in the following categories: technological space, architectural space, agency, audiences and materials. Nonetheless, we hope that concepts of relationality, affectivity and materiality in scenography will resonate throughout and in slightly different ways in each of the parts.

Technological space

The history and development of scenography has been shaped through the introduction of technologies of many different kinds including those used on stage and the technologies responsible for the spread and influence of scenographic spectacle. Now in the 21st century scenographers are also employing technology to resist globalization and the totalizing effects of spectacle in order to comment on and intervene in real-world situations. In both of these chapters, the political purpose of scenography and its extensions are foregrounded in ways that underline the relationality of the relationships between spectator and scenography but, crucially, also the wider global, political context of the work.

In '"Devices of Wonder": Globalizing Technologies in the Process of Scenography', Christopher Baugh considers how the technologies of performance and the resulting scenographies operate within wider political, economic and social structures. By examining the lavish and theatrical programme of events staged to celebrate the Medici wedding in Florence, Italy, in 1589, he exposes scenography and its attendant technologies in the service of spectacle as a 'self-portrait of power' (Debord 1983: I, 24). Baugh argues that scenography was 'effectively born out of this union between technological and political display', and has continued to exert a standardizing and colonizing influence through the form and structure of theatre buildings and the technologies they support.

However, the technologies of scenography also offer tools to resist the homogenizing effect of the spectacle, and Baugh identifies four 'scenographic extensions', that is, practices that are supported and enabled by technology which actively engage with the conditions of their production. 'New technologies', Baugh argues, 'are making and using theatre that actively challenges globalization, neo-colonial power and the control of international capital that it reflects' and in particular the widespread access to digital technologies has served to 'reconfigure human creativity – and resistance'.

Dorita Hannah's chapter, 'Scenographic Screen Space: Bearing Witness and Performing Resistance' takes up this idea of mobile technologies and resistance by examining contemporary examples that recast spectators as participants and facilitate a reflexive or critical engagement with performance. Like Baugh, Hannah sees the realm of scenography being expanded beyond the stage by the means of technology and the ways in which these technologies facilitate reflection, exchange and protest; 'the screen has become an extension of the body and lived space as well as a contemporary site for reiterating and/or challenging worldviews'.

This is significant at a time when superfluity of images delivered via screen-based media seems to distance us from real-world events and the trauma of other people. But the screens in our hand can be utilized as tools to disrupt the dissociative effect and reinstate theatre as 'a restorative site for re-enacting traumatic events'. Used in this way, screens are more than just 'transparent' facilitatory devices; their materiality starts to exert an agency that points to notions of 'thing-power' (Bennett) and the vitality of non-human things. Even objects as seemingly intransigent as the West Bank Wall in Palestine can, through the agency of the screen, be made to dissolve temporarily so that a separated community can come together and 'the violence of a patrolled borderline' can be exposed and undermined.

Architectural space

This part considers ways in which architecture performs a scenographic role both on stage and off stage. In the theatre, modernist principles of design and architectonic structure that were so influential in the development of 20th-century scenography have given way to more fragmented yet more politically engaged practices that address the social realities of urban space. Meanwhile, the potential of architecture and urban space to be animated through scenography is recognized through site-specific performance. Both on the stage and in urban spaces, expanded scenography utilizes architectural space not simply as a backdrop but as an active part of the process of inviting spectators to situate themselves with regard to their lived experience.

In 'Between Symbolic Representation and New Critical Realism: Architecture as Scenography and Scenography as Architecture', Thea Brejzek contrasts the approaches of architects and scenographers to designing for performance. Although her focus is mainly on large-scale works for the theatre, Brejzek wants to examine the move towards scenographies that exhibit 'critical realism' and designs that reflect urban space as political space. She detects an aesthetic shift in scenography that is a response to the political, social and economic realities beyond the stage which challenge some long-held principles of what might constitute 'good' scenic design. While some scenographies continue to maintain a modernist approach in the creation of 'sculptural objects of symbolic representation on stage', scenographers such as Bert Neumann and Anna Viebrock have adopted architectural 'hacking' as a subversive and critical act of scenography that is more concerned with the challenges of contemporary, 'postfordist, postmodern' life and an examination of 'inherently political, conflicted and contested' spaces. Meanwhile Performance Architecture, with its roots in 1960s art 'happenings', is primarily interested in the interaction between bodies and constructed spaces and the temporary community that forms around a 'precarious space of negotiation'.

In urban spaces, too, scenographies demonstrate and activate the interactive relationships between buildings and bodies, between symbols of power and authority that structure public space and lived experience. Marcela Oteíza's chapter 'City as Site: Street Performance and Site

Permeability during the Festival Internacional Teatro a Mil, Chile, 2012–2015' studies the different ways in which these relationships play out. Oteíza proposes that the city is composed of 'space-characters', that is urban sites and particular buildings with 'latent socio-historical meaning for Santiago's inhabitants'. During the weeks of the festival, these space-characters are brought into dialogue, through the agency of street performances, with audiences and citizens. Oteíza examines four different performances to see how they incorporate the city's space-characters and the ways that they can re-shape past experience and offer some new perspectives on the future. As a native of Santiago, Oteíza sees how the performances and their utilization of temporary structures interact with the historical and cultural significance of buildings and spaces in the city and these are then overlayed with her own memories of the Pinochet dictatorship in the 1970s and 1980s.

Agency

The chapters in this part address what scenography can do beyond traditional notions of decorating the stage and interpreting or illustrating a play text. They consider scenography as a way of doing, being and thinking and within these practices the concepts of relationality, affectivity and materiality are all strongly present. As well as considering the agency of scenographers in relation to spectators (Irwin), posthumanist perspectives help to show that the scenographer and the spectator are all situated within an interactive network of material things (Bleeker and Brooks and Collins).

The first chapter in the part addresses the use of scenographic strategies to challenge stereotypical views of cultural identity. In 'Scenography Matters: Performing Romani Identities as Strategy and Critique', Ethel Brooks and Jane Collins analyse how activists employ 'visual, spatial, sartorial and aural' methods in order to challenge prescribed notions of Romani people. Drawing on examples in London and Paris, Brooks and Collins show how these tactics can destabilize the 'concept of fixity in the ideological construction of otherness' (Bhaba 1983: 18) and 'unfix' racial stereotyping. Brooks and Collins observe how Romani culture has been neutralized by mainstream culture in, for example, the way that 'the political and social origins of flamenco are lost in sanitised and domesticated representations'. At the same time, traces of the real lives of Romani people at historical sites have been 'erased'. Through the interaction of site, scenography and activism Romani artists are able to 'reassert agency in the present by claiming back an expunged Romani past'.

Kathleen Irwin explores the idea of 'scenography as part of a complex network of creative actions and things' further. In her chapter 'Scenographic Agency: A Showing-Doing and a Responsibility for Showing-Doing', she addresses the role of the scenographer in an era when scenography has been defined as 'event, experience, and action, rather than a set of physical elements, or representational or metaphoric images' (Gröndahl 2012b: 2). With the shift from representation to action comes a new focus on the ethical position of the scenographer and their responsibility in 'not just observing the world but being part of it'. Irwin draws from Barad's theory of 'intra-action', which states that agency arises from the relationships between things, rather than being inherently given to individual things. It follows from this that the action of scenography cannot rely on the centrality of the individual scenographer and needs to be re-thought as a network or 'an organism – a whole with interdependent parts – a matrix of individuals, ideas and things' that might produce scenographic agency.

In 'Thinking That Matters: Towards a Post-Anthropocentric Approach to Performance Design', Maaike Bleeker shifts the focus further towards the agential capacity of matter and to what could be thought of as an ecological approach to the evolution of a scenography. Bleeker also refers to Barad's posthuman philosophy to think about how materials matter in scenography, that is, how they are a foundational aspect of meaning making processes and a form of 'material' thinking. She looks at the documentation of the development of Kris Verdonck's *End* (2008) to see how various kinds of materials, 'photographs, (parts of) films, documentaries, texts, events, sounds, news stories, ideas, metaphors' through successive 'tests' might coalesce with other materials to form the basis of images and ideas in a performance. The process here is not one of 'inscribing matter with meaning' in the way that more traditional approaches to scenography usually adopt. Instead, it 'proceeds through setting up intra-actions that allow matter its due in the performance's becoming'.

Audiences

As we have already argued, conceptions of audience are fundamental to contemporary scenography and the active or emancipated spectator is figured as an essential part of scenography's operation. However, the ways in which scenography stimulates and engages its audiences are currently under discussion and cognitive science and philosophies of perception have been employed to try to understand what happens when spectators encounter scenography.

The variety of spaces in which scenography is now encountered facilitate a number of different relationships between spectators and scenography. Free from the constraints of theatre auditoria and the particular ways in which the viewer is positioned there, we can re-think the role of the audience and their mode of engagement. David Shearing makes performance installations where the audience are situated within scenographic environments which they are invited to explore. His work is part of a wider movement towards what has been termed 'immersive' theatre, of which companies like UK-based Punchdrunk create large-scale work in non-theatre spaces through which the audience is encouraged to wander. However, in Shearing's work human performers are not present and the experience is focused principally on the material characteristics of the space and the inter-relationships between objects, space and the bodies of the audience members that become incorporated within the scenography.

In 'Audience Immersion, Mindfulness and the Experience of Scenography', Shearing reflects on how his work encourages a form of audience engagement that is informed by concepts of 'mindfulness'. He is influenced by Ellen Langer's definition of mindfulness as an 'awareness of automatic behaviour' and develops this to propose a mode of spectatorship based on 'embodied reflection'.

Understanding the sensual processes of our interactions with designed objects is an important development in current theories of scenography and, therefore, of expanded scenography, too. The traditional conception of theatre as either a place to see (theatron) or to hear (auditorium) has given rise to reductive notions of scenography as a wholly visual experience. This then has tended to treat scenography as a series of static images rather than to consider it as a fluid and dynamic event. The perception of scenographic materials in magic acts offers a heightened form of scenographic reception and this is what Stephen Di Benedetto explores in 'Cognitive Approaches to Performance Design, or How the Dead Materialize and Other Spectacular Design Solutions'. Benedetto shows how spectacular effects such as the recent 'resurrection' of Tupac Shakur come about as a collaboration between the propensities and materialities of objects, the sensing and anticipating bodies of spectators and the capacity of the designers and performers of magic acts to manipulate them.

Materials

Materials and what they can do are the foundation of scenography. In the 21st century we have come to recognize that the properties and potentials of the various materials, objects and things and the ways that these interact with performers and audiences are at the heart of the experience of performance. In this part, we address the embodied and phenomenological experience of scenographic materials and discuss the possibilities for both commercial and therapeutic applications. This part inevitably focuses on questions of materiality, but the positioning of spectators is especially important as part of this in Nebojša Tabački's essay, 'The Matter of Water: Bodily Experience of Scenography in Contemporary Spectacle'. In it he deals with large-scale aquatic spectacle and considers how water as a material signals new approaches to the design and engineering of new audience experiences. The use of water in contemporary spectacle demonstrates not only the spectacular effects that we have come to associate with theatrical distance and occularity but the immediacy of materials and their effect as part of the viewing experience. The technical difficulties of containing and controlling the flow and volume of water demonstrates that the performance of the technology required for these purpose-built aquatic auditoria is a significant part of the performance. In this it echoes the origins of spectacle demonstrating wealth articulated by Baugh in the first chapter, especially through the cost and effort associated with the engineering solutions that are required.

In the final chapter of the book, Melissa Trimingham offers a very different application of scenographic materials than that of aquatic spectacle. In 'Ecologies of Autism: Vibrant Space in *Imagining Autism*', she presents the findings of practice-based research where scenography becomes a medium for exploring and encouraging intersubjective and material encounters with children with autism. The scenographic environments developed for the *Imagining Autism* project provided a space where researcher-practitioners can work with children in a co-constructive way; space, light, projection, sound, costume and props are the means of exploring and developing communication, social imagination and empathy. Like Irwin and Bleeker, Trimingham draws on posthuman philosophy (Barad 2012) and the overlapping field of 'new materialism' (Coole and Frost 2010) in order to account for the active agency of materials and the 'affective, dynamic and explosive ecologies' of the project.

Expanded scenography intersections

The diverse range of material discussed in this volume offers an international snapshot of contemporary thinking in scenography from many of its leading academic protagonists. Together these examinations of contemporary performance design demonstrate an expansion and a rethinking of traditional notions of scenography and point the way towards defining and discussing a new field. As Krauss states in the conclusion to her essay on expanded sculpture, it is important to first map the structure of a new field working not from an all-encompassing historicist view of the category, but from an understanding of 'definitive ruptures' in that category. This we have tried to do with reference to key shifts in scenography in the 20th century that have precipitated what we now see as an expanded scenography. What that reveals is the potential significance of applying a scenographic lens to a range of work that involves the interaction (and, indeed, the intra-action) of humans and the non-human/more-than-human framed within the broad category of performance. As we have indicated, the reach of this work encompasses political, social, and cultural concerns in more direct and diverse ways than hitherto and it heralds new aesthetic and ethical approaches to making and viewing artwork.

This is only a beginning and there is much more that is still to be investigated with regard to the way different aspects of scenographic practice operate in expanded forms. For example, the use and adaptation of urban space, environmental and sustainable scenography, the design of museums, galleries and theme parks, virtual scenography and its use in gaming, expanded uses of materials such as costume, lighting and sound might all be considered in much more depth in order to understand the ways that design and performance intersect – and what these intersections reveal about contemporary culture. In this way, scenographic practices might not only be shown to be making a distinct contribution to our understanding of new forms of theatre and performance but to areas such as art and design, architecture and cultural geography as well. As the first volume in a new series addressing that intersection, this is a first step that we hope will work to stimulate further exploration of expanded scenography; to examine not simply what it is, but what it does and how it does it.

Notes

1   The work of artists such as Robert Wilson, Heiner Goebbels and Kris Verdonck and companies such as Societas Rafaello Sanzio, Hotel Pro Forma and Rimini Protokoll provide examples of performance that are essentially scenographic; that is, they use spatial, visual and material means to create a rich multi-sensorial experience for audiences.

2   Non-representational theory broadly describes an approach to investigating everyday life through embodied and often intangible aspects of the ways in which humans relate to their environment and which takes account of 'more-than-human, more-than-textual, multisensual worlds' (Lorimer 2005: 83).

PART ONE

Technological Space

1

'Devices of Wonder': Globalizing Technologies in the Process of Scenography

Christopher Baugh

In 1967, Guy Debord published *The Society of the Spectacle* in which he said: 'The spectacle is the existing order's uninterrupted discourse about itself, its laudatory monologue. It is the self-portrait of power' (Debord 1983: I, 24). In this chapter, I want to examine the globalization of spectacle, the role played by scenographic technologies in this process and the way in which in recent years digital technologies are extending the scenographic in ways that actively critique the 'self-portrait of power' and oppose the globalizing and colonial tendencies of international capitalism.

I hope to suggest that spectacle, along with its creators and owners, has a consistent tendency to expand and share its effects with ever-greater bodies of spectators, and that this may be thought of as a form of colonial appropriation. It is, for example, no coincidence that the expansion of the Roman Empire was closely matched by the spreading technologies of public spectacle represented by the countless amphitheatres whose remains are to be found in every corner of that empire; their geography and their relationship with Roman systems of power and control is self-evident. We may even light-heartedly refer to the Empire's need to provide circuses alongside placatory bread in order to sustain political power. Technologies and their associated aesthetics enable the replication of spectacle and, through architecture and stagecraft, establish an infrastructure of resource that facilitates and encourages further expansion. Furthermore, I want to suggest that the technologies that underpin the manufacture of spectacle are also the technologies that provide the basis for the expansion and control of economic and political capital.

In order to do this, I want to compare two historical moments in which technologies have offered opportunities for extensions of the scenographic beyond the ephemerality of parochial, live performance and the immediacy of its political and social context, and opportunities that have led to the establishment of extended national and international presence. Technologies of carpentry, canvas, rope, counterweight and painted two-dimensional perspectives developed in Europe during the late 16th century and facilitated the growth of an international network of accommodating architecture that was established throughout the Western world during the 17th and 18th centuries. Two hundred years later during the last two decades of the 20th century, the development of computer technology enabled the hitherto ephemeral elements of stage lighting and sound to become vital components of the commodified spectacle of the international 'mega-musical'. But the technologies that have enabled theatre spectacle to become as globally ubiquitous as McDonalds, Coca-Cola or Starbucks, creating 'a playground for the newly privileged, a quick stopover site on the tourist and heritage map' (Kershaw 1999: 5), have almost simultaneously enabled scenographers to explore forms and processes of community performance and theatre making that actively challenge the globalization of theatre and neo-colonial power, and the control of international capital that it reflects.

Theatre and festival have always served as companion forms through which monarchs and rulers have marked their authority and ownership. Performances of beauty and artistic achievement, often requiring sophisticated technology, offered the privilege and mystery of exclusive ownership. The combination of carnival activity alongside theatrical performance to produce the theatrical festival was one of the outstanding achievements of the Renaissance and early baroque throughout Europe. It represented a celebratory *Gesamtkunstwerk*,[1] a bringing together of the arts of social encounter, of procession, dance and music alongside the artistic and artisan practices of painting, sculpture, costume and ritual display. But they were events where all these artistic practices only became significant and meaningful, as Debord suggests, 'with reference to the setting of a constructed place, a construction which is its own centre of unification' (1983: VIII, 189).

The Medici wedding and the globalization of spectacle

In Florence in May 1589, the wedding to end all weddings took place between the French princess Christine of Lorraine and the Florentine Grand Duke Ferdinando di Medici.[2] It produced a month-long festival of theatre and public ritual performances circumscribed by politics, economics, social power and above all the desire to make Florence a centre of unification as Debord suggests. As James Saslow says, 'the various components of the enormous *festa* constitute one of the outstanding late Renaissance landmarks of artistic creativity, encompassing art and architecture, theater, music, and political-religious ceremonial' (1996: 1). Processional entries into cities and the paying of spiritual homage in cathedrals had long formed essential parts of state ceremonial and reception, but this wedding introduced innovative new arts modelled on antique precedents. The courtyard of the Pitti Palace, for example, was converted into a place of performance by enclosing and flooding it in order to stage a *naumachia* – a naval battle that remembered the Battle of Lepanto of 1571 between the catholic Holy League and the Ottoman Empire. The Uffizzi theatre was built within the palace complex as a centre-piece complete with machinery designed by the scenographic overseer and 'artificer' of the festival, Bernardo Buontalenti (c. 1531–1608). Each of the wedding events needed the design and construction of complex machinery and the making of spectacular costumes for many hundreds of singers, musicians, actors and spectators. All of this required sophisticated diplomacy and political event management. The planning and administration of the events were co-ordinated from the heart of the Medici political structure. Alongside all other aspects of the Medici civil service, Ferdinando established within the offices of the Uffizi palace a professional arts bureaucracy, headed by Emilio de Cavalieri, dedicated to achieving efficiency and cost management, but also centralizing and maximizing the considerable political investment in the event. Saslow suggests the wedding festival became a powerful illustration of the scope and complexity of Medici political economy, 'both in its overt iconography, with its claims for world hegemony and universal order, and in its "esthetic economy", by which name might be designated the social, economic, technical and managerial practices and institutions through which material culture was produced' (1996: 16). As an event, it exemplifies Debord's 'laudatory monologue' quoted above and also Randolph Starn and Loren Partridge's assertion of art making as a 'product of the triumphalist state ... controlled from the top to mobilize the display of intellectual, artistic and material resources' (1992: 211). The entire wedding festival with its multiple events of religious processions, ritual acknowledgment of distinguished guests, a decorative, spectacularly 'designed' football match (*giuoco di calcio*) played between teams of costumed aristocrats in the Piazza Santa Croce, battle-games of jousting, costume display at elaborate banquets, dance and theatre, together constructed an extended metaphor of harmonious unity. But the centre-piece was theatre and it focused upon several performances of a series of *intermedi* inserted between the acts of several comedies. The *intermedio* was a hybrid form that combined song, dance, symbolic and splendid costume and, above all else, spectacular and awe-inspiring scenic inventions, that concluded with the descent of heavenly beings to grace and bless the happy couple – all put to the service of glorifying the wonder of the occasion. The political significance of the wedding required that the festivities be illustrated and described, and for published editions to be tactically circulated as souvenirs to visiting dignitaries and to overseas ambassadors and courts. There are fifteen surviving detailed accounts of the wedding festivities. One such account by Bastiano Rossi indicates the importance placed upon the audience as performer:

> [O]nce the lights were lit, and falling on the ornaments and precious gems that the seated gentlewomen wore on their heads, hands and clothing, all the *gradi* [raked audience seating on either side of the theatre] seemed loaded with shimmering stars, which drew to themselves the eyes of all those around them, who, with unbelieving pleasure, as if their eyes had never been struck by anything like it, could not get their fill of staring at the splendor of the jewels and the beauties of these young women ... the Artificer received a sign from the Grand Duke to begin the performance.[3]

The Duke's cue set in motion the technologies that 'artificer' Buontalenti had designed to create this artistic apotheosis of Ferdinando di Medici, his bride and his territory.

Such emblems of a unified state depended upon and were developed in tandem with the growth of political control over the larger theatre of the physical and social world, particularly the bureaucratic administration of people, land and economic resources. Debord summarizes the process and function of such a political spectacle that 'presents itself as something enormously positive, indisputable and inaccessible. It says nothing more than "that which appears is good, that which is good appears"' (1983: I, 12).

Medici economic and political power shared a similar technological process to that of the spectacle. The economic power of the state was primarily established through mercantile wealth, trade agreements and especially the establishment of the Medici banking system throughout Europe. At the centre of this enterprise was its fleet of merchant ships based in the port of Livorno where Christine of Lorraine was formally received as precious political cargo on 24 April 1589. At the centre of the spectacles of change and apparition that were staged in the theatre, in palace courtyards and as heavenly manifestations in churches were the same technologies that enabled those ships to build political and economic empire: timber construction, rope suspension and complex rigging, huge areas of canvas framed with pulleys and ropes, beams, masts, spars, and counterweights. Lying at the heart of enabling the economic ambitions of the state and of justifying its conditions and goals, merchant-trading ships rapidly became ships of colonial achievement and conquest. Debord's reflection on contemporary spectacle (published in 1967) summarizes the tightness of the relationship between spectacle and political ambition:

In all its specific forms, as information or propaganda, as advertisement or direct entertainment consumption, the spectacle is the present model of socially dominant life …The spectacle's form and content are identically the total justification of the existing system's conditions and goals. (1983: I, 6)

Scenography was effectively born out of this union between technological and political display; indeed one might argue that by the middle of the 17th century the state form of the theatre festival had become Debord's 'present model of socially dominant life'. Its spectacles and its technologies were rapidly extended into the commercial marketplace of public theatres by European court patrons and the growing mercantile urban *squirearchy* who patterned their cultural values closely upon those of the courts and political power.

The content and theatrical forms of the 1589 Medici wedding developed an extended afterlife and provided the basis for a remarkable and long-lived globalization of theatre. All the scenes and machinery were carefully dismantled, inventoried and stored; costumes were catalogued, and archived; drawings and accounts were meticulously recorded. Technical components, and whole scenes were re-used many times over, and there are reports of elements of the 1589 wedding scenes being used throughout the 17th century.[4] The architectural form of the Uffizzi theatre, its performance practices, technologies and the cultural efficacy of the 1589 wedding became effectively commodified and dominated Western theatre practices for the next three centuries. In the same year as the wedding, for example, Vincenzo Scamozzi designed the *Teatro all'antica* for Vespasiano Gonzaga, the 1st Duke of Sabbioneta, which while tiny in comparison with the Uffizzi perfectly mirrored the Medici ambition in creating unified forms of architecture and spectacle as codified images of an ideal society. Giovanni Battista Aleotti undertook a similar challenge for the Duke of Parma and Piacenza, Ranuccio I, to create the Farnese Theatre in Parma in 1618, which additionally served to confirm Buontalenti's scenic technologies by constructing a permanent stage-house with a triumphal proscenium arch complete with the armorial bearings of the Duke as its framing symbol of ownership.

The artists and artisans needed to design, build and paint such theatrical events inevitably had numerous apprentices who travelled and shared their experience. For example, Inigo Jones made important trips to Italy at the end of the 16th century and again in 1613–1614, and on each occasion took detailed notes, bringing back to London quantities of material and literature relating to the Medici wedding. He met with Guilio Parigi who had been apprentice to Bernardo Buontalenti on the Wedding Festival designs, and many of his future masque designs for the Stuart Court in London bear witness to Florentine influences.[5] Costantino de' Servi, one of Jones's assistants, was among the many foreign artists and craft workers lured to work in England during the Italophile building boom that was underway in the early 17th century. In 1612, de' Servi wrote back to Italy asking a Medici secretary to send engravings and 'two or three books of inventions'[6] for various *intermedi* or other entertainments, for use in current commissions. Impressions of the spectacle of this 'socially dominant life' travelled as inexorably as the merchant ship and just as quickly required the concomitant social and aesthetic infrastructure.

But the core *new* technology that accelerated this afterlife and provided models of spectacle was the rapidly developing process of printing that enabled the widest possible distribution of ideas, aesthetic values and their technologies. There is an interesting parallel example here with the way in which the power of the printed image similarly 'globalized' (at least within a European context) the growth and development of the study of human anatomy through such major illustrated works as Andreas Vasalius's *De Humani Corporis Fabrica* (1543–1545). Costume designs, descriptions and illustrations of stage scenes accompanied by technical diagrams were engraved and many were distributed even before the performances took place.[7] Diaries, private folios of designs and post-production reflections were strategically distributed throughout Europe to advertise and celebrate the power and influence of the Medici and the Tuscan state, and in so doing they turned scenic technologies into highly desirable commodities. The skills of the scenic artist, costumier, mask-maker and lighting artist became as desirable within European courts as those of musicians and composers. The effects of this dispersal of scenography were considerable and long lasting as the Duchies of central Europe vied with each other throughout the 18th century to build their own state theatres and to use them as the focus of a decorated and a scenically politicized lifestyle.

The printed agents of this scenic commodification had begun before the Medici wedding with Sebastiano Serlio's *I sette libri dell'architettura* or *Tutte l'opere d'architettura et prospetiva* (1545), and was followed by Andrea Palladio's *I quattro libri dell' architettura* of 1570. Nicola Sabbattini's *Pratica di fabricar scene e machine ne' teatri* (1638) became a major source of stagecraft for the late masques of Inigo Jones and John Webb, and fed directly into English Restoration theatre practice. Joseph Furttenbach's *Architectura Recreationis* (1640) and *Architectura Privata* (1641) became standard sources and the influential *Apparati Scenici per il Teatro Nuovissimo dell'Opera* (1642) by Giacomo Torelli, the Venetian designer of opera, developed new stage technologies at the French court from the late 1640s. In all of these publications, the technologies that are applied to the stage are those of the merchant shipping fleets of Venice, Lisbon and the Netherlands. In London, Inigo Jones began a tradition that lasted well into the 19th century of drawing upon the skills of sailors as scenic riggers and technicians. Through the common materials of timber, canvas and rope and the shared skills of carpentry and rigging, scenic technology became codified and transferable from city to city and country to country, and the architecture and technical structure of the stage house acquired what might be thought of as a European standard format. By the last decades of the 17th century, a sophisticated network of theatrical knowledge, court theatres and international peripatetic scenic artists began to establish itself and illustrates Geminiano

Montanari's comment from his *Della moneta: Trattato mercantile* (1683): 'Intercourse between nations spans the whole globe to such an extent that one may almost say all the world is but a single city in which a permanent fair comprising all commodities is held' (cited in Rebellato 2009: 11). Mercantile empires and their trading networks and institutions, such as the East India Company, consolidated and dominated the slow transfer of power from 'the court' to 'the state' through the 18th century and scenography and associated spectacle followed this progress as theatres developed outside the courts, becoming larger and increasingly associated with the establishment of nation states and urban *gravitas*.[8]

One extended family serves to exemplify the commodified and globalizing process of scenography and theatre architecture that effectively resulted from the Florentine wedding. The descendants of the Florentine painter, Giovanni Maria Galli da Bibiena (1625–1665) dominated theatre architecture, stage technologies and scenic spectacle from the mid-17th century until the very end of the 18th century. In 1700, Francesco Galli Bibiena (1659–1739) designed a theatre in Vienna for Emperor Leopold I and was responsible for court spectacle, later designing theatres in Nancy, Verona and Rome. In 1708, his brother Ferdinando Galli Bibiena (1656–1743) organized the wedding festivities in Barcelona of Charles IV, then working on designs of scenery and decorations for court spectacle and opera in Vienna. Ferdinando's son Alessandro (1686–1748) designed the Court opera house at Mannheim. Alessandro's brother Guiseppe (1696–1757) took over from his father as chief designer and organizer of court festivities in Vienna and is noted for the publication of designs for the wedding of the Crown Prince of Poland (1740). In the same year, he published the influential *Architetture e prospettive*, which illustrated designs for court staging, alongside designs for cathedrals, spectacular funeral catafalques and monuments. Urns and arches, pillars and pediments took their place alongside theatre scenes as commodified, international aesthetic capital. With his younger brother Antonio (1700–1774) he designed theatres, scenes and festivities in Linz, Graz, Dresden, Bayreuth and Prague; from 1753, he was employed by Frederick the Great to design the iconography representing the new Prussian state. Antonio Galli Bibiena (1700–1774), Ferdinando's third son, designed the theatre in Bologna and also worked at the Hofburg court in Vienna. Francesco's son, Giovanni Carlo Galli Bibiena (1717–1760), designed the Royal Opera house in Lisbon. The last scenic artist of this remarkable family, Carlo Galli Bibiena (1728–1787) worked throughout Europe, including Germany, France, Austria and the Netherlands from 1746 to 1760; he also worked in London (1763), Naples (1772), Stockholm (1774), and St Petersburg (1778). Several Bibiena opera houses still grace the civic splendour of European cities, and with some modification, the Bibienas' international theatre architecture and their concomitant aesthetics travelled to the Theatre Royal, Bristol, designed by James Paty in 1766, and are even reflected at the tiny Richmond Theatre in North Yorkshire of 1788. Throughout almost 150 years of peripatetic scenographic practice in most of the courts and later the developing nation states of Europe, the Bibienas created an evolving paradigm of social spectacle. Their engravings served as models for the theatre, but they also served as manuals of decorative design that could provide the porticoes and friezes of the architect, the tombs of the funerary sculptor, or the arcades, follies and gazebos of the landscape gardener.

Notwithstanding the romantic aspirations and sensibilities occasioned by the inexorable transitions of political power from the court to the state during the late 18th century,[9] the globalization of theatre intensified through the 19th century with commercial theatre architecture, the stage house and its infrastructure of scenic technology becoming ever more dedicated to an interchangeable, and increasingly international scenographic approach;[10] artists would produce designs that scenic artisans could replicate on paint frames and in stage houses anywhere within the colonial Western world. By the middle of the 19th century, for example, forms of stage representation visibly demonstrated the 'civilizing' process of the new technologies of steam, gas and mineral mining, and industrial dominance of those technologies created the globalized empires of the period. Theatres in world cities become statements of civic authority and formed focal points in political geography. The location, spectacle and technologies of the Salle Garnier of the Paris Opéra (1875), for example, asserted both the civilizing values of culture and the authority and power of the state.[11] The architecture with its self-important foyers and places of display and social parade, along with the controlling panopticon view of the world offered by the stage, represented, as Debord suggests, a 'self-portrait of power in the epoch of its totalitarian management of the conditions of existence' (1983: I, 24).

Just as the 21st-century international mega-musical bursts out of the theatre into the marketing opportunities of associated merchandise and theme park attraction, so the scenographic technologies of the theatre of the 19th century expanded into the *paratheatrical* spectacles of museums, exhibitions and 'shows'. From the Great Exhibition in London of 1851, international exhibitions displayed new technologies alongside scenic representations of 'the "exoticism" of non-European cultures within a story of Europe inspired progress' (Rebellato 2009: 1). Exhibitions and world trade fairs continued to assert technological dominance, for example demonstrating the powers of electricity in transport and street-lighting during the early 20th century, thereby representing (and conquering) the world through *paratheatrical* means.[12]

But late in the 19th century, the new technology of electric light played a major part in the destruction of the scenographic language of 1589. The representations of the world that had been initiated in 1589 consisted of paint, costumes, sculpture, light and movement, and the overemphasis of any one of these could destroy the magical ability of the form to transport and immerse its spectator. The pulsing softness of tallow candlelight gently combined the seeming incompatibility of the three-dimensional performer alongside the painted 'reality' of their scenic environment. The steady glare of the electric light bulb provided a destructive overemphasis upon that incompatibility. The *relative* brilliance of early electric light exposed the artifice of the two-dimensional deconstruction of reality upon which the system was based: the three-dimensionality of the human actor, let alone three-dimensional furniture and sculpted properties began to look absurd. For three hundred years, light had, effectively, been painted upon the scene, but in the excitement of displaying the brilliance of a new technology, no scenic artist could paint a shadow as dark as that produced by the absence of light.

Mega-musicals and transnational entertainment

If electricity played a significant part in the destruction of a globalized theatre at the beginning of the 20th century, then it was the revolution in electronics towards the end of the century that produced a new globalization of theatre (globalization was now literal and stretched far beyond Europe and

North America). We might illustrate the early effects of this technological revolution through one invention that had a profound effect both on musical theatre and, eventually, the ability of cultural industries to commodify theatre product – the radio-microphone. Although invented in the late 1940s and used in a limited way during the 1960s, advances in technologies of miniaturization of microphones and transmitter packs made by companies such as Sennheisser, Telefunken and Sony, and improvements in frequency control during the early 1970s made its use in musical theatre widespread. By the end of the century, digital technologies produced DSP (Digital Signal Processing) that improved audio quality and provided sophisticated 'squelching' of background sounds such as footsteps and the rustling of costumes near the microphone, and frequency-hopping technologies that enabled the use of more easily accessible 2.4 GHz wavebands. Importantly for this discussion, the radio microphone enabled the performer to move away from the dominant point of projection at the front of the stage. The performer could whisper and be heard anywhere; the singer with a small voice could now be clearly heard. Alongside developments in the analogue technologies of amplifiers, mixers and loudspeakers, it became possible to replace cast members easily – the sound engineer could 'manufacture' vocal quality and merge the newcomer into the existing cast, voices being blended and heard through tuned and focused loudspeakers. In this way, through compound modulations of audio processing, the sounds of performance could be synthesized and accurately reproduced. By the late 1970s, the live, orchestral sound in the theatre was being compared unfavourably with the studio-engineered quality of the hi-fi long-playing disc, and tape cassette recordings, and by the mid-1980s, the emergence of digital optical audio through the compact disc. Theatres covered their orchestras, and music from live musicians was only heard through carefully focused loudspeakers. At the première performance of *Cats* in 1981 at the New London Theatre, the live orchestra was completely hidden from the audience, and their processed and manipulated sound was only heard through loudspeakers, thereby generating a distinctive break with the intimacy of an acoustic and scenographic space where the making of music is a visual as well as an auditory experience.

Neo-liberal political philosophy developed during the 1980s by the governments of Margaret Thatcher and Ronald Reagan proposed total freedom of movement for capital, goods and services, and argued that an unregulated market was the best way to increase economic growth. The globalization that was once built upon the technologies of the trading ship was now electronically reconstructed, becoming a form of digital 'post-colonial' neo-colonization. Alongside this political and economic thinking, the IBM PC 5150 (1981) represented the beginning of a parallel revolution in the ability of theatre to control and accurately reproduce states of stage lighting. Digital technologies using international equipment employing digital multiplex (DMX) communication protocols ensured that the lighting, projections and atmosphere experienced by an audience in London or New York could be comparable to those seen by an audience in Toronto or Malaysia – or wherever. Projected imagery has become an increasingly important ingredient of scenography and no longer relies upon photographic reproduction and analogue manipulation. Data projectors and the light emitting diode (LED) lamp have substantially replaced electric filament light sources. Computer-generated imagery (CGI) offers accurate and repeatable imagery – and importantly allows adjustment of the image to account for distortion enabling projectors to be conveniently placed.

Through these technologies two core and hitherto ephemeral components of performance, sound and light, can be recorded, manipulated, packaged and distributed globally. Within a timespan of little more than twenty-five years, sophisticated analogue and more recent digital technologies have permitted the performance experience to be effectively preserved, or 'cured' and prepared for transport globally. Performance spectaculars, such as *Les Misérables*, *The Phantom of the Opera*, *Miss Saigon*, *The Lion King*, or indeed New York's Metropolitan Opera 'live in cinemas worldwide', have become thoroughly globalized and form a central part of neoliberal unrestricted international capitalism. The presence of their branding and iconography in the shopping malls of the world is as ubiquitous as that of lifestyle fashion. Debord reminds us that 'concentrated spectacle belongs essentially to bureaucratic capitalism, though it may be imported as a technique of state power in mixed backward economies' (1983: III, 64). As such the mega-musical fits comfortably into the 'transnational entertainment corporation's marketing strategy' (Rebellato 2009: 46). As with similar international products, we are consistently constrained to bring to mind the brand images: the big eyed orphan, a cat's eyes, half a face-mask, an image combining a Japanese pictograph and a helicopter. No longer required, star performers form no part of the brand image, because, as Rebellato reminds us, 'in McTheatre even the biggest star is replaceable' (2009: 45). Néill O'Dwyer writes about 'the *hyper-acceleration* of processes of automation, which are now carried out, by virtue of digital electronics, at the speed of light. … Just as mechanical technological innovations found their way into the domain of art, so too now do those technologies of the cybernetic epoch along with their processes of light-speed calculation' (2015: 49). Digital interventions of light, projection, sound and computer-controlled automation serve to bind together world audiences within theatres, and through projected imagery on urban buildings and monuments within a theatrical metanarrative of stage technology and spectacular effects.

Long before the IBM PC, Walter Benjamin famously argued that the technologies of mechanical reproduction have a way of detaching the object that has been reproduced from its cultural context and tradition: '[b]y making reproductions it substitutes a plurality of copies for a unique existence' which in turn leads to 'the liquidation of the traditional value of the cultural heritage' (1992: 223). Rebellato cites Susan Russell, a former company member, who described her work: 'I was one of 37 workers who built the standard product of the *Phantom of the Opera* every night. My function was to replace the missing worker, accomplish their required task, and assemble a product without missing a beat, interrupting the flow, or disturbing the rest of the machine' (2009: 57).

Writing in 1967, Debord stated that authentic culture was being replaced by representation and he prefigured the pattern of cultural homogenization observed in contemporary globalized theatre and performance when he argued that the commodity and its image would totally colonize all forms of social life representing 'a social relation among people mediated by images' (1983: I, 4). 'It [spectacle] is the sun which never sets over the empire of modern passivity. It covers the entire surface of the world and bathes endlessly in its own glory' (1983: I, 13).

Scenographic extensions

The culturally destructive aspects of the globalization of theatre and performance are clearly evident and their effects are far reaching. However, it is significant to note that such effects are not unique to contemporary globalized theatre. John Gay's *The Beggar's Opera* (1728) and many of William Hogarth's satirical paintings and engravings mounted virulent attacks on the effects that the dominant spectacle of imported Italian aesthetics was having upon indigenous cultural forms of music, painting and performance practices. However, the digital and its cluster of associated technologies extend beyond the straightforward import/export of artistic product. Digital recording, archiving and streaming are generating new forms of ownership. Rustom Bharucha describes the way in which transnational media corporations may obtain rights to exploit for profit any piece of music, any image, any text they believe to have commercial potential. 'The consequence', he argues, will be that these corporations may become 'the exclusive owners of substantial pieces of artistic culture wherever in the world and thereby influence, perhaps even determine, the direction in which these cultures may develop' (2000: 22, citing personal correspondence with Joost Smiers in 1997).

Computer control of light, sound and scenic movement has enabled the free market to propagate its values and understanding of human interaction through spectacular theatre products. But at the same time these technologies, alongside the newer digital technologies of social media, are enabling the scenographic to explore new forms of theatre and community performance where there is a powerful ground-level resistance to the commoditizing, homogenizing and anti-democratic tendencies of globalization. New technologies are making and using theatre that actively challenges globalization, neo-colonial power and the control of international capital that it reflects. The digital – computer/mobile technology, the Internet and the smart phone – has become globally accessible with remarkable speed and offers new image and spectacle-making capabilities. But if the technology has been democratized, then so too has the ownership of the image: a YouTube posting can have the access hitherto enjoyed solely by the industrial film-maker. As recently as 2000 Bharucha considered political struggle using the digital technologies of cyberspace as little more than 'the voyeuristic stance of a privileged global intelligentsia, who can afford to surf the possibilities of resistance transmitted from the troublespots of the Third World' (2000: 149). He cautions that in many indigenous communities the availability of electricity should condition any sense of 'activist euphoria' (2000). Furthermore he suggests that regretting the globalizing impact of the digital upon the mainstream musical while simultaneously applauding new extensions of the scenographic facilitated by global access to the digital may produce what Bharucha calls 'cultural schizophrenia'. Nevertheless, it is a distinctive quality of developing technologies that what may simultaneously produce cultural destruction may also serve to produce forms of cultural regeneration.

Within the last decade, there is sufficient new work being displayed at successive editions of performance design exhibitions at, for example, the Prague Quadrennials, to suggest that digital interventions within performance making and the infrastructural provision of digital resources for research, analysis, archiving and communication are having very significant effects upon the theory and practices of scenography. New forms of scenography and performance design (the terms are significantly almost synonymous) serve both to challenge our traditional understanding of the terms of theatre design and designer and to challenge the globalizing power of the capitalist economy. I have introduced this topic and described several examples of activist performance where scenography and its use of the digital has served to create scenography as the dramaturgy of performance (Baugh 2013: 223–244). In the context of this chapter, I want to identify four 'extensions' of the scenographic that, for the greater part, directly benefit or result from digital technologies.

Scenography challenging the architectures of theatre

'Find a play. Squat a building. Steal a van. Now make a show' (Bradwell 2010). Sophisticated digital sound and light systems can exist without their being integrated within the fabric of an architectural infrastructure, thereby either allowing existing theatres to radically re-formulate their performance space, or to create performance space outwith theatre architecture all together. In this way, scenography is expanding through its rejection of the formal architecture of the theatre building. Challenging the spatial relationship between stage and audience is not of course, a new development and has been a recurring energy inspiring new theatre for over a hundred years. What is new is both the scale and ubiquity of this rejection, and additionally there seems to be a parallel rejection of the institutional establishment of theatre: the expense of maintaining and servicing high-tech buildings and their staff, and the large number of events directors, project coordinators, development managers, diversity consultants and marketing staff which the complexity of funding, sponsorship and the self-inflated apparatus of the cultural industries sector have generated.

Rejection of formal theatre architecture might, for example, involve scenographer Miriam Buether reconstructing the Young Vic Theatre in London and turning it into a court room for Kafka's *The Trial* (July 2015) or working with Sasha Wares on *Game* by Mike Bartlett at the Almeida Theatre, London (March 2015). For this, the auditorium was re-formed by dividing the audience into four 'voyeuristic' groups, each located in camouflaged 'hides' that shared 'surveillance' into the 'playing' game space. Action was also experienced via TV monitors, and headphones relayed voice-simulated instructions to the actors and live-feed dialogue. But there are more radical alternatives to the infrastructural and institutional challenges of permanent theatre architecture. Since 2010, Kneehigh Theatre have designed and developed 'The Asylum' in rural Cornwall, aiming to create what the company calls a 'flexible nomadic structure'.[13] The scenography of this is not primarily determined by the current play or performance project but responds to a sophisticated ambition to re-design the complete experience of theatre combining food, drink, music, escape, sanctuary, magic – and performance. The building combines two geodesic sections linked by a tented section; but the whole embraces a technically sophisticated environment of light and sound made possible by the flexibility of portable digital equipment.

Digital access to information about alternative design and building technologies enabled the community at Žilina-Záriečie in Slovakia to self-build the S2 Cultural Centre and theatre space beneath a motorway (see Baugh 2013: 238–239). In an attempt to assert self-sufficiency, the community project consciously avoided hi-tech building methods, maintenance and running costs by using donated plastic beer crates, straw-bale building technology and recycling a steel container to serve as a foyer. In this ironic way, the digital has revolutionized traditional practices of making theatre.

On-site scenography

The rejection of permanent theatre architectures and, in many cases, associations of institutional infrastructure almost inevitably leads to an expansion of interventions of on-site scenography. Site-specific performance has, perhaps, been most frequently associated with the making of performances that interrogate and 'unfold', as Heddon suggests (2008: 90), the biographies and autobiographies, both geographical and industrial, of their relationships with local communities. Access to the research resources of the Internet and the increasing facility of using sophisticated sound and lighting outdoors alongside developing awareness of the social efficacy of acts of shared performance significantly facilitates such work as a vehicle for remembering and (re) forming communities. As Harvie suggests, its efficacy can rest in the manner in which 'location can work as a potent mnemonic trigger, helping to evoke specific past times related to the place and time of performance and facilitating a negotiation between the meanings of those times' (2005: 42). The digital allows a new degree of flexibility to performance in and around a site with challenges to vision and hearing being explored through data projection, monitor screens and focused loudspeakers or headphones.

Simon McBurney of Complicité experimented with narrative form in *The Encounter* (Edinburgh, Conference Centre, August 2015) through an examination of identity and colonization occasioned by the contact of photojournalist Loren Mcintyre with the Mayoruna tribe of the Amazon. McBurney directly introduced his audience to the technology that he would use and demonstrated its capability. He performed to an audience wearing headphones, visibly controlling sound himself and using pedal loops to process the sound of the characters that he performed. The digital enhanced the reality of performance, but crucially also served as a direct critique of the effects of technology on indigenous communities facing deforestation and industrial colonization. Use of headphones and their ability to generate a very particular and focused sense of presence and relationship with performance is, at this time, an emergent and exciting expansion of the scenographic.

From the completion of the first continuous segment in 2003 until the present time a barrier, 'a security wall' of concrete blocks has divided Jerusalem, separating the Israeli West Bank from Palestinian East Jerusalem. Since then this barbaric wall has been the scene of a number of performance events that have focused upon the enforced separation between communities. Musicians perform on one side of the wall to an audience sitting on the other side. Timpani exchange rhythms across the divided space. Small holes designed to allow machinery to lift the concrete blocks have provided opportunity for microphones and cables to technically link communities. Musicians have conducted other musicians via TV link on the other side of the wall. In April 2008, Merlijn Twaalfhoven and fellow musicians created *Carried by the Wind*, a project that involved amateur and professional musicians from Ramallah and Bethlehem with children from Palestinian refugee camps. The project culminated with a concert of music performed from rooftops and balconies, across this wall of 'security'. Mobile phones enabled the communication necessary to bring the performers together in musical conjunction and to (re)unite divided communities (see Twaalfhoven 2008 and Dorita Hannah's chapter in this volume).

Scenographic activism

Scenography is extending its engagement with personal and community histories through the web: scenographic activism and practices have become an especially vivid part of movements for art and social change. Technologies can facilitate a wide range of interactive dialogues through digital media and, through the Internet, provide access to huge resources of information that can become available to disparate community groups, offering a virtual space of performance. YouTube and Vimeo allow for the recording, sharing and archiving of performance and personal narratives, and the design and making of web pages may serve as a record of a project achieved. The process may involve a bringing together of professional artists to work alongside indigenous artists and their communities. Traditions of performance, diurnal rituals and practices may be extended and celebrated by participants, which through traditional forms serve to enrich and empower the community. Nevertheless, Rebellato rightly warns against a form of cynical appropriation in which the artist, privileged by education and perhaps by nationality, might descend upon an indigenous community and exploit a culture by 'mining' aspects of local art practices and ' transporting them to the fringe venues of western cities, or using them as the creative basis for their own performance art' (2009: 53). Nonetheless, there are many examples of successful and politically provocative projects that have worked to make interventions that disturb everyday life, and where eventual efficacy lies in the ability to empower participant and spectator. Companies such as Mexico's Teatro OJO, Brazil's Teatro de Vertigem and the UK's Louise Ann Wilson Co. invite spectators as participants to re-experience the familiar – derelict districts, old buildings with significant political histories, moorland space, urban environments de-natured by globalized industrialization – considering identity, nationhood and the challenges of 'official history'. Dramaturgical structure frequently takes the form of a journey through scenographically mediated space and artists such as the UK's Blast Theory, or Dutch scenographers, Lena Müller, Roos van Geffen, Theun Mosk and Marlocke van der Vlugt, use portable computers or smart phones to serve as guides for the journey. The community in performance becomes inseparably participant, attendant and audience (see Baugh 2013: 235–237).

Scenography as research

In many ways, however, the most significant expansion and the most radical re-visioning of practice has been the conjoining over the last decade of scenography with academic research and scholarly enquiry. The *process* of the scenographic has become a methodology of research. Research, of course, has always formed part of the artistic process – whether studying 19th-century tailors' patterns for costume construction, or researching manufacturers to locate the right material to fulfil a particular scenic requirement. Academic research however goes beyond the straightforward 'finding out of information' to the search for new knowledge and insights. This conjoining with research represents an inevitable confrontation brought about by major changes in scenographer training that has migrated from the art college 'conservatoire', to become a subject of study within university faculties of arts. The 'conservatoire' tends to have, at the core of training, a comprehensive body of artistic assumptions and the technical skills of practical realization: a coherent understanding of 'the profession' for which it prepares its students. The universities, on the other hand, tend towards historical contextualization and theoretical underpinning of theatre and performance studies as a whole, with a particular focus, in pedagogy and in practice, on what might be called a *Gesamtkunstwerk* articulation of the act of theatre and performance: one that understands performance as a bringing together of all the qualities of acting, text, sound, costume and the visual – to make a time and site-specific artistic collaboration with an audience.

This inclusive comprehensiveness of practices has further removed scenography training from the conservatoire-like acquisition of precise skills for professional practice, and set it firmly within the questing, exploratory environment of research-led higher education. The impetus to 'do scenography' is no longer assumed to focus primarily on the interpretation of dramatic literature – designing a play. More frequently it will focus upon a research question, or series of questions for which, within the context of existing explorations of similar questions, the scenographic suggests a methodology of approach. Digital technologies and their interventions in performance are significant drivers of scenographic research, and they will certainly provide academic methodology in the acquisition of data, archiving, reporting and analysis of research. The researcher may use the encompassing breadth of the scenographic in order to explore questions embracing the entire range of the experience of performance.

Universities throughout the world have, for purposes of creating criteria for assessment and, in some countries for the external assessment of the quality of research by funding agencies, formed definitions of research in order to reinforce the forward-looking and innovative qualities of 'pure' scholarly research; and, to distinguish this from the practical 'research' undertaken, for example, when buying a new car or an item of domestic technology. Most articulations have a twin focus: upon research being a *process* of investigation, and one leading to new insights or understandings.[14] The need to share the insights of research effectively has been more recently added. What is now shared as a result of scenographic research may be the ongoing process of investigation: frequently a process for which the term 'scenographic performance' is appropriate.

Digital technologies frequently lie at the heart of methodologies of scenographic research. For example, they have particularly inspired and led research into questions of appearance, reality and 'the virtual' – the *unheimlich*[15] or the uncanny nature of human perception, into philosophical questions concerning the nature of human cognition and consciousness. Studies based upon data analysis have used scenographies to create metaphors of ecology and environmental change and to examine relationships between humanity and sites of living; and provocations have interrogated the political, economic and social effects of global economics upon indigenous cultures and performance practices. From early experiments with computer notation during the 1990s, research into choreography and dance practice has been, effectively, a product of digital technologies. Computers have transformed the way in which researchers and practitioners think about embodiment and presence and have experimented with software that can notate, sample, capture, synthesize, animate, choreograph and visualize dance movement.

Arjun Appadurai suggested the potential of such artistic research when he claimed that the 'imagination has become an original field of social practices, a form of work (in the sense of both labour and culturally organized practice), and a form of negotiation between sites of agency (individuals) and globally defined fields of possibility' (1997: 31). New modes and extensions of scenographic practice may accordingly be as extensive as the questions of research are immeasurable.

Conclusion

The first globalization of theatre used the technologies of the merchant shipping fleets of economic and political power. Theatre practices of timber, canvas, paint and counterweighted rope-craft were developed that, with inevitable shifts and developments, persisted until the close of the 19th century. The second globalization of theatre was initiated by the computing power that simultaneously created the global market-place of unrestricted economies. Understandings of the scenographic can accommodate the spectacle of an Olympic opening ceremony, illuminated public buildings or a globalized Mega-Musical, alongside a performance walk through a city guided by sound scenography and smart 'phone'. It can embrace the focused attention of a large, formally structured audience sitting within permanent theatre architecture, the immersive attention of an audience wearing headphones in a studio space, or the intimacy of personal performance in a living room. Contemporary extensions of scenography and its more recent accommodation within methodologies of research have increased its potential for engaging with humanity outside the traditional confines of dramatic literature and the architectural infrastructure of theatre buildings. While political and economic power maintains its control of institutional global spectacle, affordability and access to digital technologies have generated remarkable opportunities that not only affect communication but also in many exciting and provocative ways extend and reconfigure human creativity – and resistance.

Notes

1 Richard Wagner used this term in his 1849 essay 'The artwork of the future' (*Das Kunstwerk der Zukunft*) to describe his vision of an artwork that combined music, poetry, performance and the visual arts. The idea of bringing together multiple art forms that achieve a unity through an act of performance has made the term especially useful in developing an understanding of scenography.

2 The most comprehensive account of the 1589 wedding is in James M. Saslow (1996). However, the more detailed theatrical focus of A. M. Nagler (1964) is still valuable in *Theatre Festivals of the Medici, 1539–1637*. Two major works by Roy Strong (1973, 1984) examine the topic globally.

3 Bastiano (1589, cited in Saslow 1996: 151). The 'artificer' was Bernardo Buontalenti who was ensconced in a windowed control booth located beneath the raked audience *gradi*.

4 See especially the account in Saslow (1996: 174–188).

5 See Peacock (1995: especially 188–201) where Jones's 'Florentine patterns' are considered.

6 See Saslow (1996:184–185).

7 The 1589 wedding effectively invented the souvenir programme.

8 Consider the way in which in 1741 Frederick the Great commissioned Georg von Knobelsdorff to design a neo-Palladian public opera house for Berlin to help establish its position as a sober, neo-classical and patrician capitol city. See Blanning (2002), especially the chapter 'The rise of the nation', 185–265.

9 I consider the transition of cultural power from the courts to the state in Baugh (2012: 33–54).

10 A first-hand account of the architectural and technical resource of the fully developed mid-19th-century stage house can be found in Moynet (2016).

11 The social and political implications of the architectures of theatres and especially their frequently strategic urban locations are the main focus of Marvin Carlson's *Places of Performance* (1989). More generally on the use of cultural forms establishing the transition from court to nation, see Blanning (2002), Part II – 'The rise of the public sphere', 103–184.

12 I consider the complexity of the scenographic language of the 19th century and its demise/transformation in Baugh (2013: 11–31).

13 Kneehigh Theatre Company. www.kneehigh.co.uk/ (accessed 12 August 2015).

14 The UK Research Excellence Framework REF2014 defined research for its purposes as 'a process of investigation leading to new insights effectively shared'. Higher Education Funding Council for England (September 2009: 38).

15 *Unheimlich* literally 'unhomely' or the opposite of what is familiar. In 2005 and again in 2006 Steve Dixon named a telematic performance *Unheimlich* that connected performers and audiences virtually in Boston, USA, and in London.

2

Scenographic Screen Space: Bearing Witness and Performing Resistance

Dorita Hannah

> *Space is not one, but space is plural, a heterogeneity, a difference.*
> DANIEL LIBESKIND, 'THE END OF SPACE'

In her 1987 essay 'The Place of Crime the Place of Pardon', French philosopher and playwright Hélène Cixous wrote:

> In truth we go as little to the theatre as to our heart and what we feel the lack of is going to the heart, our own and that of things. We live exterior to ourselves in a world whose walls are replaced by television screens, which has lost its thickness, its depths, its treasures, and we take the newspaper columns for our thoughts. We are printed daily. We lack even walls, true walls upon which divine messages are written. We lack earth and flesh. (1995: 341)

Although Cixous maintained that our mediated existence was diminishing lived space to a point where we lack the material communality critical for confronting the horrors of this world, she posited the theatre as a place for remedying such etiolation via the substance of earth (stage), flesh (bodies) and true walls (architecture): a site in which to gather and, through storytelling, mutually contact the compassion required to acknowledge, forgive and actively move forward. Three decades on, live performance is still capable of providing a restorative site for re-enacting traumatic events that continue to be played out on the world stage through global media. However, newspaper columns have been replaced by the increasingly perfected thinness of glowing screens – in our hands, on our desks and in the built environment – and theatre has generally left the building; not only challenging screen space but reconfiguring performance space itself as a dispersed multiplicity.[1]

Acknowledging that media has always been a part of theatre, this chapter reflects on how the performative screen can scenographically operate alongside theatre's earth, flesh and true walls, as a spatial, social and politicized element for practising artists, designers and performance-makers to critique and engage with the pervasive geo-cultural, geo-mythical and geo-political issues of our time. No longer the planar surface upon which light, still and moving images are 'thrown', the screen has become an extension of the body and lived space as well as a contemporary site for reiterating and/or challenging worldviews: inside and outside theatre's proper sites. More critical to this chapter, it has also become the means for an embodied bearing witness in performance, collapsing time and place to reveal what Cixous calls '[t]he enigma of human cruelty, that of others and my own' (1995: 342).

Like the word 'design', 'screen' is both verb and noun: action and object. Linked to Elin Diamond's definition of *performance* as 'a risky and dangerous negotiation between a doing … and a thing done' (1996: 5), the *screen* – a fixed or movable plane that simultaneously divides and connects, reveals and conceals, upon which images and data are displayed and filtered – presents a powerful concept for scenographic performativity: especially in our highly mediated world streaming information 24/7 via smart phones, tablets, televisions, computer monitors, slideshow presentations and architectural facades; but also where bodies themselves (both visceral and virtual) are screened to vet who's in and who's out. This scrutinization is generally taken for granted in a post-Snowden world where a seemingly unending 'war on terror' sanctions invasion of personal space via surveillance to which an entire generation has generally submitted.[2] However, while the daily lives of socially networked citizens are transmitted, intercepted and controlled, there are those trying to cross borders and escape hardship for whom such monitoring is much more problematic. Exceeding cinema and television, screen space has also transcended the physical object and occupies our posthuman consciousness. What does this mean for the design of live performance? Questioning theatre's predication on 'liveness' in his essay, 'The Power of Space in a Virtual World', Arnold Aronson asks: 'Is it possible that we are also in a post-dimensional, post-spatial world in which scenographic concepts must be radically rethought? Can virtual space or non-dimensional space have power?' (2008: 29).

Preamble: Chairs, screens and troubling scenes

As a performance design scholar, investigating spatial performativity generally and performance space specifically, my tendency has been to make theoretical sense of elements in the theatre that one's own creative practice eschews, such as the proscenium arch, black box studio, projection screen and neatly organized rows of fixed seating. Having established philosophical and artistic reasons for circumventing these spaces, objects and technologies, it's intriguing to consider why they proliferate and endure. While many of last century's avant-garde artists and critics railed against these elements for their role in foreclosing on more fully embodied spatial participation within the live event – predicated on the performed visceral moment rather than a contained, technologically orchestrated image – it seems misplaced to foreclose on the potential contribution of any scenographic apparatus, as an effective micro-event within the meta-event of the received performance. The enclosed black box stage house persisting as the proscenium theatre – dependent on the frame, darkness and frontality – continues to house transformative moments for the 'emancipated spectator' (Rancière 2011)[3] seated in the auditorium, fulfilling Richard Wagner's 150-year-old objective to concentrate the view on a circumscribed and transcendent artwork.[4] Such scopic prowess is evidenced in the compelling interdisciplinary performances created by contemporary artists such as Robert Lepage (*Needles and Opium*, 1991–1992, 2013, 2015), Heiner Goebbels (*Eraritjaritjaka*, 2004–2014), The Builder's Association (*Super Vision*, 2005–2007) and Adrien M/Claire B (*Le Mouvement de l'air*, 2015): renowned creators whose productions effectively and poetically integrate live performance and projection.

However, this chapter's meditation on the active role played by the screen within an expanded notion of scenography begins by way of another element inherent to conventional theatre: the chair; adopted by the Prague Quadrennial of Performance Design and Space as a leitmotif for its 2015 global gathering. Proliferating on posters, postcards and catalogues, a range of globally familiar and seemingly prosaic sky blue chairs also featured as way-finding objects in the city; bolted to walls, hovering over doorways, sculpted as intersecting multiples and appearing via rogue seats in café courtyards. This iconic object was most effectively utilized in the various halls that held PQ's gatherings, lectures and presentations: not as an identical element locked together in rows but as a distribution of found objects; varying in design, size, colour and comfort. Nowhere was it more lyrically employed than in the splendid oval ballroom of the Colloredo-Mansfeld Palace. Set within curving marble walls, below baroque frescoes surrounding a giant central chandelier, lay a scattering of 150 chairs, cheaply sourced to present a landscape of body-objects promising to hold us up while we listened to guests from around the world. The extraordinary gesture of this hodgepodge collection, created by Wales-based designers Simon Banham and Richard Downing, was most successful when it resisted ordered organization, instead allowing the occupants to face any direction they chose: facilitated by the employment of projections upon the room's four chamfered corners: two diagonally opposite screens showing still and moving images and the other two projecting live feed of presenters and spectators. Through a de-centred view, the chair (and therefore the seated spectator) became untethered, mobile and individualized within a simultaneously unified and distributed assembly.

This multi-screen site hosted PQ's *Theory Talks*, themed on the *Scenographic Screen*, which I curated and introduced on the first of three days by referring to perhaps the most globally ubiquitous chair: the white stackable moulded-plastic seat found on all continents: in houses, parks, cafés, roadsides, beaches and public squares. I showed images of a hillside in Israel that, in July 2014, was arranged with these chairs to establish an improvised amphitheatre that faced the walled-in Gaza Strip upon which bombs were falling and lighting up a sky shared by both sides of the divide. This event, which lasted some days, was first reported on 9 July by Danish journalist, Allan Sørensen, who, while other international reporters present trained their cameras towards Gaza, tweeted an image from his camera phone of the gathering crowd with the accompanying text: 'Sderot cinema' Israelis bringing chairs 2 hilltop in sderot 2 watch latest from Gaza. Clapping when blasts are heard' (*sic*) (9 July 2014). Nikolaj Krak, Sørensen's colleague from Denmark's *Kristeligt Dagblad* newspaper, later reported that the event, which attracted 'more than 50 people' … turned the hill into something that resembles 'the front row of a reality war theatre' (11 July 2014). Such blurring of the boundaries between reality and spectacle was reinforced that evening by Sørensen who in a later tweet observed: 'Some described it as a best reality show in town. Others said it is better than the world cup [sic]' (11 July 2014). Meanwhile, on the other side of the divide, the missiles lighting the night sky killed nine young men on a Gaza beach who happened to be watching a World Cup football match on a television powered by a generator in a makeshift café, leaving twisted wreckage that included mangled remains of the same moulded-plastic chairs found gathering on the Sderot hillside.

Referred to as the 'Sderot Cinema', this improvised auditorium, which later augmented the plastic chairs with couches, cars, crates and coffee machines, co-opted the site it faced as a screen upon which live military attacks were played out as a macabre performance.[5] The border, only a kilometre away, was virtually transformed into an epic vertical surface that rendered the real-time bombardment as projected moving images with accompanying sound effects. Through such a highly mediated and deeply problematic event, we are confronted with the blurring of boundaries between performance and everyday life as well as the complex multiplicity of space in an-ever-extending field around the performing arts.

Manifestations such as the 'Sderot Cinema', where catastrophic events are aestheticized through improvised gatherings, cause one to wonder at a world that, as theorist Jon McKenzie states, 'has become a designed environment in which an array of global performances unfold' (2008: 128). In his essay on 'Global Feeling', McKenzie suggests that the complexity of our contemporary condition, folding grand narratives, theatricality and the everyday into each other, could be understood through the discursive tool of 'performance design' (2008: 176). As an expanded notion of scenography – comprising political as well as aesthetic acts – performance design is here posited as a discursive undertaking capable of exposing, critiquing and reimagining designed actions and events that proliferate locally and globally. Phenomena like the 'Sderot Cinema', which fall out of the performing arts while referring to its practices, illustrate how screen space is no longer limited to the surfaces receiving and streaming analogue and digital imagery.

What therefore follows is a discussion of how performance design, established as a mode of analysis and practice of making, offers a scenographic strategy for evaluating and utilizing the ubiquitous screen in relation to the role it plays within and without cultural venues such as galleries, museums and theatres. Performance design is proffered as one approach to expanding scenography as a critical tool, employed to creatively harness the dynamic forces in our mediated reality via the orchestrated 'event'. Those whose work I particularly focus on are Toneelgroep Amsterdam (*Roman Tragedies,* premiere 2007), Rimini Protokoll (*Situation Rooms,* premiere 2013), Omar and Osman Khan (*SEEN: Fruits of Our Labour,* 2006) and Artists Without Walls (*The Transparent Wall,* 2004), all who employ screens and render chairs contingent, mobile or redundant. Moving from the most recent productions still on a touring circuit of festivals to more minimal interventions in public space created over a decade ago, these works are discussed in relation to several themes including: intermediality as a development of multimediality; 'double-looking' and therefore 'double-shooting' by way of Rabih Mroué's 'pixelated revolution'; posthuman materialism and its relation to the screen as object; and, linking them all, empathic engagement through the screen's spatial multiplicity, determined by a mobile spectator, no longer bound to the fixed chair in a darkened auditorium.

Performance design as a mediated model
for scenography expanded

As an inherently multimedial practice – combining words, images and sounds into a unified event – theatre has always embraced the virtual through varying fields of skill that enfold mutable spatiotemporal imaginings into the staged reality. This allows the presencing of gods and ghosts, as well as 'other' peoples, places and times; often facilitated by scenography's technological devices producing a fall of light, resonant sound, moving air, flickering images – parallel realities generated through smoke and mirrors over centuries. However, live performance and its reception is not only embedded in conventional theatre with its consecrated texts, familiar architectural features and customary spatial relationships but is also moving into areas of intermedial practice. Robin Nelson maintains viewers of live performance no longer gaze at, but engage with, varying media: both 'present within' and 'aware of' their role and impact (2006: 139). This cognizance of an inter-play is inline with Chiel Kattenbelt's reference to the 'correlational' nature of intermediality (2008), which is 'more closely connected to the idea of diversity, discrepancy and hypermediacy' rather than 'unity, harmony and transparency' (2008: 21)[6], thereby replacing multimediality's homogeneity with a more dynamic, irruptive and heterogeneous inter-action between media.

Less than two decades after Cixous' comment on media-saturation, Arnold Aronson acknowledges intermedial incongruity by asking 'Can Theatre and Media Speak the Same Language?', explicating that 'the problem of film and video projection in the theatre is a result of the essentially painterly qualities of those media that clash with the unique scenographic qualities of live theatre' (2005: 5). This problematic conflict between two inherently diverse languages – the immateriality of projected imagery and the physicality of the performing body within a material environment – primarily challenges Modernist theatre's emphasis on Naturalism and mimesis, which the opposing historical avant-garde had already confronted and overcome by celebrating theatre as a hybrid assemblage of oppositions and dislocations: thereby signalling the end of scenography's 300-year history of painted perspectival scenery standing in for the real.[7] Running counter to modernism's persistence with realism – one that tended to mimetically integrate the painterly within three-dimensional scenography – was postmodernism's exploration of conflicting languages; dissolving borders, intersecting art forms and exposing mechanisms. In their effort to build a new world from the ruins of the old, post-revolutionary Russian Constructivists had already embraced new technologies on- and offstage with architectures and events that brought together the fact of the built environment with the fiction of cinema: evidenced in their assemblages – embedded with projection surfaces and designed to be set up in theatres as well as on the streets – including proposed buildings such as Vladimir Tatlin's *Tower to the Third International* of 1920, which anticipated projecting manifestos onto the passing atmospherics of the night sky. However, it was the second-wave avant-garde that signalled mediation as an inherent quality of our lived world, no longer an-other language but something embedded within the spectacle of our quotidian existence: notably described by Guy Debord in 1967 as 'not a collection of images, but a social relation among people, mediated by images' (1983: 2).

This inherent intermediation led to *Postdramatic Theatre*, predicated on what Hans-Thies Lehmann calls the 'caesura of the media society' (2006: 22), in which scenography plays a leading role as 'visual dramaturgy' (2006: 93), allowing artists and designers to question what Slavoj Žižek calls 'virtualization of our daily lives, the experience that we are living more and more in an artificially constructed universe' (2002: 19). Unable to keep the mediated exterior world at bay, even after switching off our mobile phones, we find ourselves embedded in a world of multiple overlapping performances that upstage conventional drama. Whether or not technology is employed on stage, everything is read in relation to the reality of a highly mediatized and performative existence: reinforced by Jon McKenzie's claim, in *Perform or Else: From Discipline to Performance*, that 'performance' has become our time's 'onto-historical foundation of power and knowledge' (2001: 18). No longer referring to aesthetically rehearsed productions, performance includes the cultural, operational and technological expectations of human actions, objects and environments that are manageable, measurable and appraisable. By performing (or else) our identities are formed and reinforced through iterative socialized behaviour with reality generally constructed and received via the complex orchestration of globally communicated socio-political events. This calls into question the venues designed to contain aesthetic performances, incapable of keeping our mediated reality at bay. As Aronson rhetorically asks in a more recent meditation on mediated performance, 'Is it possible that we are also in a post-dimensional, post-spatial world in which scenographic concepts must be radically rethought? Can virtual space or non-dimensional space have power?' (2012: 15). Yet the radical shifts in space-time perception that occurred over the twenty years between Cixous' plea for a grounded experience and Aronson's suggestion of post-spatiality have since developed and intensified exponentially within the last decade, so we can no longer separate theatrical performances from those occurring at varying magnitudes in our daily lives. Responding to this intertwinement of viscerality and virtuality, scenographic concepts are not only being drastically rethought but also discursively enacted.

Performance design, expanding scenography's definition and reach, establishes environments through which actions develop and multiply beyond any physical or virtual frame. Operating as a dispersed performance field it recognizes that space (immediate and distant, singular and multiple) preceding action – as action – is culturally and politically loaded. Performance designers are therefore active agents – artists, provocateurs, collaborators, activists and socio-political commentators – whose 'designs', as inventive, performative proposals, are inter-medial and inter-textual spatiotemporal orchestrations. Through an aesthetic 'acting out' – outside the proper roles of design and theatre's sanctioned sites – performance design is no longer located solely in the performing arts. Also informing spatial and visual arts practices, it enables a critique of the manifold performances in our daily lives and on the global stages of culture and politics. This reinforces the claim of architect Daniel Libeskind that '[s]pace is not one, but space is plural, a heterogeneity, a difference' (Libeskind 2000: 68).

The messy interface between mass media as channels of global communication and the attendant irreality of the catastrophes they convey – witnessed through events such as the Sderot Cinema – is something many artists are currently engaging with via their transversal practices. Harnessing the arts to critique contemporary politics they show that although technology may have advanced – allowing us to destroy more in less time and from greater distances – the human animal has continually manipulated power and desire to destroy societal and biological ecologies while waging perpetual war. William Shakespeare's 500-year-old political dramaturgy on wars past and present remains valid today and, since 2007, Dutch theatre company, Toneelgroep Amsterdam, has mobilized over fifty cast and crew to stage three history plays within one event, performed at international festivals in conventional proscenium venues. *Roman Tragedies*, a technologically and visually complex six-hour-long production, is dominated by a media storm, which includes war reports, scrolling information, close-ups, live-streaming, screenshots, social commentary, rules of engagement, countdowns to events and security warnings: mediated action that is bracketed by an introductory invitation to leave your phones on and the final list of questions, projected above the stage as credits, asking a departing audience about freedom, principles, reason, power and honour.

Roman Tragedies

Shakespeare's *Coriolanus*, *Julius Caesar* and *Antony and Cleopatra* were adapted and amalgamated into *Roman Tragedies* (Figure 2.1) under the successful partnership of director Ivo Van Hove and his long-term collaborator Jan Versweyveld, whose innovative design is predicated on the lack of necessity to remain in our seats over the six-hour duration. Instead the audience in the auditorium is invited to occupy the stage where video monitors, distributed amidst bland corporate furniture, show live action subtitled in the language of each hosting country. Technicians hover and camera operators move discreetly about, following the action of performers embedded within the onstage spectators who eat, drink and use their phones to record the show or communicate through social media (some of their texts returning as streaming data on the *news ticker* above). While a series of clocks show the current time in various world centres, cameras and microphones are constantly mobilized to record the highs and lows of politics, power and desire being played out by the leaders, officials and lovers whose actions are as relevant today as they were in ancient Rome or Elizabethan London. Pre-recorded footage and streaming LED texts intermix with dramatic action while real-time world events enter the auditorium. The mediated stage briefly spills out onto the street when Caesar is chased from the theatre pursued by his rivals and cameramen: exposing an unsuspecting public to violent action, which, difficult to differentiate as real or staged, is projected back onto the multiple onstage monitors and the large proscenium screen that faces the auditorium. Reviewing *Roman Tragedies*' 2009 iteration in London, *Guardian* critic Lyn Gardner wrote:

> We the audience are part of this performance. We both watch the play and we are in the play, invited on to the stage to loll on the sofas, check our email on the computers or buy a drink from the on-stage bar. We are the nameless citizens of Rome; we are implicated in the action. (21 November 2009)

Roman Tragedies' fragmented, multimodal production refers directly to ubiquitous news networks – such as BBC, CNN and Al Jazeera – that beam political conventions, press conferences, global politics, neoliberal agendas and celebrity affairs into our homes, hotel rooms, airport waiting rooms and urban sites. Here design 'acts out' on an ever-shifting trajectory between conventionally staged scenography and the provocative actuality of events in public space. Versweyveld states: 'What interests me is to create a new stage reality that is not an illusion or illustration. Everything

FIGURE 2.1 *Roman Tragedies:* Toneelgroep Amsterdam (Jan Versweyveld).

you see on stage is real and present … you see bars, TVs, cables and the technology…. We are here together, now, not in Rome or Alexandria' (2014).

As a 'living organism' (Versweyveld 2014), the streaming text from world news and social media is absolutely specific to the time and place of each performance. Interweaving the play's events with current affairs and audience responses, the harsh reality of continual conflict and political struggles is brought directly into the theatre. Throughout the decade *Roman Tragedies* has been touring, geopolitical clashes have come and gone in the world, while some are still being played out on the global stage in the never-ending theatre of war. The spectators who restlessly move between stage and auditorium are as at home as one would be in the anonymous space of a hotel conference centre: in transit they become part of the performance and therefore complicit as history's bystanders. The audience itself initiated the inclusion of social media commentary during the 2009 London run and this became an incorporated feature. Versweyveld's highly mediated performance landscape of many intersecting texts (visual, aural, written and spoken) – co-created with director, dramaturge and video-artist as well as composers, translators and technicians – emphasizes Shakespeare's proposition that the most critical and complex stage is the global one we occupy here and now.

Screen as body extension in *The Pixelated Revolution*

Roman Tragedies employed screens at varying scales: with live projections onto large panels in the auditorium and foyer; a scattering of television monitors on the stage; and smaller devices in the hands of the spectators who are encouraged to contribute to the production through social media. While the use of phone cameras is a common feature in events such as rock concerts – held high and radiating light like votive candles – their infiltration into conventional theatre is relatively recent. Although experimental companies have explored the connectivity and inherent use of mobile phones in performance for many years, miniature displays glowing in the dark still tend to signal a refusal or inability to 'power down'.

Our current tendency to simultaneously watch, record and share unfolding moments through an intervening screen renders the device an extension of body and space. This is in keeping with posthuman discourse – advanced by thinkers such Donna Haraway and Rosie Braidotti – that recognizes the hybridity of our contemporary cyborgian reality in which corporeal and spatial instrumentation is taken for granted. Technologies designed to focus and enhance our senses, increase our comfort, augment our anatomy and advance communication are becoming progressively digitized and imbedded in body and environment. Protocols originally established to deal with mobile phones in public space are diminishing as the device is increasingly taken for granted as a supplemental body part through which we are able to see twofold. Companies such as UK-based Seven Sisters Group – headed by director, Susanne Thomas and designer, Sophie Jump – play on this doubled view through their staged site-specific video-walks in museums (*Asterion*, 2008–2009 and *Atlanta,* 2010) and London's lidos (*Like a Fish Out of Water*, 2012), where the audience walks around holding small screens in front of them that overlay the lived space they inhabit with one of enchantment, peopled by mythical characters from other times and places.[8]

Lebanese visual and theatre artist, Rabih Mroué, advances such double looking – in which we simultaneously gaze at digital screen and immediate environment or use the devices to persistently record unfolding events – as a 'double-shooting' in his notable 'non-academic lecture', *The Pixelated Revolution* (2011–2015), which presents the visual chaos of media through still and moving images culled from the Internet. Assembling material created and utilized by Syrians to document the revolution in its early stages, Mroué compares their revolutionary tactics with the strict cinematic rules adopted by the Danish film movement, Dogme, in the pursuit of authentic representation. However, unlike the fictional films of Lars Von Trier and his contemporaries, these images of war in a war of images can end up with the amateur cinematographers, 'armed' with cell phones, recording themselves being fired on and even killed by snipers: hence the double-shooting. Rather than immerse or enchant the viewer, Mroué scrutinizes the use of digital tools to document and own events in the absence of foreign journalists with their 'proper' media. He also reinforces discourses around the posthuman by stating that it's 'as if camera and eye have become united … the camera has become part of the body. In other words, cameras are not cameras but eyes implanted in their hands'. Pointing out a conflation between shooting images and shooting bodies, the lecturer asks, 'how many mobile phones have been lost? How many digital eyes have been extinguished?' (Mroué 2014).

Berlin-based theatre collective Rimini Protokoll (Helgard Haug, Stefan Kaegi and Daniel Wetzel), working with designer Dominic Huber, has incorporated such digital eyes in *Situation Rooms*, a 'multiplayer video piece' that questions and presents the globalized arms trade and those affected by it.

Situation Rooms

Situation Rooms (Figure 2.2) was provoked by one of the most haunting media images in this century; Pete Souza's photograph of the United States' top military and civilian leaders, including President Barack Obama, gathered in the White House 'Situation Room', receiving updates on the tracking and killing of Osama Bin Laden. The screen they are watching is out of frame and assumed to be streaming live video feed from drones hovering above Bin Laden's compound in Pakistan: marking what Rimini Protokoll describe as 'the end of a manhunt that was pursued with all possible weapons' (2014a). Their response was to create an inter-medial installation virtually inhabited by twenty people they interviewed from varying continents who are implicated in, and affected by, the international arms trade. From refugees to rulers, these protagonists include a child soldier, arms manufacturer, lawyer, sniper, peace activist, gunship pilot, member of parliament, surgeon, war photographer and hacker:

In the globalised world of the arms trade, the coming together of members of governments and refugees, of profiteers and victims, and of demonstrators and soldiers leads to unexpected overlaps and new questions. Free of simplistic moralising, [we offer] the listener the chance to adopt the different positions as if they were character masks, trying them on and seeing how it feels to be inside a particular individual's skin and inside their logic. (2014b)

FIGURE 2.2 *Situation Rooms:* Rimini Protokoll (Jörg Baumann).

In a set constructed like a cinematic sound stage – far from the proscenium venue required for Toneelgroep's *Roman Tragedies* – twenty spectators, each clutching a handle attached to a digital tablet and wearing headphones, follow onscreen instructions, respond to visual prompts and navigate allocated trails within the labyrinth of *Situation Rooms* – all of the time matching the POV (filmic point of view) on their iPad with the scene before them. Each spectator engages with ten of the possible twenty characters; donning costumes, assuming physical positions, deploying objects and undertaking covert actions that bring them closer to the stories of the real protagonists. The stories become interlaced through brief interactions with other participants: 'The audience does not sit opposite the piece to watch and judge it from the outside; instead, the spectators ensnare themselves in a network of incidents, slipping into the perspectives of the protagonists, whose traces are followed by other spectators' (2014b). The work aims to entangle the audience in the virtual and material spatiality of its labyrinth. Echoing Mroué, Rimini Protokoll aim for each individual to become 'part of the re-enactment of a complicatedly elaborated multi-perspective "shooting"' (2014b).

Žižek discusses mediatized images as dissociative phenomena in which 'the distance that separates Us from Them, from their reality, is maintained: the real horror happens there, not here'

(2002: 13). Working with double-viewing, *Situation Rooms* provides a theatre-based strategy to come to know the other in ways that mainstream media tends to withhold. Rimini Protokoll's strategy of humanizing and bringing into view those who are distanced by culture, politics or lack of visibility was behind *SEEN: Fruits of Our Labour*, an interactive installation designed by Omar and Osman Khan for the ZeroOne San Jose Festival in 2006.

SEEN: Fruits of Our Labour

To initiate their project the Khans approached members of three concealed communities that constitute San Jose's Labour force – 'Silicon Valley's technology workers, undocumented service workers and outsourced call centre workers' – asking them one question: 'What is the fruit of your labour?' (2008: 296):

> Their responses are displayed back to San Jose's general public on a 4' x 8' infrared LED screen that can only be viewed using digital capture devices like cell phone cameras, digital cameras, DVcams, etc. This is because the image capture technologies on these digital devices are sensitive to infrared wave-lengths that are invisible to the naked eye. Our interest in using this alternative communication spectrum was in response to the evermore spectacular media that constantly accost our attention. By presenting the public with a 'visibly' silent screen, the audience is solicited to consciously participate or labour to interact with the information. (Khan 2008: 282)

Although technology has radically transformed since 2006 with the advent of smart phones, the Khan's project preceded Rimini Protokoll's objective to utilize digital eyes as a way of seeing those out of sight and out of mind. Omar (architect) and Osman (media artist) created *SEEN: Fruits of Our Labour* (Figure 2.3) by way of a shiny black monolith that appeared unannounced in the public square. This inscrutable monument was designed to harness the moment by fleetingly materializing the presence of the region's invisible workers while 'deal[ing] with their projected hopes and the "American Dream" in light of globalization' (2008: 282). Considering Silicon Valley's global dispersion of fruit, technology and labour, the Khans briefly revealed and cohered an isolated and generally overlooked community of workers whose expectations and desires were streamed to those who unsuspectingly held their cameras up towards the blank object, which magically transformed into a screen transmitting concealed information. Playing into people's curious desire to document even the most banal sights, the revelation produced a briefly cohered gathering of strangers who, sharing hitherto intimate devices, appeared as an enthusiastic group of shutterbugs incomprehensibly focusing on a passive object:

> During its installation *SEEN* instigated vibrant interactions between people who shared their viewing devices with total strangers, discussed its streaming messages and telematically communicated their viewing experience with others in their phonebook. It also brought voices, like the badly stigmatized un-documented workers, into the public arena (Khan 2008: 283).

FIGURE 2.3 *SEEN: Fruits of Our Labour*: Omar and Osman Khan (Omar Khan).

FIGURE 2.3 *(continued)*

FIGURE 2.3 *(continued)*

Tapping into Marshall McLuhan's pre-digital notion of the 'global village' – later articulated by Manuel Castells and Howard Rheingold as the 'electronic agora' now expressed through a socially networked Internet – the Khans briefly returned the ancient *agora* to the public piazza as the democratic site for open assembly, encouraging political and philosophical debate. This was facilitated by the monolith's enigmatic presence, recalling the mysterious slab as machine-object featured in Arthur C. Clarke's book, *2001: A Space Odyssey,* concurrently released as a Stanley Kubrick film in 1968. At first recalling Henri Lefebvre's reference to the implacable *objectality* of a mute artefact and its inherent oppositional force (1991: 57), the San Jose monolith is digitally mobilized into what Gilles Deleuze names an *objectile* – constantly becoming as and through the event: exceeding its material boundaries and annihilating its own representational frame (1993: 37). The agency and effect of this streaming 'object/event' (Eisenman 2007: 16) is predicated as much on its unavoidable materiality as its instrumentality.

The screen as material object is critical to all intermedial performances discussed in this chapter. Just as the posthuman body is rendered a cyborgian hybrid, so the screen as object-event becomes what Haraway calls 'a condensed image of both imagination and material reality' (1991: 50). Neither a passive plane upon which to throw the image nor an inert surface emitting pixelated light, the screen is acknowledged as a performative player in its own right. This was enacted in two New York projects commissioned by Artangel and the Public Art Fund in 2000: Pipilotti Rists's *Open My Glade* and Tony Oursler's *The Influence Machine*; both of which have since been adapted for urban sites in international festivals. Rist co-opted Times Square's NBC Screen in order to disrupt its endless stream of advertising with one-minute appearances every hour where her face presses up against the surface and smears it with makeup; interrupting the surrounding media frenzy with an uncanny image that counters the colossal figures of sleek heroic models and actors peddling products from architectural facades. For Oursler, the trees, fences and buildings surrounding Madison Square Park provide projection surfaces upon which to communicate with the living and the dead: streaming text via internet messages also determines the pulsations of light from lampposts; and projected characters morph on moving foliage or drift by on clouds of smoke. The effects and affects of both these New York projects are predicated on the inescapable reality of the existing built environment transformed into dialogic screen space, which is inherent to the final project discussed here.

The Transparent Wall: Opening a window

There is a danger in opening a window in the wall, for ultimately what we want and what we came together for, is to do away with the wall altogether the wall is merely an expression, in a concrete form, of what is already there, a high degree of segregation and wish for separation, a mentality, a feeling which is widely present in the public … so to work against the wall means working against this, changing the mentality … the question is what it means to work against it, in both publics, both the Palestinian and the Israeli … it means to know that public, and to know how to bring the issue of non-separation in a way that still moves them. (Artists Without Walls 2004)

We return to the troubled region where this chapter began; this time the contentious and constructed border of the West Bank Wall: an object both mobile and immovable, representing what Mike Davis calls 'the interlocking system of fortification, surveillance, armed patrol and incarceration' that 'girds half the earth' (2005: 88). Although an emphatically fixed object constructed of eight-metre high concrete panels, originally following the abstract boundary demarcated by Moshe Dayan as the 'Green Line' after the 1948 Arab-Israeli War, this shifting barrier that constantly reconfigures ownership and public access is also a technological object; incorporating electric fences, trenches, cameras, sensors and military patrols.

Artists Without Walls are an interdisciplinary group of Arab and Israeli artists and architects who meet in Ramallah and East Jerusalem to devise alternative means to what they see as the repeatedly failed protest strategies against the separation wall, described by them as 'a monument to failure and a testament to pessimism' (Artists Without Walls 2004). In 2004, they selected Abu Dis as a site for creative rebellion: a Palestinian village suddenly and violently split by the wall, making it impossible to access services in Jerusalem without a permit or a time-consuming, convoluted and demeaning journey. They intended to highlight that although the wall aspired to construct a sense of security for Israelis by separating them from Palestinians, in effect 'the real separation created is between Palestinians and their families, neighbours and communities as well as jobs, hospitals and schools' (2004). Setting up video cameras on either side of the barrier, the activist-artists passed the technology through the small holes designed to allow machinery to lift the heavy units into place and then projected the live transmissions from each sector on the opposite side of the wall, briefly reuniting the village's inhabitants who gestured ecstatically and moved together rhythmically while speaking to each other on mobile phones. In his essay 'Primitive Separations', Dean McCannell described witnessing this event:

> When both sets of images were projected simultaneously the effect was a very large virtual hole in the wall. We were able to protest together, singing, dancing and cheering as though the wall was not there. With a prodigious act of the imagination, even this most forbidding wall can be used as a device to bring people together. (2005: 44)

Artists Without Walls were working with what political theorist, Jane Bennett, would name the barricade's 'thing-power'; encouraging us to rethink our 'habit of parsing the world into dull matter (it, things) and vibrant life (us, beings)' (2010: vii). Maintaining that our 'analyses of political events might change if we gave the force of things more due' (2010: viii), Bennett's theory is influenced by Bruno Latour's 'actant': a participatory source of action (such as the wall) that, responding and requiring response, is implicated in a complex and epic network. In this case, the wall's brutal objectality – momentarily undermined by rendering it a digital interface – represents global complicity towards the development and maintenance of a barrier built in the name of one regime's security while interlinked to Western neoliberal values and a thriving, well-fabricated 'war on terror' designed to condition the competence and performance of communities and subjects.

Made under the watchful and hostile eye of Israeli authorities, *The Transparent Wall* enacted subtle manoeuvres with formidable effects (Figure 2.4). By adapting the wall into a double-sided screen, its existing relationship to technological surveillance was exposed through the artists' covert employment of cameras and projectors, which allowed a small unwillingly divided community to briefly cohere in a

FIGURE 2.4 *The Transparent Wall*: Artists Without Walls (Oren Sagiv).

FIGURE 2.4 *(continued)*

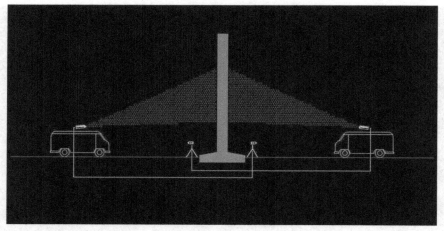

FIGURE 2.4 *(continued)*

moment of celebration. Speaking to power, the strategy worked with the wall's inherent rigidity and implacability to temporarily undermine the violence of a patrolled borderline. As a radical borderline act, it exposed an inherent vulnerability within the wall itself as well as the symbolic order.

Photographic and video documentation of this event at the West Bank Wall show people talking to each other on mobile phones and waving towards the large projections through which they coordinate dancing, clapping and singing. Amidst these celebrating bodies are the moulded plastic chairs previously mentioned in relation to the Sderot Cinema: mobile and dispersed within another improvised auditorium, this time spontaneously established on both sides of the divide. The performative screen tends to untether the chair and its occupant from the ordered rows of theatre's dark and disciplinary environs: no longer an indispensable element designed to immobilize the viewer before a distant image. Instead the material and proliferating screen facilitates a more immersive and embodied engagement with the performance environment, while calling attention to spatial multiplicity in a world of intersecting (ir)realities. Screen space provides the potential to awaken us from a mediated reality into a 'real reality' via intermediation.

Conclusion

The challenge, then, is not only to elicit such emotions, but to sustain and interconnect them with the feelings of people in different institutions and other, far-distant places, not only places in the margins of societies and cultures, but also in the more centralized nodes of high performance sociotechnical systems. (McKenzie 2008: 127)

The scenographic screen is no longer predicated on a fixed onstage textile nor even a flat surface for receiving or emitting background images. It is increasingly adapted to any number of environments: seen in the proscenium theatre necessary for Toneelgroep's *Roman Tragedies*; the controlled soundstage environment required for the construction of Rimini Protokoll's *Situation Rooms*; a seemingly benign urban environment for the Khan's *SEEN: Fruits of Our Labour*; or an overtly contested space upon which *The Transparent Wall* was contingent for the Artists Without Walls – where, in all four projects, a universal language of visuality and embodied experience prevailed.

Aronson's questioning as to whether media and theatre can speak the same language relates to digital scenography, which tends to operate as a backdrop generally confined to the prescribed multimedial stage, as opposed to the visual dramaturgy of a hybridized intermediality predicated on a complex spatiality as well as a more mobile and participating public. As he maintains in his subsequent article, it is key that 'two or more vocabularies are intentionally combined with a keen awareness of how one informs the other' (2008: 94). No longer predicated on a shared language, this correlational dialogue between varying media (as multiple agencies of action)[9] depends on disrupted and intersecting space-time realities that adapt 'the raw material of this generation's world' (ibid). This is achieved through ever-developing, ever-changing and ever-redundant sources acknowledged by the editors of *Mapping Intermediality in Performance* as 'an inexorable refunctioning at work - of the spaces, bodies and media of performance, and not least of our own expectations and experiences in the face of such developments' (Bay-Cheng et al. 2010: 124).

Activating the scenographic screen is predicated on the assumption that performance is not just limited to the stage or even the human subject, but that *spaces and things perform* with their particular set of unfolding forces. However, at the very heart of my argument is what Jill Bennett calls 'empathic vision': 'the artist's capacity to transform images' and 'specifically, to open up a space for empathic encounter for others to inhabit' (2005: 142). This involves a type of bearing witness described by documentary artist John Di Stefano as 'an embodiment of doubling … through the *performance* of witnessing' (2008: 263). Di Stefano maintains that 'witnessing also implies an empathetic stance that somehow "binds" witnesses to what they see unfolding before them, whereas observing lacks that subjective positioning' (2008: 261). Rather than cruel immersion (expounded by Antonin Artaud's *Theatre of Cruelty*) or distanced observation (encouraged by Bertolt Brecht's theatre of alienation), such witnessing requires the viewer to be simultaneously connected to and separated from the event, inhabiting 'a space of *betweeness*' (Di Stefano 2008: 261).

By the time this chapter is published much of the mechanisms mentioned will be redundant, as devices and bodies become more integrated. However, technology is only ever the tool by which artists express their ideas – a Heideggerian poetic, 'challenging-forth' (1997: 16). The performances discussed have worked with the digital screen to explore a productive interrelation between seemingly separate elements and their capacity to alter spatiotemporal perspectives as well as object and event structures: creating hybridized and distributed performances that reveal and expand a troubled relationship between embodiment and the real where 'fixity of meaning is continually in jeopardy' (Bay-Cheng et al. 2010: 123).

In discussing a performative politics of global feeling and feeling global, McKenzie proposes that 'a resistant performativity cannot do without a global feeling of political love' (2008: 119). Referring to Michael Hardt and Antonio Negri's demand for 'a more generous and more unrestrained conception of love' (2004: 351), operating beyond romantic and familial ties, McKenzie introduces the concept of being 'a/part' – 'feeling a part of the world and feeling apart from it at the same time' (2008: 129). This approach equates with Di Stefano's inhabitation of *betweeness* that requires 'the ability to *feel* or empathize as well as the sense of not fully embodying the event' (2008: 261). The artists in this chapter have – operating a/part – adopted the proliferating digital screen as a reflexive and performative means of productively contacting the terror and pity, previously withheld by old and new media. Their short-term aesthetic interventions play out the need for longer-term participation. In working with fleeting acts of liveness – both immediate and mediated – perhaps they have come close to McKenzie's conception of loveness (2008: 127) as something that necessarily persists beyond the transitory event; echoing Cixous' claim that the very heart of the matter lies in our own hearts.

Notes

1   This theatrical diaspora can be seen in the rise of site-specific and immersive theatre as well as performance installations and events in public space: on and offline.

2   Such covert scrutiny refers to Edward Snowden, former CIA employee and US government contractor who publically disclosed numerous global surveillance programmes, facilitated by communication companies working with various governments. With a proliferation of surveillance technology, we have generally acquiesced to pervasive scrutiny *in the name of security*.

3   French philosopher Jacques Rancière argues that despite spectators being physically distanced from the stage they are still active agents within a communal performance.

4   As Chiel Kattenbelt notes, 'Wagner's aim for the "artwork of the future" of his day was for the spectator to be immersed into the represented world' where the varying elements and their skilled artisans (performers, musicians, designers etc.) served the composer's vision rather than advocating a dynamic and variable interplay found in the proposals of the ensuing Historical Avant-garde (2008: 26).

5   Cited in *The Independent*, Sunday 13 July 2014: 'Israel-Gaza conflict: "Sderot Cinema"' image shows Israelis with popcorn and chairs "cheering as missiles strike Palestinian targets"'. http://www.independent.co.uk/news/world/middle-east/israelgaza-conflict-sderot-cinema-image-shows-israelis-with-popcorn-and-chairs-cheering-as-missiles-strike-palestinian-targets-9602704.html: the original page is no longer accessible, despite being an *Independent* article. Images, videos and reports still on the web suggest that this gathering occurred over several days.

6   As Kattenbelt maintains, a more correlational intermediality undermined Wagner's multimedial *Gesamtkunstwerk* (total work of art) in favour of the dynamic interplay, expounded by last century's historical avant-garde, particularly the constructivists with their dynamic compositions and irruptive interchange (2008: 24–26).

7   As early as 1896, Alfred Jarry's infamous backdrop, co-created by a group of late 19th-century artists, worked against mimesis by standing in for multiple times and places. This break with history was exacerbated by the advent of gas and then electric lighting on stage, which exposed the disjunction between three-dimensional performer and two-dimensional painted backdrop.

8   Of course this notion of location-based augmented reality has concurrently been adopted in public gaming strategies, most explicitly played out during mid-2016 with the worldwide craze of *Pokémon Go*.

9   Through intermediality, media is no longer limited to intervening technological transmissions but refers to the agency and means of action; thereby encompassing performing and receptive bodies, built and virtual environments, sound, light, projection and so on.

PART TWO

Architectural Space

3

Between Symbolic Representation and New Critical Realism: Architecture as Scenography and Scenography as Architecture

Thea Brejzek

While architecture and scenography share a common history, their mainstream functions are fundamentally different, and the primary aim of architecture, namely to provide shelter, is typically posited against scenography as providing the decorative backdrop for frivolous entertainment. In her framing of the interdisciplinary relationship between architecture and scenography, Juliet Rufford rightly points to their formal dissimilarities: architecture's task is the creation of stable and durable built structures while the time-based art of scenography is concerned with the ephemeral qualities of transformation, atmosphere and effect (Rufford 2015). Of particular interest to Rufford, however, are the links and seams where architecture and theatre meet and how the notion of performance may push architecture beyond its traditional parameters of programme and tectonics towards more fluid states of production.[1] This chapter contributes to this debate from a scenographic perspective through close readings of the architectural scenographies and performative architectures by some of the major players in contemporary practice. In doing so, the assumed dichotomy of theatre's ephemerality and architecture's durability following Vitruvius[2] and their seemingly mutually exclusive aesthetic possibilities and restrictions is questioned. The notion of architecture's durability is shown to be predominantly upheld by architect-scenographers, that is architects who primarily practise architecture but occasionally venture into set design through singular sculptural objects of symbolic representation on stage, reminiscent aesthetics and style of the architects' built projects. On the other hand, the fixedness and object-character of architecture is more likely to be subverted by scenographer-architects, that is scenographers who see themselves as working architecturally on the stage. It is established that while the majority of the superstars of architecture tend to avoid detailed depictions and interpretations of contemporary urban life by resorting to symbolic representations when designing a set, their scenographer-colleagues embrace what I define as a new 'critical realism'[3] through techniques of collaging and fragmenting identifiable architectural elements, interiors and objects to present an acute view on the urban condition and to reframe domesticity as not private, but inherently political. Ultimately, this chapter demands the dissolution of traditional binary theatre-architecture classifications into the emerging genre of performance architecture in public space, where the built structure comprises a new kind of situated scenography, seeking participation and pursuing a distinct political and social agenda.

Prize-winning German scenographer Anna Viebrock, during a 2010 Basel public forum on the relationship between scenography and architecture, delivered a surprise provocation aimed at iconic Swiss architect Jacques Herzog, pointing to a fundamental difference between scenographic and architectural aesthetic practice: 'On stage, maybe it's possible to construct more intense atmospheres, i.e., uncanny or terrifying spaces. As an architect, one is not allowed to do that' (Viebrock and Herzog 2011: 73). Viebrock's statement implies that an architect cannot transgress the limits of a generally accepted aesthetic and that it is therefore not a question of 'not doing' but rather 'not being able to' work beyond beauty. As a result, so Viebrock claims, architects are unable to realize contested atmospheres that may evoke fear or aggression, and consequently are unable to create architectures of intensity. Herzog, perhaps surprisingly, not only agreed with Viebrock's provocation but also extended her argument, referring to what I will call here 'architecture's aesthetic imprisonment'. Jacques Herzog's own interest, as an architect working on the stage is the uncensored possibility to spatialize a narrative through scenography, made possible, he argues, by the convention and knowledge of the performance's temporality. Conversely, the 'horror' of architecture, Herzog suggests, is its durable, built reality:

But actually people make the stories. This is something you can tell in a stage design; you can be wickedly evil. In architecture that is not possible. But the true horror exists only in the real world [of architecture]. In the theatre it is only for approximately two hours. (Viebrock and Herzog 2011: 74)

Viebrock's and Herzog's contention completely aligns with Vitruvius' three classical principles of architecture. However, the seemingly universal validity of Vitruvius' triad has long lost serious ground. While the architectural ideal of the design and construction of a harmonious whole still resounds in the architecture critic Ruskin's mid-19th-century notion of architecture contributing to 'pleasure' (Ruskin 1849: 13), modernism has since reframed aesthetic effects as qualities emerging from function rather than ornament, and postmodernist architecture has provocatively embraced the vernacular. In the vocabulary and the emerging practices of performative and performance architecture since the 1980s and 1990s, it is not the architectural object that lies at the centre of investigation but rather a disruption of conventionalized practices. Such a focus brings with it an emphasis on process and participation and a rethinking of tectonics and materials towards a responsive or interactive architecture.[4] Equally, the practice of scenography has progressed from its beginnings as a backdrop with merely decorative function, towards practices that interrogate and deconstruct the assumed spatial unity of the 'set' as a result of the postmodern fragmentation and disorientation of the subject-individual in a globalized post-Fordist society. It is not surprising that the highly aestheticized approach of scenographies by the superstars of architecture should strike Viebrock as alien to her own practice, one based on the contrary agenda of scenography as a heightened mirror to social reality. I interpret Viebrock's provocative generalization as a call to architect-scenographers to fundamentally question the value of the Vitruvian *venustas* in favour of a stage practice that is as engaged as it is irreverent of tradition and commonly shared notions of beauty. In this chapter, I take up the provocation that architectural convention limits the social impact of scenography by interrogating recent architectures on the stage by scenographers and scenographies, and in public space by architects.

Architecture as performance

Media theorist Chris Salter points out the contributions to performance that some of the iconic deconstructivist architects have made in their uncompromising application of materiality and technology to contemporary scenography. His argument, however, goes beyond the description of a move away from modernism's rigid form–function duality, a development which undisputedly has migrated to the stage with the involvement of some of the prominent protagonists of deconstructivism:

> Even if many of the projects that Hadid, Libeskind, Gehry and Coop Himmelb(l)au were most of the time one-off opportunities, what these architects brought to performance was not just the specialized architectural discourse of program, event, strategy and movement, but an aggressive challenge to modernist discourses of form versus function advancing the role of technology in the process of construction, and examining the political relationships inherent in the perceptions of space. (Salter 2010: 77)

Yet, while Salter is in many ways correct to bundle Hadid, Libeskind, Gehry and Coop Himmelb(l)au together, it must be noted that it is only the Viennese Coop Himmelb(l)au that has, right from its inception in 1968, radicalized the notion of architecture through performance as an integral part of its practice.

From the passionate manifesto *Architecture must burn* (Coop Himmelb(l)au 1980), coupled with the flaming outdoor installation *Blazing Wing* to their projects documented in the 1983 publication *Architecture Is Now* (Coop Himmelb(l)au 1983), Coop Himmelb(l)au used site-specific performance, installation and built projects to underscore their belief in the immediacy and emotionality of architecture itself. While the notion of hegemonic forces inherent in space and spatial production pervades Coop Himmelb(l)au's early and highly provocative practice, it is perhaps harder to see how other iconic architects have articulated scenographic positions relating to a politics of space, especially as they progressed to international fame. Indeed (as this chapter will confirm) a close look at the stage works of some iconic contemporary architects reveals their continued interest in scenography, yet a preoccupation with abstract and symbolic form-making refuses detail and shuts out the gritty reality of urban life. While the architect's daily practice engages deeply with the city, its infrastructure, social and cultural contexts and issues, disengagement with the urban fabric (with dwelling at large and the domestic in particular) is evident in their excursions into stage scenography. Rather, it is the architects' notion of the theatre and the stage as a controlled and controllable machine, operating at the will of its creator, that underlies many fascinating yet ultimately reductive scenographic inventions, typically comprising a large singular object or environment of objects with a sculptural quality and volume that showcase the architects' known formal and material language. Machine-like constructions and the showcasing of the perfection of their operation on the stage, as designed by architects Herzog and de Meuron, Daniel Libeskind, and Zaha Hadid among others, point back to the formal and material experimentations of Russian constructivist architect-scenographers such as Konstantin Melnikov, Vladimir Tatlin and Alexander Vesnin, and, notably, the Austro-American architect-scenographer Friedrich Kiesler's electro-dynamic *Space Stage* from 1924.

The architect as scenographer: Symbolic representation and the 'theatre as machine'

In the project notes to their 2006 scenography for *Tristan and Isolde* at the Berliner Staatsoper, architects Jacques Herzog and Pierre de Meuron point to 'experimentation' as the main driver and methodology for their scenographic work, and to seeking not to represent actual objects but rather to spatialize the *appearance* of things. They sought to achieve this by designing an amorphous rubber membrane with wall-like dimensions for their Berlin *Tristan* that would act as an autonomous organism with ever-changing features, using negative pressure in a tailor-made built pressure chamber (see Plate 1). Fascinating and continuously drawing attention to itself and its workings, the single object of the membrane operated as a symbolic representation for the psychological states of the two protagonists, Tristan and Isolde, and their doomed love for each other. The singular object's presence with its intricate surface seemed to be breathing with – or for – the tragic pair, and, while dominating the stage did engage with its narrative through its symbolic significance rather than through its engagement with the opera's narrative.

Herzog and de Meuron, being highly critical of the theatre, opera and dance designs realized by their colleagues, were unlikely addressees of Viebrock's assumption:

> The stage sets created by architects or even by artists are perfectly dreadful – we thought, in view of so many failed attempts. The pitfalls of simply transferring one's own style, one's typical trademarks from construction site to proscenium stage seem almost inescapable. (Herzog and de Meuron 2006)

Renowned in their architectural practice for the reassertion and reframing of ornament within a minimalist framework, Herzog and de Meuron continue to extend their trademark architectural, material and formal aesthetics in scenographic practice towards a new and distinctly ephemeral spatial expression. This practice is based on their understanding of the theatre as machine, as in their *Tristan,* thus allowing for a complete yet object-oriented re-articulation of the stage's seemingly fixed parameters. Their approach points back to the radical 1920s theatre experiments by Austro-American architect-scenographer Friedrich Kiesler as exhibited in his 1924 *Internationale Ausstellung neuer Theatertechnik* in the Vienna Konzerthaus. Kiesler's *Railway Theatre*, constructed as a 1:1 model and prototype of the *Space Stage* (Raumbühne), comprised a scaffolded spiral ramp leading up to a circular performance area that could be accessed by a staircase from ground level or via steel ladders from the performance strip below the top tier. The *Space Stage* was to form one of the stepping-stones of Kiesler's theory of correalism (from 1930 onwards) as a convergence of art, life and the sciences. Design, Kiesler proclaimed, would be radically redefined through specific mathematical relations between stage, its elements, and speed: 'Design = Stage + Elements x Movement' (Kiesler 1939: 60). Kiesler's correalist equation is exemplified by his description of the model of the *Railway Theatre* in the catalogue to the Vienna exhibition:

> The Space Stage of the Railway-Theatre, the contemporary form of theatre, is floating in space. The ground floor is only the support for the open construction. The audience is circulating in electro-magnetic movements around the core of the stage. (Kiesler 1924: n.p.)

Although never fully realized for performance, a modified, static version of the *Space Stage* was trialled in 1924 where Kiesler proposed a mobile and kinetic stage that fully encompassed audience and performers and is thus a utopian space where the act of looking and the space of action become permeable and converge as a dynamic experiential space (see Plate 2). While Kiesler had conceptualized the *Space Stage* as an active and self-organizing object comprising stage, scenography and auditorium at the same time, Herzog and de Meuron's *Tristan* adhered to the basic spatial organization of proscenium stage and auditorium as two separate entities. This does not constitute as radical an invention as their description of the machine seems to promise.

As organism and constructivist machine at the same time, Kiesler's *Space Stage* proved to be highly influential for future visionaries in architecture and theatre, notably the iconic architects of the 1960s to 1990s such as British architect Cedric Price.[5] Price's collaborative performance machine *Fun Palace* (1960–1961, unrealized) developed with theatre director Joan Littlewood, embraced Kiesler's concept of the autonomous theatre machine. It aimed to combine the built elements with new and emerging media technologies that would enable a kinetic, adaptive and performative architecture where the spectator as participant can:

> Learn how to handle tools, paint, babies, machinery, or just listen to your favourite tune. Dance, talk or be lifted up to where you can see how other people make things work. Sit out over space with a drink and tune in to what's happening elsewhere in the city. Try starting a riot or beginning a painting – or just lie back and stare at the sky. (Littlewood 1961 cited by Duffy 2013)

Price's and Littlewood's kinetic architecture, that operates as a machine while keeping the architectural programme (function) and spatial configuration fluid and changeable, finds an echo in the experimental practice of Dutch architect Rem Koolhaas and Partners' Rotterdam-based OMA office, which specializes in performance and event. OMA, however, while articulating the notion of the theatre as machine convincingly in their 2012 scenographies for three Greek dramas in the summer season of the amphitheatre Teatro Greco in Syracuse, Sicily, designed three highly symbolic architectural objects rather than being concerned with devising a *Fun Palace*-like performative architecture (see Plate 3).[6] This is conceptually more aligned with the scenographic practice of Herzog and de Meuron yet without their formal rigidity. OMA termed the three symbolic architectural objects they created for Syracuse: the Ring, the Machine and the Raft. Each intervention adapted and reinterpreted core elements of the antique Greek theatre on its very site.

Conceptualized as architectural interventions into the body of the amphitheatre, the Ring construction provided a complete circumference of the theatre from semi-circle to circle via a scaffolded passage at the theatre's highest point. Further, it offered additional entry and exit points for the performers. The Machine mirrored the incline of the amphitheatre's seating area in the form of a wooden disc at the upstage end of the orchestra. The raked disc could rotate and split open in the middle to allow for entrances and dramatic exits while a second flat disc, the Raft, operated as OMA's 'reimagined' orchestra and acting area with the disc's very centre positioned in the traditional location of the altar of Dionysos. Together, the three scenographic interventions both increased the antique theatre's interior technologies and expanded the theatre's historic architecture to create a highly controlled and controllable environment. The machine-like character and physical real-time transformations of OMA's Syracuse project allowed for the stage to act as a precise scenographic entity able to anticipate, act and react physically on the drama's action, thus suggesting a multitude of spaces. The abstracted sculptural and architectural objects by architect-scenographers thus are able to realize what Foucault calls 'heterotopias', and of which theatre is one, namely, a place that is comprised of several unrelated spaces and temporalities[7] (Foucault [1967] 1984: 6). The iconic architects' scenographic, symbolic 'machines' introduced here, though, remain in the purely symbolic realm and refuse an in depth engagement with the relationship between dramatic narrative and social reality.

Similarly, Polish-American architect Daniel Libeskind has designed symbolic scenographic machines that were able to produce a 'space (that) is not just one space, but a plurality and heterogeneity of spaces' (Libeskind in Salter 2010: 60) and that were, in an expansion of scenography towards the urban condition, a 'paradigm of the city' (Libeskind in Wise 2003). Libeskind's architecture, his set designs and 'machines', are both symbolic and narrative and demand to be read as texts that are often the outcome of the architect's intense engagement with the 'historical destiny of architecture' (Libeskind 1985). The sculptural elements of Libeskind's set design for Olivier Messiaen's rarely performed opera *Saint François d'Assise* at Deutsche Oper Berlin in 2002 point back to a much earlier work by the architect, namely the construction and installation of three machines at the 1985 Venice Architecture Biennale. According to Libeskind, the four-sided wooden cubes of the Venice *Writing Architecture* machine as the third of his three architectural lessons[8] 'industrialize the poetics of architecture' (1985) (see Plate 4). The rotating cubes that comprise 2,662 mobile parts, entire 'cities, types of buildings, gods, signs, saints, imaginary beings, forgotten realities' (1985) reappear as central scenographic elements in his 2002 Berlin staging of *Saint François d'Assise* forming an insurmountable topography:

In response to Messiaen's musical text, I used the text of architecture generated by the constellation of rotating cubes. By moving the matrix of the 'foursome' as physical objects, I felt a connection with their 'non-physical' presence. Thus I understood that just because something is a non-existent reality, doesn't obliterate the fact that it is a reality nevertheless. The parallel yet independent relation between music/story and the architecturally spiralling score is for me the core of this fact. (Libeskind 2002)

For Libeskind, both architecture and music draw their emotional impact from the treatment of a chosen narrative, which marks the foundation of both practices. Scenography and architecture meet in their ability to invest space with meaning through the creation of a readable, almost text-like construction of a spatial narrative.

Famously, Libeskind a trained pianist drew his competition entry for the Berlin Jewish Museum on music manuscript paper and called it 'Between the Lines'. The building itself was conceptualized as an architectural articulation of the last, unwritten act of Schönberg's opera fragment *Moses and Aaron* and is designed around a void, from which four axes represent the forced journey of the Jewish people into exile. Libeskind's Jewish Museum is a highly narrative and scenographic architecture and a spatial narrative of charged emotion. His opera work on the other hand has been criticized for its disengagement with the subject matter.

Reviews of Libeskind's scenography for *Saint François d'Assise* lamented the overall bleakness of the set and questioned Libeskind's actual engagement with the subject and narrative of the opera (focused on the events in Francois' life after his conversion to Christianity), but could not help being fascinated by the monumental materiality of Libeskind's stage architecture and the transformations it offered, in this case through ever-changing constellations of the cube and intense coloured lighting. Thus, far from creating a generic set design, Libeskind achieved an 'uncanny space' and an 'intense atmosphere' – exactly the kind of space that Viebrock argues that architecture cannot manage on the stage, and that is related to Herzog and de Meuron's and OMA's approaches in its formal rigidity and 'machine' metaphor as opposed to aesthetic expression.

In contrast to OMA's and Herzog and de Meuron's relatively recent scenographic projects, American architect Frank Gehry, labelled as a 'deconstructivist' alongside Libeskind, has a relationship with the stage that goes back to 1983 when he collaborated with choreographer Lucinda Childs and minimalist composer John Adams on the dance piece *Available Light*.[9] His somewhat modest admission to not being a theatre expert has led to him listen intently to the needs of the dancers and to the choreographer's conceptual vision. In a reprinted interview from 1983, Gehry described his working relationship with Childs as one of a common search:

Just because you are an architect and make decent buildings does not mean that you can suddenly become a set designer for one of the best avant-garde dancers in the world.... It has not been easy in that we are searching for something. We want to make something that none of us would have done alone. That is the essence of collaboration. When you agree to collaborate, you agree to jump off a cliff holding hands with everyone, hoping the resourcefulness of each will insure that you all land on your feet. (Lazar [1983] 2015)

These days, however, according to Gehry's office partner Craig Webb, the continued interest of Gehry's office in scenography arises from the possibility of experiencing the building from the user's perspective[10] rather than the architect's engagement in an artistic collaboration. Time pressure and responsibility for the running of several parallel projects and the running of a large office means that, typically, a sought-after international architect like Gehry will no longer spend time in the theatre to experiment but rather design the set in isolation and send a partner to test, rework and optimize the set during technical and lighting rehearsals.

Gehry's *Don Giovanni* from 2012 was such an example of a typical Gehry look, very aesthetic but rather generic and in no way related to Mozart's narrative (see Plate 5): a single all-white set of large mounds of crumpled paper, strongly reminiscent of his trademark deconstructivist techniques of creating architectural form from the twisting, bending, folding, wrapping and subsequent extrusion of unusual materials such as titanium, corrugated iron, chain link and raw plywood. While Gehry is quoted as saying that *Don Giovanni*'s sculptural paper elements are not meant as symbolic representations, they repeatedly have been described in reviews as resembling icebergs, waves or marble.[11] As shown in these examples, Gehry's and Libeskind's scenographic language strongly affirms the architectural language that both are renowned for while at the same time embracing experimentations in formal and material approaches but without engaging in the spatial interpretation of the narrative, psychology or social context of the dramatic text.

In contrast, OMA, as a collective practice that is not defined by a singular look or approach, engages with theatre, performance and event most strongly as spatial designers with strong site-specific concepts. The notion of the theatre (and scenography) as a massive machine which operates as a single, symbolic entity rather than as an ensemble of autonomous scenic elements links the work of OMA, Libeskind and Herzog and De Meuron, with OMA most successfully extending the machine's operations to performance landscapes. Frank Gehry, possibly due to his more experimental collaboration with Childs, clearly understands the stage to be different from a building, and has avoided the placement of a single architectural, monumental object on the stage yet his work, as the works of the other architect-scenographers introduced, remains highly abstracted and explicitly symbolic, refusing the engagement with narrative, temporality and social reality.

The scenographer as architect: New critical realism and the reframing of domesticity

Parallel to the continuation of the scenographic tradition of abstraction and symbolic representation since Adolphe Appia and Edward Gordon Craig at the turn of the century, the late 20th century has seen a reappearance of highly detailed sets comprising functional interconnected rooms, passages, and even building levels. A close look reveals that the domestic architectures presented on the stage have been manipulated, compacted, densified, cut and pasted to convey the frenetic and overall disoriented biographies of the postmodern subject. While realistic, this realism, following the socialist, critical realism developed by Bertolt Brecht and Erwin Piscator in the 1920s together with their scenographer-collaborators, namely Caspar Neher and Teo Otto, is fuelled by a political view to the domestic and its representation. I identify this trend in scenographic practice since the 1990s as the development of a new critical realism that provocatively reinstates the fourth wall both metaphorically and architecturally in the form of functional, practisable living spaces as the peephole into the politicized domestic life of the neoliberal citizen.

Leading in the development of a new critical realism on the stage, German scenographer Bert Neumann and Swiss scenographer and director Anna Viebrock engage with subversive acts of hacking architecture to construct new forms of contemporary inhabitation in the post-Fordist society. Their scenographies refute the notion of a stable identity of the contemporary subject and the present-day object. This notion lies in stark contrast to the scenographic concepts of the iconic architect-scenographers' introduced here with their focus on the representation of monumental, abstract, symbolic and singular machine-like objects that draw their seductive power not through their relatedness to a social reality, but rather through an apolitical, purely experimental and innovative material aesthetics. In contrast, Viebrock, as one of a new generation of leading European scenographers, asks for an engaged and positioned scenographic practice beyond aesthetic delight.

Since her early work with Swiss director Christoph Marthaler, known for his slow-moving productions – that taught audiences to look ever more closely at the lives and behaviours of Marthaler's eccentric characters as they moved, danced and sang through Viebrock's hermetic interiors – the German scenographer has continued to bring spatial relicts that had been shaped by past ideologies of East and West Germany onto the stage. The spatialization of perceived ingrained national habits and preoccupations such as order, cleanliness, hierarchy and surveillance form recurring visual motifs in her work across the genres of theatre, installation and opera. Typical Viebrock settings are the many 'non-spaces' (Augé 1995) of modern life: hotel lobbies, train stations, dreary office buildings and non-descript apartment blocks. Viebrock herself stands for a critical scenographic practice and her own 'trademark': relentlessly detailed and large architectural constructions. For *Medea in Corinto* 2011, her scenography comprised a hybrid two-storey 1900s/1950s building with a neo-classicist stucco gable, crowned by a miniature house modelled after the Vienna parliament's sheltered roof constructions. Similarly, the exterior facade and nested interiors for her 2009 *Riesenbutzbach, Eine Dauerkolonie (Riesenbutzbach, A Permanent Colony)* were modelled after several unrelated real spaces. Viebrock names the characteristics, genres and atmospheres of the spaces she sought in her research notes for *Riesenbutzbach* as: 'Bourgeois interior, single family-owned home, hybrid spaces, inside/outside, control space, light, private/public, suburbia, technical apparatuses, uncanniness' (Viebrock and Herzog 2011: 93).

The found architectures of *Riesenbutzbach*, typically for Viebrock's methodology and aesthetics, rarely comprise a single building or rooms, but rather inscrutable and inescapable labyrinthic networks of seemingly recognizable interiors and exteriors, staircases and overhead window panes – where the performers never seem quite at home but appear rather as displaced figures in a game yet unknown to them: 'The liberty of the theatre consists in creating a kind of parallel universe. I equip the stage with objects trouvés from the real world because that is the material available to us' (Viebrock and Herzog 2011: 8). And thus, while Viebrock's built structures appear functional at first sight, they prove to be as dysfunctional as the production's protagonists themselves, mirroring their psychological imprisonment, their obsessions with orderliness and structure, or their fruitless search for individuality and self-determination.

Bert Neumann's constructions of temporary cities and hotels, obstructive and hybrid interiors, are another form of hacking but they behave in a distinctly different way from Viebrock's structures. Modelled on the aesthetics of B-grade Hollywood films and soap operas, Neumann's interiors exhibit the hysterical and pathetic vignettes of domestic life where the characters are under constant media surveillance. As Head of Design at Volksbühne, the East German had, from 1992 until his untimely death in 2015, developed the specific Volksbühne aesthetics that succinctly echoed the *Zeitgeist* of Berlin's creative communities after the fall of the wall.

Not wanting to be labelled as a set designer or scenographer, Neumann insisted he was an architect, literally as his sets both simulate and comprise architectural constructions, but also, I argue, in the Brechtian understanding of the set designer as set builder, and as a builder of (alternate) worlds. Neumann's core strategies comprised hacking and recycling in a critical yet subversive 'imitation of life' (Neumann 2001: 31) by constructing the realistic architectural, object and costume details out of the realities of living in the former oppressive political regime of socialist East Germany (GDR). This practice sought to bring onto the stage a subversive reframing of the official histories of the two Germanies (East and West) and their conflicted unification in 1990. At the same time, as Neumann explained in a 2001 interview, his idea to resurrect and stage a kind of hyper-real GDR at the Volksbühne, had originated from a pure reflex: 'Suddenly we turned into the Super-GDR – citizens that we had never been before' (Neumann 2001: 33).

Together with the Volksbühne's Artistic Director Frank Castorf, Neumann had turned the institution of the state theatre into a social and political laboratory where the notion of the fourth wall was literally reinstated with the same vehemence, as was its subsequent complete destruction. In a relentless rehabilitation of the fourth wall, much of the stage action would happen inside completely enclosed spaces only partially visible through video transmission (see the descriptions of *The Demons*, below), while in another configuration, and in a complete annihilation of the fourth wall, temporary inhabitable environments across stage, auditorium, foyer and surrounding rooms formed one acting and living area for performers and audience (see the description of *Hotel Neustadt* below). Within the unique Volksbühne situation of artistic freedom through flexible production processes, Neumann typically designed the scenography before conceptual talks with director and creative team had even started. In rehearsal, Castorf expected Neumann's uncompromising spaces to offer both a challenge and productive resistance to director and actors. Since Castorf's 1999 adaptation of Dostojewski's *Demons,* Neumann had started to build closed interior spaces such as entire bungalows, which held most of the action. Microphones and cameras inside the house, in conjunction with loudspeakers and video screens outside, served to deliberately mediatize the action and words. At times the audience experienced echo and delay, and this stuttering appeared to be due to technical issues. As a result both performance and relayed transmissions were incomplete. The interior and exterior surveillance set-ups and their faulty communication rendered the iconic image of the house fragile and uncertain, unable to guarantee privacy. Dramaturge Matthias Pees described *Demons* as a transnational and transcultural dystopic travesty:

> Frank Castorf stages the *Demons* with set and costume designer Bert Neumann in a last house just behind Russia's western border, somewhere between *Paris Texas* Cindy Sherman, *Dogma 95* and *Duma 2000* as a kind of post-soviet-panslawist panopticum. (Pees 1999)[12]

Neumann re-used the bungalow from *Demons* in the 2001 production of Dostoevsky's *Erniedrigte und Beleidigte* in collaboration with Vienna Festwochen, but this time in a more built-up version where the interior was only visible through video transmission (see Plate 6). Visually, the technique of video transmission allowed for close-up shots that both turned the viewer into a voyeur of a private drama and emphasized the characters' alienation in a world where privacy is gone.

Media philosopher Boris Groys described the oversized video screens that in many of Neumann's productions loomed precariously in the midst of scaffolded multi-storey environments (e.g. *Forever Young* 2003; *Nach Moskau Nach Moskau* 2010) as

> always somehow referring to their transmission into an afterworld or afterlife.... We assume that what is shown on the screen is being shown post mortem. The actor on the screen is being thought of as already dead and what remains of him is his transformation into a virtual figure. (Groys 2007)

In the first instalment of Neumann's, Castorf's and Rene Pollesch's *Neustadt* series (2002), the entire theatre building was transformed into a *substitute city* (Ersatzstadt) with ten-metre-high scaffolding and the invitation to the audience to participate in *Neustadt*'s private and public life for two days and nights in total: hotel, public square, hair salon, employment office, supermarket; in short, a multitude of alternative temporary micro-economies and impromptu businesses had been set up. The first four *Neustadt* marathons of four weeks each, quickly became an obsession for Berliners who seemed to fervidly anticipate the call to enter a theatre with a forty-eight-hour ticket and their sleeping bags. In the midst of Berlin's growing economy and global *hipness,* they were in effect queuing up to participate in Neumann's spatialization of a post-industrial urban survival camp. *Neustadt* became synonymous with a radical departure from the constraints of the proscenium arch theatre. This was extended to the Volksbühne's alternate location, Berlin's oldest beer garden, the *Prater* (2002–2010), with its adjoining former cinema. Here Neumann built sequences of fully furnished and practisable rooms, as well as exploiting the cinema ground plan to transform the space into a film set where, it seemed, performances occurred almost incidentally.

Neumann's preference for being called an architect rather than a scenographer becomes clear when we understand architecture to both connote the design and construction of buildings, and more widely as a connective system that combines construction elements into a complete built structure. In his years at the Volksbühne, Neumann did several key things: he designed and constructed temporary built environments that brought to the fore a kind of vehement naturalism, and he rehabilitated the fourth wall as a confronting, excluding and isolating spatial element through closing off the action from the gaze of the spectator. He had also, with the *Neustadt* series, devised systems of spaces that allowed for yet-to-be-invented narratives and public participation throughout the theatre building.

The architect as performance architect: The staging of participation

The recent term 'performance architecture' belongs to an architectural discourse and extended practice that is firmly situated in the spatial and performative analysis of everyday behaviour. Performance architecture has its origins in the happenings and performances by artists and architects from the 1960s on, and the term is realized today as performance installations and participative temporary constructions.

Performance architecture understands domestic behaviour, scenarios and narratives as shaped by politics. It also recognizes the way in which the private and domestic is directly connected to urbanism. It does this through performance installations and temporary constructions, both of which typically involve local residents in the building process and performance, and with the aim to 'complicat(e) the distinction between occupying subjects and occupied subjects' (Schweder 2014). As an emerging genre, performance architecture is associated most strongly with the Spanish architect Andrés Jaque and his *Office for Political Innovation*, the kinetic and participative architectural installations of American architect Alex Schweder, and the French architecture collective EKYZT.[13]

Jaque's practice spans the genres of built architecture, performance and temporary architecture while Schweder has to this date sited his permeable and changeable architectures in galleries, a theatre and public space.

The 'performance of architecture' or the notion of buildings that 'perform themselves' is not a new concept. Its many points of departure reach back to Russian utopian constructivist architectures and to performance art by architects and visual artists, notably the Vienna architecture collective Coop Himmelb(l)au[14] and the body architectures of Vito Acconci since the 1970s. In an interview from 2007, Acconci describes his performance experiments as a 'play or practice architecture' the nub of which is the body, that causes or activates architectural construction while at the same time probes architecture's historic need for stability:

> Work of mine had always been connected with the body, so in the beginning of the 1980's, I did a number of pieces that, in retrospect, were a kind of play architecture or practice architecture: A person sits in a swing, and the action of sitting in a swing causes walls to come up. I wanted to make a body be the cause of architecture. Can a person's action make a shelter? (Acconci in Rousseau 2007)

In the main, performance architects and their predecessors have not sought out designated performance spaces as spaces of encounter, but have rather occupied such spaces as galleries, museums and urban space as these explicitly help to rearticulate the private domain and its associated concepts of domesticity and shelter in the public realm. Alex Schweder's site-specific piece *The Rise and Fall* for the fourth Marrakesh Biennale in 2012 is an exception that took place in the unfinished Théâtre Royal de Marrakech in Gueliz. After twenty-five years of construction, the exterior façade, the outdoor theatre and the foyer had been opened in 2001, yet the centrepiece of the opera house, the auditorium and stage remained in a raw, unfinished state. Schweder chose the ruin as a dual site of architectural and political tumult and a metaphor for Morocco's uncertain future since the Arab Spring and the Moroccan independence protests in 2011–2012 (see Plate 7).

Schweder constructed a wooden bridge between the stage and the orchestra pit that was fixed to one wall yet tilted across a five-metre height difference between the two entry points. The audience began to clamber rather carefully across the bridge structure once they became aware of both its fragility and the impact of each other's movements on the structure. This activity acted as a spatial catalyst for the structure to 'rise' to one side while 'falling' to the other, activating one of the two record players on either side. Inserted into a site of political failure manifested in an unfinished architectural object, the fragility of community allied to the effects of deliberate yet playful actions were enacted in Schweder's performance architecture. At the same time, *Rise and Fall's* placement in a theatre building temporarily transgressed the apparent fixity of the border between auditorium and stage – the space of action and the space of reception – towards one precarious space of negotiation.

The structures resulting from a performative approach to the housing of a temporary community within an existing structure or in a public space straddle the genres of scenography and architecture, yet transgress both. As staged models of inhabitation where numerous scripts of behaviour arise and are reframed, Schweder's work links to Jaque's performance *IKEA Disobedients* from 2011 in the construction of temporary environments for daily behaviour (see Plate 8).

Restaged by MoMA in 2012, Jaque's performance interrogates and subverts the reality-producing sanitization of domestic behaviours as shown by the idealized families in the pages of the annual worldwide IKEA catalogue. In a video accompanying the performance, the female voice-over's first sentence, the premise of the overall work, claims: 'IKEA delivers societies' (MoMA 2012) thus emphasizing the existence of a politics of the domestic, which is produced and affirmed by global companies worldwide. In both iterations of *IKEA Disobedients*, Jaque invited local residents (from inner-city Madrid in 2011 and from Queens, Brooklyn, New York in 2012) to perform their everyday home-based activities in the public arena of the gallery.

> Most of the time when you see a public square there's not much that could actually happen there. But when you see a house, you see that the possibilities are far greater: You could watch TV, you could cook, you could read, you could listen to music, you could talk to people or argue with them, you could swim in the swimming pool. (Jaque in Hawthorn 2013)

The temporary construction of Jaque's IKEA *Disobedience* could have been the very beginnings of one of Neumann's transgressive scenographies at Volksbühne Berlin. Yet, while Jaque's performances of domestic behaviours emphasize the political impact of the transference of domesticity into the public realm, they ignore the ways that any staging might be a manipulation of the real.

The performances of the unspectacular behaviours of local residents occur in an environment that has been subversively assembled and constructed from IKEA furniture through a hacking methodology. To Jaque, the perceived non-political reality of the private home and its activities is given agency through its public performance. Architecture, for the performance architects Alex Schweder and Andrés Jaque, thus becomes an arena for participation as much as a platform for the reinvention of the discipline itself. And it is precisely this kind of aesthetic and disciplinary irreverence, this political premise and formal invention, that Viebrock laments when architectural aestheticism, however innovative, meets with the bourgeois convention of the proscenium arch theatre.

Architecture as scenography: Scenography as architecture

The representation of architecture has always been a major feature of scenography, and this chapter has set out to undermine the assumed binary classification, following Vitruvius, of the ephemerality of theatre and the durability of architecture.

The chapter opened with German scenographer Anna Viebrock's provocation, namely that a clear distinction exists between the scenographer's freedom in the setting of intense atmospheres and aesthetics that disregard dominant aesthetic ideals, and the limitations that an architect is faced with, namely adhering to what is generally regarded as 'good taste'. Viebrock's addressee, Jacques Herzog of the Swiss architecture firm Herzog and de Meuron, endorsed Viebrock's assertion and explained the gap between the boundless aesthetic and formal possibilities open to the scenographer, compared with architecture's limited choice between the temporality of theatre and the durability of architecture. Close readings of scenographies on the proscenium stage by Herzog and De Meuron, OMA, Daniel Libeskind and Frank Gehry revealed that their engagement with urban reality and detail has been marginal compared with these architects' focus on material and formal explorations. Rather, abstracted and symbolic representation, articulated through the notion of the theatre as machine and monumental object, comprise the bulk of their design propositions and echo the Vitruvian notion of 'firmitas'. These findings support Viebrock's and Herzog's verbal exchange on the fundamental difference in the practices of scenography and architecture and further confirm that in an architect's occasional practice of scenography in parallel to his daily architectural practice, the language of architecture with its aim for an overall harmonious whole allied to a disciplinary historic prevalence for the claim (and merit) of singular authorship comes to define the scenographic decisions made. From Kiesler and Tatlin in the 1920s to the scenographies of the most publicized architects of today, architect-scenographers continue to privilege the often-experimental singular, sculptural object on stage – which refuses detail as well as scenic transformation (Kohlhaas' OMA is the notable exception here). The singular object reliably conveys the architect's formal and aesthetic signature as identical to his or her built structures in the urban environment, and thus positively reaffirms the architect's authorship and 'brand'.

While also instantly recognizable, the architecture-hacking and reality-hacking practices of scenographers Anna Viebrock and Bert Neumann neglect any coherent formal and material language in order to speak of the political which pervades the private, through the recycling and adaptation of both found and official architectures and architectural elements. In addition, the constructions of participatory environments in the theatre and beyond blur the borders between private and public, and invite the audience to test new forms of temporary inhabitation. The emerging genre of Performance Architecture sees architects embracing the performative as an inherent spatial condition that is well-suited to uproot architecture's assumed durability, and instead to propose material, aesthetic and political counter-positions.

In current scenographic practice, and in contrast to many of the iconic architect-scenographers' scenic propositions that are purely reliant on symbolic representation, a new critical realism comes increasingly to the fore in opera, theatre and performance design. In an acknowledgement of the failure of the modernist grand narrative, the detailed domestic scene, rather than the symbolic object, is established as an inherently political, conflicted and contested space of failed interaction and miscommunication. The scenographic representation of the private dwelling in this way, formerly a symbol of identity, security and ownership, has clearly become the spatialized representation of a hypercapitalist society, so that across the re-established fourth wall we watch the hysterical writhings of the post-Fordist, postmodern subject.

Architects, on the other hand, need to leave the safe and aesthetically pleasing territory of symbolic representation on the stage behind and embrace the politicized domestic as a mirror of society, a conceptual move that would allow for the urban city-builders of today to finally become world-makers in the theatre.

Notes

1   The term 'programme' in architecture denotes a building's function, that is as a school or a theatre, whereas the term 'tectonics' describes the organization of material and structural forces into a meaningful whole (for a discussion of the 'scenographic' and its counterpart, the 'tectonic', see Brejzek 2015).

2   The 1st-century Roman architect Vitruvius' claim of architecture's three main principles, namely *firmitas*, *utilitas* and *venustas*, generally translated as durability, convenience and beauty (Vitruvius 1960: 17), has held long authority over architects and scenographers in how to build a theatre, how to construct a bridge or how to design a harmonious column. Vitruvius's *Ten Books of Architecture* aimed to record and codify the past architectural achievements of the Hellenistic period and those of his present-day Rome and outlined several building types including the Greek and Roman theatres, architectural compositional orders and construction principles. Long-lost but rediscovered in 1414 and translated and published in 1486 in Florence, Vitruvius' normative treatise continued to influence architects and scenographers alike well into the late Renaissance, notably with Leon Battista Alberti's first theoretical treatise on architecture since antiquity, *De Re Aedificatoria* from the middle of the 15th century that extended the Vitruvian tradition to a future of building rather than its past and developed a perspectival theory that should become seminal for the fixed scenographies of the Renaissance stages such as the perspectival street scape of Palladio's *Teatro Olimpico* (1580).

3   For a detailed discussion of my definition of 'new critical realism' in scenography, see Brejzek (2017).

4   Examples of performative architecture include Kolarevic and Malkawi (2004), Liu (2011), Schwarte (n.d.) and Mulvey (2012), and for a first articulation of responsive architecture, see Negroponte (1975).

5   Incidentally, Price was the prize winner of the Third Austrian Friedrich-Kiesler-Prize for Architecture and Art in 2002.

6   The three plays staged by the Instituto Nazionale del Dramma Antico with scenographies by OMA were, Aeschylos' *Prometheus Unbound*, directed by Claudio Longhi, Euripides' *Bacchae*, directed by Antonio Calenda, and Aristophanes' *The Birds*, directed by Roberta Torre.

7   'The heterotopia is capable of juxtaposing in a single real place several spaces, several sites that are in themselves incompatible. Thus it is that the theatre brings onto the rectangle of the stage, one after the other, a whole series of places that are foreign to one another' Foucault ([1967] 1984).

8   Lesson A: Reading Architecture, Lesson B: Remembering Architecture, Lesson C: Writing Architecture.

9   *Available Light* was premiered at the opening of the des Museum of Contemporary Art, Los Angeles, 1983 and restaged for the Disney Concert Hall, Los Angeles in 2015.

10 Webb in Wise (2003).

11 Pastier (2012) and Webb in Wise (2003).

12 'In einem letzten Haus kurz hinter der Westgrenze Rußlands, irgendwo zwischen Paris Texas, Cindy Sherman, Dogma 95 und Duma 2000, inszeniert Frank Castorf im Bühnen- und Kostümbild von Bert Neumann die "Dämonen" als eine Art postsowjetisch-panslawistisches Panoptikum' (my translation from the German)

13 EXYZT write in their 'manifesto': 'The collective conceive and organise each project as a playground in which cultural behaviours and shared stories relate, mix and mingle. Each project always strives to involve different constituencies of the local community in a social network that is invited to inhabit a temporary space' (EXYZT 2015).

14 For example, Haus Rucker Gordon Matta-Clark (e.g. *Conical Intersect*, 27–29 rue Beaubourg, Paris Biennale 1975).

PLATE 1 Herzog and de Meuron, *Tristan and Isolde*, Staatsoper Berlin, 2003 (Monika Rittershaus).

PLATE 2 Kiesler's *Space Stage* in rehearsal, Konzerthaus Vienna, 1924 (Austrian Friedrich and Lillian Kiesler Private Foundation, Vienna).

PLATE 3 OMA, *Prometeo*, Teatro Greco, Syracuse, 2012 (OMA).

PLATE 4 Daniel Libeskind, *Writing Architecture* Machine, Venice, 1985 (Studio Daniel Libeskind).

PLATE 5 Frank Gehry, *Don Giovanni*, Walt Disney Concert Hall, Los Angeles, 2012 (Autumn de Wilde).

PLATE 6 Bert Neumann, *Erniedrigte und Beleidigte*, Vienna, 2001 (Thomas Aurin).

PLATE 7 Alex Schweder, *Rise and Fall*, Gueliz, 2012 (Alex Schweder).

PLATE 8 Andres Jaque, *IKEA Disobedients*, New York, 2011 (courtesy of wikicommons).

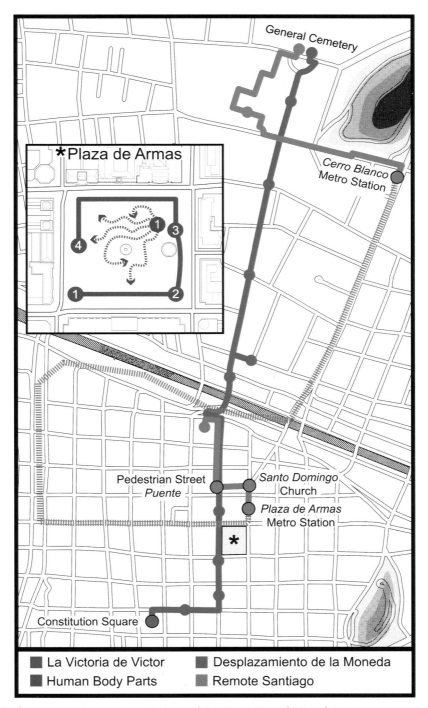

PLATE 9 Performance trajectory maps in central Santiago (Daniel Maseda).

PLATE 10 *La Victoria de Víctor*, Santiago, 2012 (Marcela Oteíza Silva). Clockwise from top left: (1) Truck arrival, bringing four guitarists that each impersonated Víctor Jara. (2) Víctor Jara perched on litter chair. (3) Chorus standing on a wheeled platform. (4) Actor impersonating a Chilean official stands on the truck high above the audience, the cathedral's facade as his backdrop.

PLATE 11 *El Desplazamiento del Palacio de la Moneda o Minga:* Immigrants voice their demands, Santiago, 2014 (Marcela Oteíza Silva).

PLATE 12 *Remote Santiago:* protest at Pedestrian Path *Puente*, Santiago, 2015 (Marcela Oteíza Silva).

PLATE 13 La Voix des Rroms placard, Hotel de Ville, Paris, April 2015 (Ludovic Versace).

PLATE 14 Giant puppet burning outside Basilica St Denis, Paris, May 2015 (Ludovic Versace).

PLATE 15 Romani Triangle Walking Tour, Hoxton Square, London, June 2015 (Alice Clark).

4

City as Site: Street Performance and Site Permeability during the Festival Internacional Teatro a Mil, Chile, 2012–2015

Marcela Oteíza

Street theatre performances activate the city, layering their meaning into the places where they are staged. Conversely, the city adds its own social and political history to the performances. In this chapter, I focus on the exchange that occurs between the city of Santiago, its inhabitants and festival street performances. The analysis is conducted from the perspective of stage design, as well as through the lens of site-specificity, in order to examine the different levels of permeability of a given site, taking into consideration the contemporary context of trans-disciplinary spatial practices in scenography.

The Festival Internacional Teatro a Mil[1] (FITAM) takes place every year in Santiago, the capital city of Chile. For several years now, I have attended the festival's street performances. Through my ethnographic research into the scenographic spatial significance of the festival's city, I have been considering how the occupation of iconic urban sites has the potential to reveal the many layers of the socio-political history of Santiago, as well as the curatorial insight required from the festival's organizers in support of each production's dramaturgy. The connections between the city, its inhabitants and the theatrical explorations of national and international companies raise questions about Chile, a country marked by geographical isolation and a history of government-imposed censorship.

FITAM aims to promote contemporary Chilean and international theatre, and to provide affordable and equal access for all audiences. Starting in 1995, the festival has offered free outdoor performances of music, dance, digital spectacles, urban interventions and street theatre, in addition to paid productions in theatres and alternative spaces. As its core mission, FITAM aims to expand local audiences' perceptions of contemporary performing arts. This is evidenced by their curatorial choices where diversity and breadth seem to define their programming. Street performances reveal the diverse ways in which the festival re-shapes the city in itself into each production's scenography. Consequently, the city becomes a site that has been intervened upon. Utilizing Santiago as a site draws forth its socio-political history and its aesthetic urban composition. The socio-political history of Santiago is linked to that of its inhabitants. Thus, the city as scenography is layered with meaning that permeates through the reception of the street performances.

One cannot consider Santiago's history without considering the role it has played during the years of Chile's military dictatorship. During that time, Santiago's inhabitants occupied the city's public sites as they struggled to reclaim both their city and their right to self-governance. The Chilean dictatorship, led by military general Augusto Pinochet, was in power from the coup d'état on 11 September 1973 until 11 March 1990 – the inauguration day of the first president elected after the coup. The military regime was characterized by systematic suppression of human rights violations that were unprecedented in the history of Chile.

I grew up in Santiago during Pinochet's regime, at a time when gathering in public spaces was at first illegal, but later in the 1980s was seen as an act of resistance. Civilians had to abide a curfew for most of those years. I remember how my generation participated in acts of civil disobedience to reclaim the return of democracy in the county. In that process, streets, neighbourhoods, plazas and buildings became characters that were our partners in that struggle. For example, each time a protest began on the main street, Alameda, the aim was to reach La Moneda, the seat of the President of the Republic of Chile and, therefore, a representation of the military regime's power and oppression. Even if the protest dissolved before reaching it, the crowd would still shout: 'A La Moneda' ('To the Moneda').

Other areas in the neighbourhood of Alameda and La Moneda are also significant, and they all depart from Santiago's central plaza, the Plaza de Armas. Built in the 16th century, Plaza de Armas has long been the political, economic, social and religious heart of Santiago. Adjacent to the cathedral on the west side of the Plaza sits the Vicaría de la Solidaridad (Vicarage of Solidarity), which provided a safe haven from heavy police repression during times of protest. My generation knew the ins and outs of the city as a matter of survival: we knew from which direction the police water cannons would emerge, which streets connected to possible exit routes and where to re-group in case the manifestations (protests) were disbanded.

Protests in the Plaza de Armas are not solely events of the past. In 2012, Chilean high school and university students protested in the plaza against the decreasing level of the quality of public education (Vergara 2012). The Plaza de Armas also has its everyday users, such as workers looking for a green patch of grass in central Santiago, and with passers-by that mingle with puppet shows, evangelical preachers, shoe shining and souvenir stands. Thus, the plaza's adaptability to different uses and many populations makes it permeable to multiple readings.

Upon these buildings and spaces that are charged with history, FITAM productions add new layers of meaning to them. At the festival's outdoor performances, Chilean audiences experience a renewed connection with the space-characters of central Santiago. I use the term 'space-character' to refer to a specific urban place or architectural iconic site that has a latent socio-historical meaning for Santiago's inhabitants and that are used as recurrent theatrical spaces for the Festival, thereby rendering the space-characters a role within the construction of meaning of the festival's productions. For example, Plaza de Armas and La Moneda both intersect with the dramaturgy of traveling productions. Even if the festival's productions are usually conceived for touring and, therefore, for other sites and audiences, at the moment in which they are transposed to space-character locations that are also home to Chilean audiences, these performances' visual compositions assume particular meanings in relationship to those spectators' collective memory. In turn, these productions actually recover and reaffirm the mnemonic qualities of Santiago's public spaces. During the festival, Santiago's central square, the Plaza de Armas, becomes a prime example of how collective memory is recovered at a public space.

Consequently, the occupation of Santiago's space-characters by FITAM productions expands the notion of the scenographic from a traditional stage design to a trans-disciplinary engagement with the performative space (Brejzek 2011: 8). This allows us to understand performance design as an 'idea' or as a model, enabling us to see and experience the city anew through the blending of theatre, urban architecture and history within a particular performance.

As I recorded and interviewed practitioners and spectators of FITAM's performances at different outdoor sites between 2012 and 2015, I examined how the notion of place and the spectator/actor relationship can transform the urban architecture into a stage. I was often reminded that independently of the type of site – be it a street or a park (transitory or permanent site of convergence) – the performance interventions cause the surrounding architecture to become part of the performance's *mise en scéne*,[2] and conversely, the dramaturgy is layered onto the city space-characters, thus addressing in a twofold fashion: first, the permeability of site and, second, the level of openness of the event.

To analyse the levels of site permeability into a given production, I utilize site-specificity as a point of entry. Kaye states that 'site-specific art [functions] as articulate exchanges between the work of art and the places in which its meanings are defined' (Kaye 2000: 1). This view, therefore, accounts for the space and the context in which each performance takes place. This view also takes into consideration Fiona Wilkie's assertion that site-specific performances foreground spatiality as a locus of performance meanings (2004: 2). Furthermore, Jen Harvie writes that site-specific performance can be especially powerful as a vehicle for remembering and forming a community (Harvie 2005: 42). By integrating the notions of Wilkie and Harvie into my analysis of the performances, I intend to re-define the street performances here presented as site-oriented performances, underscoring the performance-space relationship (Kwon 2014: 34). I will argue that the site (the city of Santiago), and in particular the 'space characters' (Plaza de Armas, La Moneda, etc.) where the street performances of Santiago a Mil are staged, interconnect the meaning of the productions with the ones of the site, even though some of the touring productions are not necessarily created for the places where they are shown.

I consider the street performances discussed here to be site-oriented works because they intervene into the public space and incorporate the context of their surroundings into viewers' construction of the production's meaning. In the description and analysis section that follows below, I will offer an account of the 'space-characters' Plaza de Armas (city central plaza) and La Moneda (Chilean presidential palace) within the socio-political context of Santiago, Chile, and describe how the street performances interconnect their own meaning with the particular historical, political, and religious significance of urban sites that they occupy.

Plaza de Armas

During the festival, Santiago's central square, Plaza de Armas, becomes a prime example of how collective memory is recovered at a public space. Architect René Martinez Lemoine explains the history of spatial organization of such spaces in Latin America:

> We, in Spanish America, understand the city, beginning from a central, empty square. We 'know' that in the centre of the pattern there is a block missing, an empty square we will always find the Cathedral, the Municipal building, the Post Office, the central governmental office, the bank or a least a bank, and the main hotel. This is simply a 'fact', something that is the natural order of things. (Martinez Lemoine 2003: 367)

The Plaza's adaptability to different uses and many populations makes it permeable to multiple readings. In 1976, the Vicary of Solidarity (La Vicaría de la Solidaridad[3]) operated next to the cathedral. This left-leaning branch of the Catholic Church supported human rights during Pinochet's dictatorship. Activists held protests in front of this organization's building and throughout the Plaza. Currently, groups advocating for animal and ecological causes, or immigrant, gay and lesbian rights, mingle with its everyday users. As Marvin Carlson points out:

> The absence of a specifically theatrical structure from the medieval city's repertory of architectural objects by no means indicates that the physical situation of theatre performance within the city was devoid of symbolic significance. On the contrary, a situation allowing those producing a performance to place it in whatever locale seemed more suitable meant that the theatre could use to its own advantage the already existing connotations of other spaces both in themselves and in their placement within the city. (Carlson 1993: 14)

La Victoria de Víctor

The performance's use of the city's pre-existing symbolic significance is certainly the case in the staging of *La Victoria de Víctor* (*Victor's Victory*) by the company La Patriótico Interesante (FITAM 2012). Utilizing a sequence of visual vignettes, the performance conveyed the story of Víctor Jara, a Chilean songwriter, theatre director and political activist that was tortured and killed due to his opposition to Pinochet's military regime. Its dramaturgical structure mirrored the stations of a liturgical medieval play. *La Victoria de Víctor* (see Plate 9) took the shape of a parade that led the audience through the corners, crossings and buildings of the Plaza de Armas, as the company director Ignacio Achurra states, 'The production has a structure built on the base of stationary and itinerant points. It has five stationary scenes and six itinerant or transit scenes' (I. Achurra, personal video interview, 7 April 2015). Therefore, the performance connected Víctor Jara's political martyrdom to the '*Via Crucis*' stations. The structure of a religious procession has been embedded in the performance's mechanics; for example, in the manner by which the actors introduced scenographic elements, such as litter chairs or carts. Achurra comments that these objects were stationed in different locations, usually within two blocks of the performance's main focal point at a given moment. The actors moved these structures into the next scene as the parade developed, bringing with them new audiences of passers-by that were attracted to the performance and that may have curiously followed these design elements.

> For the Plaza de Armas [to] work for the production… [the performance] [had to move] circularly around the plaza. The audience doesn't see, [the different scenes] because it turns on its axis. But instead [the audience] advances like in a line [alongside] with the litter chairs. [The performers] go into different streets to [eventually] form … a procession. (I. Achurra, personal video interview, 7 April 2015).

The performance of *La Victoria de Víctor* began when a group of actors wearing guerrilla masks appeared at the Plaza's south-eastern corner. They moved the crowd to the sides to open a path (see Plate 10). A truck arrived bringing the four guitarists that impersonated Víctor Jara, playing his famous song 'El Aparecido' – except that the arrangement distorted the melody. The scenes that followed included a depiction of Jara's relationship with his father and mother; a fictional meeting between Jara and songwriter-and-activist Violeta Parra; and the re-enactment of Jara's political life by a chorus standing on a wheeled platform. In another moment, actors dressed as the Chilean police arrived from the Plaza's north-eastern corner to re-enact Víctor Jara's imprisonment and murder. As the sun set, spectators turned their attention to an actor playing a Chilean official: standing on the truck, high above the audience and with the cathedral's facade as his backdrop, the official delivered an overtly demagogical discourse. This final moment was *La Victoria de Víctor*'s strongest example of how architecture, history and dramaturgy intersect. The Chilean audience could, therefore, experience the Cathedral as a space-character that was historically charged. The speech symbolized the alliance between the Catholic Church and the military dictatorial regime. It was an ominous reminder of the audience's national history.

Indeed, the symbolic significance of each cardinal direction and architectural feature at the Plaza in the context of specific dramaturgical events of the production prodded the Chilean audience to identify different power relationships. In the scene between Víctor Jara and Violeta Parra, the two arrived from opposite corners of the Plaza on litter chairs held high above the audience. Jara entered from the south-eastern corner where the cathedral is located, while Parra arrived from the Plaza's commercial southeast side. The choice highlighted the opposite but complementary ties between religion and economics. This scene placed masculine and feminine facing each other from opposite directions. The two characters connected, but held onto their distinct kinds of power.

The scene in which Jara was arrested unfolded on the ground. Audience and performer met at eye level. The shift in the spatial relationship underscored that the military regime had not only crushed Jara but also that the entire country had experienced disempowerment. *La Victoria de Víctor* was not specifically created for Plaza de Armas, but it became a site-specific performance because the performance incorporated the architectural buildings into the production's construction of meaning. As Achurra explains, the performance makes a deliberate use of iconic architectural sites:

> [In street theatre] When you [visually] compose the street for performance, in some ways, the street is a [pre-existing] picture that has been already painted – it's hyper-populated by

signs. Therefore, any signs that you add will enter into a dialogue with [the previously existing] signs.... In other words, to set the final scene in front of the cathedral, that was a decision [for this particular production]. (I. Achurra, personal video interview, 7 April 2015)

La Victoria de Víctor uses the company's understanding of the Plaza as a public site to effectively juxtapose the performance's dramaturgy and Plaza de Armas' history and current urban life to awaken the audience's social and political memories of a space axiologically charged. As a result, *La Victoria de Víctor* transforms Plaza de Armas into a 'site-oriented place', a term coined by Miwon Kwon to explain how street performances may act as relational events:

> Moving beyond the inherited conception of site-specific art as a grounded, fixed (even if ephemeral), singular event, the works of these [street theatre] artists are seen to advance an altogether different notion of a site as predominantly an intertextually coordinated, multiple located, discursive field of operation. (Kwon 2014: 33)

Such perception of the theatrical event as a field of intertextual operations views the performance always in a communication with its context. In these cases, the notion of intertextuality exceeds considerations of the text to include an understanding of the performative that is a composition of interconnected layers of visual and other signs. In *La Victoria de Víctor*, the field of operations at work on the audience gathered together the texts created by the plaza's history, iconic buildings and urban significance, the arc of the production's dramaturgy, and the inherently transient nature of theatre and its spectatorship.

La Victoria de Víctor made tangible the idea of multiple mobilities, because the production moved through present and past time, travelling across physical space, and as the audience circulated throughout the plaza to follow the action. Here, the theatrical event is no longer understood as a repeatable rehearsed work, but instead as one that is always immediate and that, during its course, is formed through the co-presence of performers, place and spectators in an ongoing process of the production of meaning. In this light, the construction of meaning of *La Victoria de Víctor* at Plaza de Armas is constituted by the author's intentions, the specific location, social-historical context and the particular reception of its varied types of spectators, particularly perhaps for Chileans.

Human Body Parts

At the Plaza de Armas in 2013, the puppet performance *Human Body Parts*[4] established a different relationship between the audience-performer's co-presence and place and, therefore, the construction of meaning of the piece does not rest on the historical context of the site, but instead on the physical use of the plaza. The site of Plaza de Armas becomes recycled into a social space that functions as both auditorium and stage by confounding the roles of spectators and performers.

The performance of *Human Body Parts* erases socio-political history of the Plaza. Instead, the performance physically interferes with the plaza's normal usages, dismantling the geometry of its paths, as well as the everyday activities of its occupants. The performance creates a new place for its participants through its occurrence, because places are in a permanent state of change as they are inhabited and, as such, their residents engage in the act of dwelling and, by their relationship, transform them. As Mike Pearson states:

> [It is] because places are about relationships, about the placing of peoples, materials, images and the systems of difference that they perform.… A place owes its character to the experiences it affords to those who spend time there – to the sights, sounds and indeed smells that constitute its specific ambience – and these, in turn, depend on the kinds of activities in which its inhabitants engage. It is from this relational context of people's engagement with the world, in the business of dwelling, that each place draws its unique significance. (Pearson 2010: 514)

Australian Snuff Puppet Company's *Human Body Parts* takes over the entire plaza to alter the behaviours of its usual passers-by. The playful giant body parts roam around the plaza interrupting and interacting with bystanders. The festival website explains that:

> The Ear and Eye [are] still and pensive; [they follow, watch and listen]. In contrast, The Mouth … [is] quite articulate, chomping, snarling, devouring and licking with its giant tongue. The Hand [creeps] its way down the footpath, touching everything, holding people, tapping, slapping and generally gesticulating its way around town, while the giant Foot hops along trying to keep up. (Human Body Parts 2013)

At the beginning, the puppets were stationed in a gated space northeast of the plaza. The performance started from north of the plaza's gazebo taking the path towards the southwest corner (Compañía and Bandera street corner). Hundreds of people, including children, followed the puppets, trying to touch and interact with them. The dramaturgy followed no particular storyline, in that in the performance, each body part behaved and intermingled independently. The puppets got caught on park benches and trash cans, as well as on people and traffic. Daniele Poidomani, a member of the company, comments on the audience engagement with the piece:

> It's something everyone can relate to because of course we all have body parts, but it becomes immediately surreal and abstract, having body parts acting on their own will, out there and being extremely giant… The people … Oh! They scream, and they're happy … normally we get pushed around a lot and kicked and, yeah they do everything to us. (Poidomani, personal video interview, January, 2013)

The plaza's symmetry seemed to dissolve; its functionality and architecture no longer organized the flux of passers-by, since the audience ran hectically around chasing the different body parts for a better glimpse or interaction. The plaza's space, usually organized and filled with socio-historical meaning, had been transformed into an unruly playground. The Australian company disrupted Plaza de Armas by creating a spontaneous celebration; a space, primarily, for performer–spectator interaction.

Central Santiago

My next examples took place across a number of sites across the city centre. Santiago was designed during Spanish colonization in the traditional chessboard layout, starting from Plaza de Armas and continuing with eight blocks from north to south and ten blocks from east to west, in a pre-occupied *Picunche*[5] settlement, a native indigenous group. The Spanish-imposed grid layout, as Martinez Lemoine states, became Santiago's centre where the city would develop from its colonial architecture to neoclassic buildings. The cathedral, the opera house, the National Library and other edifices dating from the 1800s, currently blend-in with modern skyscrapers and other historic architectural buildings. Libertador General Bernardo O'Higgins Avenue, popularly known as La Alameda, serves as the main artery of the city and is where La Moneda is located (Aranguiz 2004: 56). La Moneda and the surrounding areas, such as the Plaza Cívica (Civic square) and the Plaza Constitución (Constitution Square), are used yearly as sites for FITAM's performances, as are other locations of the city, such as the general cemetery. The cemetery is the resting place for some of the most influential people in the country, among them President Salvador Allende,[6] and it has a vast green area and serves as a park. It also hosts a memorial in honour of those 'disappeared' during the military regime.

El Desplazamiento del Palacio de la Moneda o Minga

El Desplazamiento del Palacio de la Moneda o Minga (*Displacement of the Moneda Palace or Minga*)[7] is a procession-style performance created by the Spanish artist Roger Bernat in 2014 specifically for the city of Santiago. It made evident use of the city's iconic sites and its communities as part of its dramaturgy by moving a replica of La Moneda governmental palace from its location to Allende's tomb at the General Cemetery. As Roger Bernat states:

> To deviate from our path towards la Legua[8] to go through the cemetery was an act of justice. The circumstances in which Allende was torn from La Moneda deserved it, it will not happen very often that La Moneda moves from its place, and we will make the effort to end the first round in front of his grave. (Bernat in Inostroza 2014)

Bernat thus utilizes the palace's symbolic power, as well as overlaying into the performance the Chilean tradition of la Minga, a custom from southern Chiloe Island, where communities work together towards a shared goal. The Minga usually entails moving a house from a current location to a better one. As a way of payment, they celebrate the completion of the work with a communal meal. *El Desplazamiento del Palacio de la Moneda o Minga* was also a long processional journey through the centre of Santiago, involving the multiple and varied communities who live there. The route started at Plaza Constitución behind La Moneda and crossed through Plaza de Armas, to arrive at the city's main cemetery.

The performance focused on a miniature wooden replica of La Moneda approximately two metres tall.[9] Wooden poles extended from the base of the square structure, so that this miniature

La Moneda could be carried like a processional altar. Community groups from along the route alternated in the carrying of the model and a ladder so that it could be used as a podium. Each community group used the Moneda podium to state their demands.

The approach to audience participation was key to the realization of this performance and to intervening in the city. As Jens Roselt states, 'The simultaneous presence of performers and spectators, which marks it as a cultural performance, generates and shapes specific forms of attention' (Roselt 2013: 265). The collective procession stopped at twelve locations, each highlighting a different community group. The structure of the performance allowed people from these communities to actively participate. For example, at Plaza Constitución, a political group stated their demands by addressing not only their own groups, audiences and creators of the piece but also the miniature of la Moneda Palace itself: 'This is a house [pointing to the palace miniature] of lies, where the people are not able to get in to build a better society' (*Santiago (en) Vivo* 2017). As Rancière underscores:

The precise aim of the performance is to abolish this exteriority in various ways: by placing the spectators on the stage and the performers in the auditorium; by abolishing the difference between the two; by transferring the performance to other sites; by identifying it with taking possession of the street, the town or life. (Rancière 2009: 15)

Later, at Plaza de Armas, in front of the cathedral, another group stated its demands:

I am a night-building-concierge representative and I am bringing our demands to the house of la Moneda. Even though we work in buildings, we are not part of the property. We cannot continue to be sold as property parts ... We want dignity and a living wage. (*Santiago (en) Vivo* 2017)

As Bernat explains, the audience involvement in his work went beyond spectators becoming performers and extended to the idea of active actors:

The audience is led to become a sort of spectator of his/herself and to simultaneously be actor and spectator. They are productions in which spectators take responsibility not only of becoming the performer but also to bring the action of the performance to the end. This means that our shows never have the same form. It will depend on how each spectator interprets the rules of the game. (R. Bernat, personal video interview, January 2013)

While the community leaders voiced their demands, the intervention moved through the city, gathering more and more groups and onlookers, until it arrived at Allende's tomb at the cemetery. This processional intervention was particularly poignant to Chileans because, as scholar Jan Cohen-Cruz writes, 'witnessing supposes a connection between knowledge and responsibility' (Cohen-Cruz 1998: 65). The procession established an intimate relationship between audience and performance, because spectators fully participated in activating Santiago's mnemonic potential. Furthermore, it made visible the links between the city's political and religious powers and manifested the political unrest of entire generations as it stopped at each iconic site; it tied the city's architecture to its religious past; and it reminded all of the value of Chile's long history and belief in the power of community. Ultimately, the intervention allowed spectators and performers alike to bear witness to their own past and to see anew the present of the urban space they occupy.

> Site-specific performance can be especially powerful as a vehicle for remembering and forming a community for at least two reasons. First, its location can work as a potent mnemonic trigger, helping to evoke specific past time related to the place and time of performance and facilitating a negotiation between the meanings of those times. (Harvie 2005: 42)

Jen Harvie's words became particularly pertinent many times during the processional intervention *El Desplazamiento de la Moneda*, but more clearly when the procession arrived at Paseo Puente where Peruvian immigrants, now a strong and thriving community in Santiago, took their turn on the la Moneda podium. They voiced their frustration with Chilean immigration laws and 'nominated' their own children as possible future presidents of Chile (see Plate 11). A representative of the Peruvian refugees Committee demanded:

> Thank you for this beautiful gesture. We receive and reaffirm that we want to be one nation. We are committed to Chile and its future; We are committed to the changes required by history. We do not want a constitution that excludes children because of their nationality, because we are all equal. As part of the immigrant community, I present to you Estrella who will state the demands of the children: Nobody should be Stateless. (*Santiago (en) Vivo* 2017)

The performance foregrounds the significance of the Paseo Puente site. This is where generations of Chileans took to the streets to voice their own discontent with the government. During the performance, the actual site acted as a backdrop where the immigrant community voiced their current demands. The performance happened in the present, but the mnemonic qualities of the site were brought forth and, by such, facilitated the understanding and negotiation between new communities.

Remote Santiago

Site-specific performance can also be a vehicle for understanding the notion of place. For instance, the superimposing of an external reading to a familiar place such as your hometown can bring light to its idiosyncrasies. In 2015, Stefan Kaegi (Rimini Protokoll) adapted *Remote X* specifically for the city of Santiago. *Remote Santiago* was an auditory journey for an audience of fifty, who were guided through the city by a disembodied voice delivered through headphones. *Remote Santiago* took its audience on an 'anthropological' tour in order to induce the local audience to experience their city, customs and traditions as a computer being would if it was investigating the city through time and space in relation to its physical character, environment, social relations and culture.

The audio guide led the assembled audience through the city, allowing them to relinquish control and self-determination to the guiding technology, coupled with a sense of eerie disorientation and finishing with a liberating view from above (Rimmele 2013: 1). The sites were no longer only what we see, but what we are led to experience. This touring performance travelled through many of Santiago's iconic sites. Here, I will focus on the meanings created by its use of the cemetery as a point of departure; and the neighbourhood of Plaza de Armas as the performance's mid-points.

At an Italian mausoleum in the General Cemetery, the audience gathered and put on headphones. The audience members were greeted by a GPS-style, computer-generated, female voice. 'Rosa' explained that her speech had been made by putting together syllables derived from 2,500 hours of female-voice recordings.[10] Rosa instructed audience members to become aware of the cemetery surroundings, and to focus their attention on a particular crypt, and the photographs and dates of the deceased buried inside. Rosa's voice through its narration invited the audience to draw parallels between the life of the unknown person inside the crypt and their own. The performance underscored individual histories and pointed the audience towards a 'nostalgic' view of the past. Later, when Rosa referenced Allende's tomb while a passage of Pinochet's discourse taking control of the nation during the days that followed the 1973 coup d'état was played, the audience had already been thinking of the past in reference to the themselves. This brought their own individual and subjective history to their current moment, to the performance present, becoming perhaps, as Rancière stated, an emancipated spectator. The use of the recording within this particular context had the effect of bringing forward specific individual memories to the audiences. However, a sense of detachment occurred while the audience crossed from the cemetery, where it had just left Allende's tomb, the adjacent monument to the detained and the disappeared during the military regime, back to the street. The GPS-style voice recording compelled the audience to somehow distance themselves and to create a moment devoid of actual feeling.

The audience continued to listen and to take its directions from Rosa, through streets and public transportation, until arriving at the Plaza de Armas metro station, where they walked into Santo Domingo's church. There, the audience sat in the pews of the dark and cool church nave where the group listened to Rosa's transformation into Rodrigo, a male computer-generated voice, while he gave instructions to divide the audience into two groups. Here, the religious culture of Santiago is highlighted in two ways in juxtaposition to the performance as a site occupied simultaneously by the audience and everyday church goers, and by the content of the performance narration that invoked the presence of the religious icon as possible embodiment for the computer-generated voice. This evoked in the audience important themes, such as trans-gender issues and the position of the Catholic Church in these matters, as well as an important shift in the performance structure as the group was divided for the first time. However, this moment of the performance doesn't become a pivotal one. Instead, it is accepted and experienced by the audience as an intellectual fact, as we kept following orders. *Remote Santiago* thus succeeded in superimposing the computer's point of view and provoking the audience to relinquish control and self-determination. This was made even clearer later when, out in the street, the voice of Rodrigo directed audience members to choose one personal object, to raise it over their heads and to shake it. While the recording shifted into an old recording of a political protest, a police escort appeared (see Plate 12). The march became a staged silent protest. It functioned as an imposed reminder of Santiago's past history, but it did not necessarily resonate in that specific present. The experience had a sense of present emptiness.

The superimposed GPS narrative with its anthropological perspective prompted the participants to experience the city with a sense of detachment, since the self had been replaced by the group, and the group was propelled by a programmed view of space and place. As Helmuth Höger, a member of the *Remote Santiago* company, asserts:

I think *Remote X* is an invitation, at least from my point of view; an invitation to pause, an invitation to rediscover your city … and to enjoy it, to know it from a different perspective, from other angles. (Höger, personal video interview, January 2015)

As such, the city and its landmarks are no longer what the audience has in front of their eyes; what they know and what it normally would experience. Instead, it is a myriad of possibilities, of possible realities that are heightened by the performance narration; possible realities that are latent and waiting to be awakened by the relational experience that each inhabitant has with its city and the construction of meaning of the performance narration.

Remote X is both 'site-specific', as it was in *Remote Santiago*, and a mobile project that moves from city to city. Here, then, it is important to consider the multiple mobilities embedded in this project. *Remote Santiago* was also a performance that moves in time, past and present. An example of its past could easily be seen in the use of historical recordings, and its present in the multiple locations that the performance occupies with their current uses, such as the Santo Domingo Church; but also its audience mobility, as they are actually moving, walking, riding the metro and other activities. This is in addition to the project that moves throughout the world. Wilkie writes that '[i]t is important that we think of [a] project as both mobile and site-specific. By emphasizing the mobility of place, makes the political argument that places need not be accepted as given but can be actively changed' (2012: 40).

Remote X has been conceived as a highly adaptable work, as it is inherently a site-specific work wherever it is performed. In this regard, the use of cultural memories, political history and landmarks of the city that it intervenes, activates the storyline of the journey and makes it site-specific. In *Remote Santiago*, the church, the cemetery, Allende's tomb and political and riot soundscapes are some of these elements.

I would like to emphasize that the way that these everyday spaces can be experienced by *Remote Santiago*'s audiences will depend on their own individualities, such as generational and cultural differences, even within a 'homogenous Chilean' audience. Street performances, and the majority of theatrical performances for that matter, address their audiences as a group. '[Street performances] address themselves to whole communities. Already conceptualizing their audience as a united collective, a valuable pre-condition for social change, these performances take place in public by-ways where people tend to congregate' (Cohen-Cruz 1998: 65). By providing individual headphones, *Remote Santiago* is no different, as everyone in the tour knows that every other participant, like himself or herself, are listening to the same recording, except when otherwise indicated. However, the individual agency is present as part of the personal power that each spectator brings to the shared experience, thus translating their perception in their own adventure.

Conclusion

The performances that I analyse here utilized different modes of interrelational mobility and intertextuality. These interrelational modes refer to audience-performer-site interconnectivity, where the co-presence of actors and performance at a particular space-character co-creates layers of meaning or intertextuality. For example, in *Human Body Parts,* the interrelation established by performers and audience, and their shared-space, effectively balanced the power dynamics of the theatrical event, where Plaza de Armas ceased to operate as a place of memory, but instead, as a place where a community could co-create a new history through the course of the performance.

In contrast, in the *Desplazamiento de la Moneda*, scenography is layered with meaning that can be perceived through its audience's socio-political knowledge of its own community and city, coupled with the audience's active role that carries the performance forward. *Desplazamiento de la Moneda* was a deliberately open performance with a structure and mechanics that functioned as a catalyst for its participants, where its clear modes of intertextual narratives became a powerful vehicle of remembering, while forging new bonds of complicity within its communities.

Remote Santiago and *La Victoria de Víctor* were street performances that utilized a specific storyline and script. In *Remote Santiago* for example, the script was an amalgam of historical recordings and site narrations by a computer-generated voice. In *La Victoria de Víctor*, the script was composed of Jara's songs and other devised texts. Here, the audiences that participated in these two performances contextualized the story to the physical, social, political and historical aspects of place and text. The audience's collective ability to understand the production's permeability and its socio-historical context in relation with Santiago's space-characters and its history was crucial to activating the mnemonic qualities of these performances.

The productions discussed here turned the centre of Santiago into a 'space of another nature' as they intervened into the city's daily life and rhythm. As Erika Fischer-Lichte writes, 'performances do not transmit pre-given meanings. Rather, it is the performance which brings forth the meaning that come into being during its course' (Fischer-Lichte 2009: 8). As I have documented, these productions performed at places that I identify with Chile's political past, gave my hometown a sense that was both fictional and real. The Festival reshaped the space-characters that I knew growing up during Pinochet's regime without robbing them of their historical significance. Audiences relived their collective memories and discovered new meanings in well-known streets and corners. The street performances at Festival Internacional Santiago a Mil re-contextualized the city's architecture in their usage of iconic sites; turned spectators into players and witnesses of the city's transformations; and in doing so, reshaped residents' experiences and perceptions of Santiago de Chile.

Notes

1   The name 'Santiago a Mil' is Spanish for 'Santiago for 1,000 [pesos]' and refers to the low entry price of 1,000 Chilean pesos for events in the festival's early years. It is also a play on the phrase 'trabajar a mil por hora', Spanish for 'working a full one thousand per hour'. Prices for some events have risen over the years, but affordability is still a central factor, with several free performances and many low-cost tickets at the 2015 edition of the festival.

2   The *mise en scéne* creates experimental and ludic spaces which allow for unforeseen and unpredictable events to take place (Fischer-Lichte 2008: 189).

3   La Vicaría de la Solidaridad (1976–1992) was an agency from the Chilean Catholic Church. Its function was to assist the victims of the military dictatorship of General Pinochet. During this

time, the Catholic Church in Chile served both the government and its victims (Arzobispado de Santiago 2014).

4 *Human Body Parts* by Snuff Puppets, Co., Australia. Original creator Andy Freer; designer and puppet builder Nick Wilson, Santiago a Mil 2013. Location: Plaza de Armas.

5 *Picunches* is the name of the indigenous group that inhabits the valley of Santiago. From Mapudungun language: north people (*pikun*, 'north', y *che*, 'people').

6 Salvador Allende Gosen, Socialist Chilean President, who was democratically elected and governed from 4 November 1970 until 11 September 1973 (the date of the coup d'état).

7 La Minga (*mink'a* o *minga* in quechua, 'collective work done in favour of the community'; *minca* from quechua *minccacuni*, 'ask for help offering something in return'; or *mingaco*) in Chile 'Tiradura de Casa' (to move and transport a house). The house is attached to yoke of oxen, bulls or tractors and dragged to wherever it is going. Sometimes, particularly around Chiloé Island, it is also necessary to carry the house through the sea.

8 La Legua Santiago neighbourhood is named after its location, as it is one league from Plaza de Armas. La Legua was originally established in the 1930s by a group of unemployed miners coming from the north of the country that occupied the land. It is politically considered as a bastion of the left.

9 The replica of La Moneda Palace was made by la Legua carpenters, father and son, Jose and Patricio Saavedra. It is made of pinewood, measures 2 metres in length and is 2 metres wide. The whole structure has a height of 2.36 metres or 7'7", it weighs about 80 kilos and needs at least eight people to transport it.

10 'My words are created by more than 2,500 hours of a female voice. The words were divided into syllables by a computer. I form my words with these syllables. For example, I form the word 'identity' in four parts IN comes from the word *inauguración* DEN *densidad* comes from the word IT comes from *tiempo*, DAD comes from *dado*. My identity is composed of four syllables'. Transcribed and translated from video source (Fundación teatro a Mil (FITAM) 2015).

PART THREE

Agency

5

Scenography Matters: Performing Romani Identities as Strategy and Critique

Ethel Brooks
and Jane Collins

This chapter employs scenography as a framework to analyse examples of site-based performance currently being produced among Romani Communities in Europe. It draws on the findings of the 'Performing Romani Identities: Strategy and Critique' (PRISaC) network.[1] Along with creating interconnections among Romani artists, activists and scholars working in performance in key sites in Europe; Alicante, Bucharest, Budapest, Paris and London, the network had a remit to:

> Look to the future place and practice of [Romani] performance in multiple venues, including traditional arts institutions, Romani neighbourhoods and diverse public spaces, acknowledging the particular challenges around the site specificity and target audience of each performance. (AHRC Application 2013 Ref AHM000044/1)

From the outset one of the foci of the research network was to extend the analysis of well-known and established modes of Romani performance that feature in mainstream venues and the media, such as Gypsy Jazz, Balkan Brass and Flamenco, to ascertain how these performance modes were being used strategically by Romani activists in sites outside of building-based theatres. We didn't begin with a specifically scenographic agenda. However, as the project progressed, the manipulation of these mainstream representations – visual, spatial, sartorial and aural – emerged as one of the key methods employed by activists to challenge prescribed notions of Romani people and communities. This became evident through our observation of the performance work we encountered as we moved around Europe and underpinned our own performance experiments in London.

This re-encoding of Romani identities in performance, through interventions in public space, employs definitions of performance design as an 'interdisciplinary and collaborative field', falling as Dorita Hannah argues:

> '[B]etween' theatre and other performing art forms. Emerging as an interstitial space for extending scenography's influence ... avoiding terms such as 'scenery', 'costumes' and 'lighting' in order to focus on how objects, environments, garments, bodies and the intangible elements of sound, light and media *perform*, that is, how they are all active agents in the performance event. (Hannah 2015: 128)

Romani culture is marked by a history of critical performance and performativity. Romani survival in Europe, over the course of a millennium, has been contingent upon the adoption and practice of a number of performance strategies, including oral history, storytelling, music, dance and theatre, as well as upon everyday narratives that perform intelligible Romani identities for both the community itself and for non-Roma. This chapter discusses how Romani artists are harnessing the potential of this 'performativity' by engaging 'objects, environments, garments, bodies ... sound, light and media' (2015) in order to destabilize what Homi Bhabha in his seminal essay on stereotypes and colonial power calls the 'concept of fixity in the ideological construction of otherness' (1983: 18). Bhabha points to this concept as the sign of difference in colonialism; it is the fixity of difference that is disrupted through the performance practices we discuss in this chapter. According to Bhabha:

> Fixity, as the sign of cultural/historical/racial difference in the discourse of colonialism, is a paradoxical mode of representation: it connotes rigidity and an unchanging order as well as disorder, degeneracy and daemonic repetition. Likewise the stereotype, which is its major discursive strategy, is a form of knowledge and identification that vacillates between what is always 'in place', already known, and something that must be anxiously repeated. (1983: 18)

Bhabha stresses the importance of not submitting these representations, 'to a normalising judgement' arguing that 'To judge the stereotyped image on the basis of a prior political normativity is to dismiss it, not to displace it, which is only possible by engaging with its *effectivity*' (1983: 18–19, italics in original). In other words, we must engage with the way these representations are jointly constructed between colonizer and colonized and address why they endure. This chapter addresses this joint construction through analysis of two case studies in Paris and London and argues that one of the methods employed by Romani artists and activists, to move beyond straightforward critique and to actively engage with the 'effectivity' of negative and dehumanizing depictions of Roma, is the strategic use of performance design. From the position that Bhabha calls the 'space of "otherness"' (1983: 19) through the conjunction of site, scenography and activism, Romani performance sets out to 'unfix' the production of difference.

In her introduction to *Artificial Hells,* Claire Bishop suggests that the rationale behind collective artistic projects that engage with the social is a response to the 'repressive instrumentalism of capitalist production' (2012: 11). Referring to Guy Debord and *The Society of the Spectacle* (1967), Bishop describes 'an art of action, interfacing with reality – taking steps – however small to repair the social bond' (2012).

[T]he artist is conceived less as an individual producer of discrete objects than as a collaborator and producer of *situations*; the work of art as a finite, portable commodifiable product is reconceived as an ongoing or long-term *project* with an unclear beginning and end; while the audience, previously conceived as a 'viewer' or 'beholder' is now repositioned as a co-producer or *participant*. (2012: 2 italics in the original)

Such collaborative endeavours push the limits of scenography as an expanded field where responsibility for the spatial, material and aural elements of the project or situation is shared among a range of people, including the audience. For Romani artists, scholars and activists, this necessitates a new form of knowledge production, one that centres Romani subjects as both performers and audience, and which disrupts the objective, objectifying gaze of the (non-Romani) spectator. This collective artistic practice and its work to reposition also signifies the re-centring of Romani knowledge, history and practice – against the figure of the Gypsy reproduced as, for and by *gadzhe*[2] (non-Romani) fantasy. It disrupts the logic of distinction between Romani and *gadzhe*; this logic runs parallel to Orientalism, defined by Edward Said as 'a style of thought based upon an ontological and epistemological distinction made between "the Orient" and (most of the time) "the Occident"' (1979: 2). Said understands Orientalism as a set of academic, imaginative and corporate institutions and practices. Here we see a striking parallel to the production of Romani subjects through academic, imaginative and corporate discourses, and through practices and structures. While the majority of Roma are located in 'the Occident', Romani subjects nevertheless are categorized as part of the ontological and epistemological 'Orient'.

Romani collaborative practice is marked by an eclectic, provisional aesthetic, with multiple contributors and a porous relation between performer and audience. With no singular artistic vision or apparent aesthetic coherence, how are these events framed and recognizable as performance? This blurring of boundaries between the quotidian and the theatrical is part and parcel of a Romani performance strategy that aims to disrupt these dominant regimes of representation. What we are working with, in fact, in these multi-practice, site-specific performances is an engagement with what Spivak has called a 'position without identity', a 'position *from* which to view' (in Yan 2007: 430; emphasis in the original) that calls into question the fixedness of position, the divisions between Orient and Occident, between Roma and *gadzhe*, from which one can posit a critique. By taking this 'position *from* which to view', Romani activists disrupt the circulation of essentialist identities with regard to Romani communities precisely through their reproduction in performance and performativity. In other words, they play on and with these essentialist identities in both performance practice and in the embodied subject positions and slippages of everyday life (Butler 2006: xiv).

Performance, site and history

Romani people number more than 12 million and are spread across the globe, from Europe to the Americas, the Middle East, Africa, Asia and Australia. Romani communities have been in Europe for nearly a millennium, with the first records of Romani presence in the Balkans dating from the late 1200s in Constantinople (Hancock 2002: 15). Romani settled in various sites across Europe, and became known as 'Egyptians' or Tsingani – the former because of the prevalent conception that they had come from Egypt and the latter deriving from the Greek term for 'untouchable', also the name for a 'heretical' sect (Al-Issa and Tousignant 1997: 259). While the word 'Roma', derived from the Romani word for 'people', and 'Romani' are the words that Romani groups use for themselves, 'Gypsy' and its variations – *Tsigan*, *Zigeuner*, *Cigano*, *Gitano* – come from these two derivations. In many parts of Europe, the appellation is racist in its connotations and has been the subject of linguistic contention. There are a number of subgroups within the Romani diaspora, which self-identify with other names, such as the Sinti, a Romani community from German-speaking areas of Europe who live in Germany, Austria, Switzerland, France, Czech Republic, Slovakia, Poland, Hungary; *Manouche* in France, *Kalé* in Scandinavia, *Gitanos* in Spain, *Ciganos* in Portugal, and others. Despite centuries of persecution, Romani culture, language and identity are rich, diverse and extremely resilient, and throughout the Diaspora, Romani people recognize each other across the borders of nation states, across oceans and across varied geographies and histories. Romani culture – including performance – continues to flourish.

To activate the PRISaC network, we set up a series of three-day workshops, conducted over six months, working with performers, activists, stakeholders and academics to map current Romani performance practices, including the use of technology, in the four European cities.

In Alicante, the UK network team worked with the Federación Asociaciones Gitanas de Alicante Comunidad Valenciana (FAGA) who use the web as a performance 'site' to catalyse the abject and/or romanticized representations of Romani people that dominate the Spanish imaginary and counter the appropriation of Romani performance as a symbol of Spanish nationalism. FAGA is a real presence across Southern Spain and its website has extended this reach internationally with projects such as *Gitanízate y Participa* (Gypsify yourself and Participate) and performance interventions such as *Flamenco Electrodoméstico* (Electrodomestic Flamenco) in which a washing machine 'performs' in surreal conjunction with Flamenco to produce a sardonic political critique.[3] In Bucharest, we visited Romano ButiQ, the museum of Romani Arts and Culture which serves as a community centre, performance and exhibition space, and restaurant, featuring Romani artists and craftspeople from across Romania. In Budapest, we were hosted by Gallery8 who ground their work in the context of the city of Budapest. Gallery8 is located in a central square of the historic Roma 8th District and features the work of contemporary Romani artists as well as running community programmes for adults and children.

The two case studies we have selected, sited in Paris and London, both employ multi-disciplinary modes of performance, including the strategic use of social media, to reclaim, re-historicize and re-activate public space and collective memory to incorporate Romani history and Romani presence. Both these events triangulate site, scenography and activism, and through close analysis, we will show that the materials that constitute the performance design of these works, while they do not cohere into an overarching scenographic vision, nevertheless act as important framing devices that both separate and imbricate these performances in the quotidian. Performance design becomes a crucial marker to delineate performance space and segregate performance acts, staking out the performance territory on city streets. First some clarification of what we mean by the triangulation of site, scenography and activism, as a literal mapping of space in the London work and as an ongoing strategy in both cities.

Re-claiming the vanguard

In her introduction *to One Place After Another, Site Specific Art and Locational Identity*, Miwon Kwon discusses how 'vanguardist, socially conscious, and politically committed art practices always become domesticated by their assimilation into the dominant culture' (2002: 1). She cites the ubiquitous rise in the so-called 'site-specific' projects in the latter part of the 20th century that have become 'weakened and re-directed by institutional and market forces' (2002: 2) as one example of this process. Kwon's introduction articulates two distinct but interrelated problematics in the 'spatial-cultural' discourse for Romani performance. Firstly, expressions of opposition to dominant political processes in 'vanguardist' art practices very often derive their inspiration from the 'outsider' status and romanticized ideas of 'freedom' associated with nomadic life, including those of the itinerant artist, *le flâneur* and the bohemian. Mike Sell in his extensive study 'Bohemianism, the Cultural Turn of the Avantgarde, and Forgetting the Roma' examines the relationship between bohemia and the avant-garde, both of which 'came into being around the same time and place – Paris in the 1820s' (2007: 42). While drawing attention to the differences in these movements, Sell posits 'bohemia's function as one of a handful of cultural, political and ethical tendencies out of which [came] the avant-garde' (2007):

> To be a bohemian is to be a memorialist. To remember in a certain way is to be authentic in a certain way. This combination of memory and authenticity is a hallmark of bohemian otherness and a wellspring for the critical-creative minority movements conventionally understood to be the *avant-garde*. (2007)

Sell goes on to cite the performance historian Cynthia Carr, who, despite her 'precise descriptions of the kinds of racism, sexism and homophobia that are integral to that … bohemian tradition' (2007: 43), nevertheless harbours nostalgia for a bohemian past. Carr concludes her survey of late 20th-century performance by reminding the reader of the 'great sites of bohemian resistance' but fails to mention until the very last lines of the book 'the original bohemian':

> We've come full circle, back to the original meaning of the word bohemian: 'gypsy *(sic)*.' Of course, bohemia was always part of the exile tradition, the place where the lost ones went to find each other. But it was exile from one tangible place to another. Now there *is* no place, the exiles have become nomads, and there's a whole culture of the disappeared. (Carr in Sell 2007: 43)

This dispersal and dilution of the efficacy of radical art and performance chimes with Kwon's more general description of the fate of 'vanguardist' art practices. However, as Sell is quick to point out, Carr couches this in terms which are 'weirdly disembodied, ahistorical and naïve'.

> For the Roma, finding a place for community has always been a life- threatening quest, their 'disappearance' not just a consequence of mass-media hypocrisy and the malign neglect of federal funding agencies, but of 'gypsy hunters,' Nazis, and skinheads. (Sell 2007: 43)

For the majority of Romani communities, notions of 'site' are always temporary, contingent and dangerous. Even in sedentary communities,[4] the threat of violence, expulsion and re-settlement is an ever-present reality. And yet – and this brings us to the second point raised by Kwon and demonstrated by Sell – Romani cultural practices are often invoked as 'sites of resistance' even as they are appropriated into the mainstream, where the realities of Romani life are written out. In mainstream productions of Bizet's *Carmen*, for instance, aestheticized, sexualized depictions of Romani bodies, male and female, occupy the stage; the political and social origins of 'flamenco' are lost in sanitized and domesticated representations touring the globe. As audiences shed tears in the final aria of Puccini's *La Bohème* in opera houses around the world, traces of 'the original Bohemians' are nowhere to be seen.[5] Sell argues that a close study of this 'simultaneous invocation and erasure', this process of 'forgetting', what he terms 'certain enabling dimensions of that [Romani] consciousness, that identity, that authenticity … that might provide a more complex understanding of cultural activism' (2007: 43), is also an important strategy in understanding the roots of racism.

The two works we now focus on acknowledge this collective amnesia and the racial and cultural hierarchization it has produced. The artist collectives that produced these works in the Saint Denis area of Paris and Shoreditch in London see performance as a means of talking back; as a 'process of recuperation' (Gilbert and Tompkins 1996: 205) and as a method of publically establishing a Romani presence in all its 'enabling dimensions'. These performance events are fashioned through the dynamic interaction of *site* – where Romani presence has been historically both invoked and erased – *scenography,* materials, maps, processes associated with Romani identity and productivity – and *activism* – actions through which Romani subjects reassert agency in the present by claiming back an expunged Romani past.

Paris, May 2015

Fête de l'Insurrection Gitane, 16–17 May 2015, was a multi-disciplinary performance event to commemorate the Roma and Sinti uprising, on 16 May 1944, in the so-called *zigeunerlager*, or 'Gypsy Camp' of Auschwitz II-Birkenau. This act of resistance has until recently been written out of Holocaust histories, and one of the ongoing preoccupations of the collective La Voix des Rroms,[6] the organizers of the event, is recognition of the Roma and Sinti who, with the help of Jews, Poles and others, averted the imminent murder of thousands of men, women and children. The recuperation of this history for Roma and Sinti communities, and remembrance of all those who died despite this intervention, is only now, some seventy years after the event, being marked by acts of commemoration in France and other parts of Europe. In Paris, in the run up to the commemorative activities, a series of disruptive visual interventions at iconic sites across the city took place in April and early May. On 8 April – International Roma Day – stencilled graffiti cardboard placards decorated the walls and monuments around the Hôtel de Ville (City Hall). The stencil image was of a woman with a defiant stance; arms raised, holding a pick-axe. She is contemporary – she wears a Lara Croft type t-shirt – but she also evokes romantic images of past revolutionary leaders. This female figure is reminiscent of the Marianne and the Statue of Liberty, whose torch, in this instance, is replaced by the pick-axe, indicating a call to arms. This female figure was the poster image for the 16–17 May festival, designed to appear in different modes and materials, as costume and as theatricalized props in the form of 'gifts' that were distributed throughout the city during the five weeks prior to the festival. Set against the Hôtel de Ville, the provisionality of the cardboard placards was in stark contrast to the 'monumentality' of the building and statues in front of it (see Plate 13). In *The Production of Space*, Henri Lefebvre lays out not only what 'monumentality' reveals but also what it hides:

> [I]t says what it wishes to say yet it hides a good deal more: being political, military, and ultimately fascist in character, monumental buildings mask the will to power and the arbitrariness of power beneath the signs and surfaces which claim to express collective will and collective thought. (Lefebvre 1991:143)

These acts did not so much '*counter* the monuments' authority' (Kaye 2000: 40) as draw attention to the 'disorder' that authority is trying to control. 'Space lays down the law because it implies a certain order – and hence also a certain disorder' (Lefebvre 1991: 143). Monuments and statues also prescribe who will be remembered and who will not. The placards will not last; they can easily be cleaned up and disposed of. However, the recurrence of these 'disorderly' images of insurrection at different sites, in different materials and at different times attests to the resilience of a community that won't be so easily swept away.

Three days later, the image of the female figure appeared on a poster as part of an anti-racist demonstration in conjunction with Amnesty International in Place de la Bastille. Two weeks after that, the image re-appeared on the t-shirts of an 'International Esmeralda Flash Mob' beneath Notre Dame, when over 100 local and international Roma and Sinti, young and old, male and female, converged on Place du Parvis, the vast square in front of the Cathedral. Breaking into dance, they offered an alternative narrative for Victor Hugo's beleaguered Esmeralda, the desired and demonized figure of the adopted Gypsy girl who becomes the repository of all the sexual fantasies of the male protagonists in Hugo's story. At the end of the novel, Esmeralda is hanged by the authorities in Place du Parvis, her murder reflecting the fate of most fictional Romani heroines. In many ways, it is a symbolic murder of the possibility of Romani women's subjectivity, sexuality and authority. The dancers reclaimed the space presenting a synchronized routine to the song 'Asfalt Tango' by Fanfare Ciocarlia[7] that renounced this victimhood and offered alternative forms of embodiment that challenge the gendered, racialized stereotype of Esmeralda as 'Gypsy temptress.'

The power and poignancy of the image was demonstrated again at the end of the month when it was printed on hand bills which were bound with yellow ribbon and decorated with a fresh red carnation to become part of a performative gesture called 'This is a gift'. Organized by La Voix des Rroms, members of the Romani and Sinti community from all generations offered these carefully crafted invitations to the public as gifts on buses, trains and in shopping malls and parks across the city. This reversal of expectations – not selling or taking, but giving – was played out in different areas of Paris three times over the next month. It was this extended temporality and persistent shape shifting of image and materials that constituted one of the key elements of the performance design of this event. The gift giving continued, and on May Day they handed out small bunches of

Lily of the Valley to the passing public and decorated the inside of buses with yellow ribbons on which the image had been miniaturized to spread awareness of the forthcoming festival across the city. A few days later, a video trailer featuring the image was released online. The giving of gifts not only reversed dominant expectations about Romani communities but also called upon the public to recognize Romani subjects as engaged members of society. Jacques Derrida has pointed out the aporia of the gift – in that it is never really a gift if acknowledged or brought into economic circulation – arguing that:

> [I]f the figure of the circle is essential to economics, the gift must remain *uneconomic*. Not that it remains foreign to the circle, but it must *keep* a relation of foreignness to the circle, a relation without relation of familiar foreignness. It is perhaps in this sense that the gift is the impossible. …Not impossible but *the* impossible. (1992: 7)

The gifts given to the residents of Paris in the time leading up to the 16 May celebration of *Insurrection Gitane* were anonymous – left on bus seats and in public spaces, or given without expectation of recompense. The multiple and diverse ways that these materials performed to reinstate Roma into the narrative of the Parisian past while simultaneously promoting a forthcoming event draw paradoxically on strategies of mass advertising under neoliberal capitalism; image saturation, multi-media campaigning, the use of transport systems to disseminate information. In La Voix des Rroms campaign, however, the materials remained outside the currency of commodification; flowers die, and handbills and ribbons have no resale value – at least not yet.

Romani Resistance Day is on 16 May but *Fête de l'Insurrection Gitane*, 2015, was spread over two days and attracted over a thousand spectators to the square outside the Basilica St Denis and between 15,000 and 30,000 followers on various social media. Symbolically significant, Basilica St Denis is commonly known for housing the tombs of the royal families of France, but this site was specifically chosen because it also happens to be where the presence of Romani people was first documented in France, in 1427, according to the French National Archives.

The event organizers called it a 'show' in the sense of multiple activities happening simultaneously across the site. There was a fully equipped stage with a lighting rig and sound system erected directly in front of the Basilica. On this stage, international Romani dancers and musicians performed over the course of the two days but it was also a site of public debate. The stage was the largest structure and dominated the space but all round the perimeter of the square were stalls selling food, books and 'traditional' costumes and artefacts, including promotional posters and T-shirts as memorabilia. A number of transit vans lined the other side of the square used as portable cinemas for film screenings and classrooms where seminars and language lessons were held. A photographic exhibition was set up on a makeshift metal fence, while in the adjoining park a house constructed of found wood and cardboard acted as a critique of the evictions of Romani families currently happening in France but also as a source of information about Romani life and culture.

The 'show' started with a parade along the main thoroughfare leading up to the Basilica. A local Romani brass band played up-tempo celebratory music accompanied by dancers and jugglers who gathered people along the way. Site, scenography and activism coalesced as the parade was dominated by a gigantic puppet carried high above the crowd. The figure was clearly female and reminiscent of Alfred Jarry's 'Ma Ubu' from his play *Ubu Roi*, first performed in Paris in 1896. She has been made from 'found' materials, assembled by local children, including members of the boxing club that La Voix des Rroms organize for Romani and non-Romani young people in Saint Denis. With over-sexualized breasts and lips, the puppet was designed to evoke disturbing feelings of ambivalence in the viewer. Brightly painted in yellows, blues, green and red, she exuded a carnivalesque air that chimed with the music and rhythms of the dancing that accompanied her, especially with the female dancers who were also wearing brightly coloured skirts. At the same time, this was a personification of all the warped fantasies heaped on the figure of 'the Gypsy' amplified for the viewer and performed by the puppet in the parade. The figure was both abject and desirable, the bright colours attracting while the grotesque form repelled. Confronting this 'object' the look of the viewer was turned back on itself; as the eye was drawn from puppet to dancers and back again, the viewer, however, did not see himself or herself reflected in the 'fixed' stare of the puppet but rather the disturbing reality of racism. On arrival outside the Basilica, the puppet was placed in a pen to the right of the stage.

In front of the stage, the Romani theatre group, Les Enfants du Canal, had marked out a playing area with a few folding tables and props – suitcases full of old clothes, hats, helmets, washing up bowls and dolls which acted as babies. They fought to be heard initially but soon an audience gathered, made up of Roma and non-Roma, who attentively engaged with the action which depicted the crisis of eviction currently affecting the community. The 'joker' figure (Boal 1979: 167–190) sought ideas from the audience about ways of dealing with this problem and those with suggestions were encouraged to join the group and act out their solutions. This was 'rough' and 'immediate'[8] political theatre that ended with calls for 'solidarity' but it was followed by the refined aesthetics and virtuoso performance of a sophisticated international band of Romani dancers and musicians.

In the evening of 16 May, as darkness fell, a man appeared on stage wearing a mask and directly addressed the puppet in the pen. He read out 'A Romani Resistance Manifesto':

I'd like to have a word with you to explain the meaning of what we are doing today – Romani Resistance day. Here in front of you, I shall address the monstrous effigy standing there: the Racism of the State. If it is with joy and pride that we show you the power residing in the gestures and voices of the musicians, singers, and dancers of the 'Terne Roma'[9] and the beauty of those who will follow in subsequent performances; it is not because we are duped by the hypocrisy that makes us appear beautiful as we perform in front of a world that grudgingly makes us ugly every day. Seduction, among Romani people, as among other subjugated peoples, is a way to avoid being beaten by turning yourself into something pleasing to the master. Without wanting to spoil anyone's fun, I have to confess that in any colonial imagination, exotic pleasure is the flipside of the coin of racial hatred.[10]

Manifestos – political and artistic – are associated with the avant-garde of the 19th and 20th centuries and their deployment as both artistic provocation and strategy of resistance in the present could be read as form of nostalgia for a more coherent past. As Hans Ulrich Obrist describes it, '[a] "contemporary" manifesto could perhaps be perceived as a naïvely optimistic call for collective action, as we live in a time that is more atomized and has far fewer cohesive artistic movements' (2010). In the process of attempting to re-historicize a European past that includes Roma and driven by the political expediency of the dire conditions of Romani subjects in the present, the artists, intellectuals and activists that constitute La Voix des Rroms see the manifesto as a means of a binding together these dual imperatives through political and artistic actions. As Obrist puts it, '[the]' striking commonality between artistic and political manifestos is their intention to trigger a collective rupture' (2010). Within the artistic/activist community in Paris there was a growing awareness that socially engaged art works depicting suffering and exclusion as the only experience of Romani subjects in Europe was producing a kind of aesthetic fatigue. At best indifference from those outside the community, at worst downright hostility and violence, and this is compounding a lack of self-esteem within the community itself. A 'rupture' in both form and content from past modes of representation was required. This underpins the ongoing artistic strategy of La Voix des Rroms and was one of the main drivers of the performance design of *Fête de l'Insurrection Gitane*.

At the end of the reading of the manifesto the grotesque puppet, the travesty of the Gypsy, was set on fire after which the music and celebrations continued into the night (see Plate 14). This striking juxtaposition between the socio/political and the artistic was characteristic of the entire performance event spread over the two days, a multi-modal sensory experience manifested through scenography in which, reiterating Hannah, all the constituent elements of the design 'perform' as 'active agents' (Hannah 2015: 128).

London, June 2015

When the Oil Runs Out People Will Need Horses[11] was a site-based performance in the form of a guided walk, that took place in London in June 2015. It was planned to coincide with Gypsy Roma Traveller History Month, which happens every June across the UK with strong support from local councils, and Roma, Gypsy and Traveller organizations. This performance, collectively authored by members of the research network, was a tour, led by Ethel Brooks, around 'The Romani Triangle' located in Shoreditch in London's East End. The aim of the performance was to reclaim the hidden Romani history of this area while at the same time critiquing the way history as hegemonic knowledge is constructed. The strategic use of materials, including props and costumes, as well as 'gift giving' was an integral part of the design, linking it to the Paris work, and like the manifesto performed at *Fête de l'Insurrection Gitane*, this London work also drew inspiration from the early 20th-century avant-garde.

On 14 April 1921, as part of *Grande Saison Dada*, Andre Breton and fellow members of Paris Dada invited members of the public to meet in the churchyard of Saint Julien-le-Pauvre to go on a walking tour, the aim of which according to the fliers advertising the event 'was to set right the incompetence of suspicious guides' (in Bishop 2012: 67). Breton read out a manifesto while another member of the group played the role of the guide who 'holding a large Larousse dictionary in his hands; in front of particular sculptures and monuments, he read definitions from the book, chosen at random' (2012: 69). This attempt 'to make nonsense of the social form of the guided tour' (2012) had to be curtailed because of heavy rain and as the audience dispersed they were given 'surprise envelopes' (2012: 70) as parting gifts. Breton considered the tour to have been a failure but it marked, according to Bishop a change of tactics and tone in Dada's mode of performance, less 'antagonistic' and more 'participatory'.

> Rather than operating within the proscenium frame with all [its] connotations of escapism ... Breton implied that viewers should find a continuity between the work of art and their lives: 'taking to the streets' would thus be a way to forge a closer connection between art and life'. (2012: 71)

The Romani Triangle is roughly equilateral and designates an area in Shoreditch of approximately a twentieth of a square mile (eighth of a square kilometre) with Old Street running along its northern perimeter, Great Eastern Street lies to the west and Shoreditch High Street and St Leonard's Church mark its most easterly edge. It is made up of a series of narrow streets intersected by Curtain Road where in 1576 James Burbage built The Theatre, the first playhouse in England. During the 17th century, the area was a refuge for Huguenots escaping persecution in Europe who established a thriving textile industry there and by the 19th century Shoreditch was renowned for furniture making as well as supporting profitable market gardens. By the end of the 19th century, the area had gone into decline with overcrowding, poverty and crime. Dominant historiographies cite Jewish and Huguenot immigration to the area but there is no mention of the Roma who have been living there for centuries. However, Romani and Traveller organizations, including teachers and academics, have drawn from parish and council records to excavate a historical narrative that includes the area's Gypsy, Roma and Traveller residents.[12]

Shoreditch is now a byword for 'hipsterfication', the kind of gentrification that brings with it trendy bars, galleries, cafes and shops. The factories and warehouses have become artist studios, offices or 'loft' apartments. The narrow streets are packed with delivery vans and slow moving traffic, while the bars and public houses spill out onto crowded pavements. Towards the northern edge of the Triangle, the walking tour began at Rivington Place, the gallery and performance space of PRISaC partner Autograph-ABP.[13]

The first task for the participants of *When the Oil Runs Out People Will Need Horses* was to put on bright yellow hi-visibility jackets, a rather overzealous health and safety requirement that was used to advantage. 'Romani Triangle Walking Tour' was printed on the back of the jackets in black block lettering and they therefore acted as a form of costume that united the participants and separated them from the quotidian activities in the area, as well as validating the tour with a kind of 'official' status. This status was however simultaneously undermined by the tour leader Brooks, who spoke through a large 'Dadaist' cardboard megaphone, designed and made by one of the PRISaC team Daniel Baker, decorated in the red, blue and green colours of the Romani flag. Negotiating the narrow streets, the tour drew considerable interest from those passing by as the participants themselves became 'objects' of attention promoting the Triangle and Romani presence in the area.

Brooks's topography pointed out the precise relations of Romani subjects to specific buildings and sites. In Mills Court, for instance, a tiny passage-way between Curtain Road and Charlotte Road, the Victorian signage of Hudson's Furniture Company is still clearly displayed. Hudson were makers and exporters of furniture, brass and metal products throughout the world, and a large sign on the brickwork on the side of the building attests to their links to the great ports of London, Liverpool and Glasgow. Brooks pointed to the importance of Romani craftspeople to the furniture and metalworking industries, both as producers of intricate metal work and as horse-breeders, traders and blacksmiths; horse-power still being widely used as a means of transportation to the ports in Victorian times. It was also Romani traders who would have taken the scrap metal away at the end of the manufacturing process. Along with Romani presence in the furniture trade, Brooks pointed out the Romani links to the ports featured on the wall and the transportation of Romani subjects as slaves, indentured servants and criminals from the British Isles to the Americas, Africa and Australia under the Egyptians Act 1530. The Act, 'to expel the outlandish people calling themselves Egyptians', was not repealed until 1856.

Brooks's re-mapping and recounting of these local features was augmented by a series of interventions by other members of the PRISaC group. As the tour turned to leave Mills Court, they encountered the figure of Delaine Le Bas framed in the narrow archway leading out of the factory courtyard into Charlotte Road. She was wearing an ornately decorated dress, heavy silver jewellery and carrying a multi-coloured parasol; these clothes set her apart as 'the Gypsy', the 'exotic Other', but in contrast to Chopinaud's description in the Paris manifesto of 'subjugated peoples', there was no 'seduction' in her gaze; staring straight ahead, she exuded a powerful presence. However, as the tour moved closer, this statuesque demeanour was compromised by the crude cardboard sign around her neck with 'Romani Embassy' roughly handwritten on it. In Rivington Street, as Brooks recounted the relations between Romani workers and the 19th-century market gardens in the area, a young man[14] led a brown mare in working livery across the road in front of them. In Hoxton Square, on the edge of the Triangle, the tour came upon Daniel Baker, dressed in black with a red neckerchief, seated next to a post box at a small table on which were placed postcards bearing the Romani flag (see Plate 15).[15] There the progress of the tour came briefly to a halt as Brooks distributed Baker's cards and asked participants to write a message and post them in the post box. As in Paris, Baker was not selling; these were gifts and the cards were already franked. These costumed 'apparitions' went unremarked by Brooks; they occupied the site, delimiting the space of performance but they also blurred the boundaries between the fictional and the real. Le Bas was subjected to derogatory comments from some young men in passing cars; the horse also 'costumed' in her livery, 'slowed down time' as the traffic waited for her to pass and the incongruity of a Belgium cob in this gentrified part of the East End caused people to pause and stare.

As people finished writing their postcards, Collins unexpectedly burst into song, an enthusiastic rendering of Eydie Gorme's 1957 popular classic, 'Gypsy in My Soul'. The anodyne rhythm and apparent innocence of the song's lyrics belies its inherent racism. This unsettling intervention was also ignored by Brooks as she led the group to the final stopping place on the tour, St Leonard's Church.[16]

In a reversal of Breton's walk in Paris, this tour ended in the churchyard, or more precisely, on the steps outside St Leonard's. Famous for being the actors' church – many of Shakespeare's company are buried there – St Leonard's was also a popular site for the marriages and christenings of the many Romani living in Hackney and the surrounding area in the 19th century. Brooks took the participants inside the church where the early 18th century font is still in use. Leaving the building they encounter Le Bas once more sat on the church wall with the same implacable stare (see Plate 16). A basket containing handmade pegs was positioned beneath one of the four vast columns of the Tuscan portico. These carefully wrought objects[17] fashioned out of willow and bound with re-cycled tin were specially commissioned for the project and distributed by Brooks as a parting gift to the participants at the end of the tour. 'Material objects matter,' Ann Smart Martin argues, 'because they are complex, *symbolic* bundles of social, cultural and individual meanings fused onto something we can touch, see and own' (in Taylor 2002: 72). These were real pegs – part of the productive economy of Romani woman for centuries. As performance design the 'symbolic meanings' of these materials become attenuated by their function in the narrative. In *When the Oil Runs Out People Will Need Horses*, Brooks's generous gift-giving is counterpointed by Le Bas's implacability, however the gift also ensures – or attempts to – that the currency of the Romani histories constructed through the performance continues to circulate.

The Romani Triangle is also a 'construct', a portable scenography invented by the PRISaC collective that can be transposed and reconstituted in any city in Europe and other parts of the world where Romani presence has been erased. Brooks pieced together a Romani past in Shoreditch, which, while it is based on factual evidence, statistical data, census, birth and baptismal records and death certificates, was performed as historical fiction. While the 'fact' of Romani presence in the area is undisputed, its attachment to the specific streets and buildings identified by Brooks, like the Triangle itself, is conjecture. The performance departed from Breton's in that it did not set out to make a 'nonsense' of walking tours, so much as a re-instate them as a form of political critique that exposes the constructed nature of history itself.

This 'destabilizing' of the fixity of identities, monuments and histories is wrought in both projects through the dynamic interaction of materials, bodies and sites. The projects in Paris and London inserted into the buildings, streets and monuments of these cities' alternative narratives of history through what Polish artist Krzysztof Wodiczko has described in relation to his own work as 'a different repertoire of iconography', where in the event of seeing one 'myth' through another 'there is the possibility of challenging both' (Wodiczko 1986, in Kaye 2000: 36). These insertions not only question histories that exclude Romani presence, but they question the way knowledge itself is produced. In the drawing, mapping and (re)presenting of Romani experience, quotidian activities merge with staged situations that re-historicize Romani presence and illuminate Romani resistance. These events exploit the mutability of materials in different contexts while the position of the audience oscillates *between* Bishop's binary descriptors; in one moment as 'viewers or beholders' and in the next as 'co-producers and participants'. The work of materials as a means of extending the life of the performance after the event in London mirrors in reverse their function in Paris as a prelude. In London, the postcards, pegs and hi-visibility jackets continue to circulate as reminders and prompts for reflection. One hi-visibility jacket worn by an audience member who is also a cyclist has attracted the attention of London cab drivers, who have incorporated The Romani Triangle into their mental map of the city known as the 'London Knowledge'. Thus, while film recordings and video give the works a virtual presence on the web, it is the items themselves that continue to circulate as tangible traces of the ideas embedded in the performances: a concretization that ensures the continued narration of invisible histories, with each re-telling a small step, a challenge, a strategy of resistance and a critique.

To conclude we return to Said's definition of Orientalism and what he designates as its third meaning:

> Taking the late eighteenth century as a very roughly defined starting point Orientalism can be discussed and analyzed as the corporate institution for dealing with the Orient – dealing with it by making statements about it, authorizing views of it, describing it, by teaching it, settling it, ruling over it: in short, Orientalism as a Western style for dominating, restructuring, and having authority over the Orient. (1979: 3)

Said argues it is the third aspect that becomes the most dominant and the most difficult to challenge. In response to the institutionalization – and literal embodiment – of Romani subjects as 'Oriental Others', the performance practices carried out by what we might term the new Romani *avant-garde* are calling into question all three aspects of this formation: the academic, the imaginative and the corporate. Collaborative work – marked by multiple performance interventions that deliberately engage with site, history and embodiment – has become a prime strategy for challenging the bio-political production of Romani communities as subjects to be managed and maintained by the state, while at the same time serving as its abject *outside*. A key factor in these engagements is the imaginative application of the materials of performance design 'as active agents' to counter 'the limitations of thought and action' (Said 1979: 3) that have become embedded in the dominant regimes of representation. Romani artists and activists conjunctional application of site, scenography and activism is one way to talk back to racialist stereotyping; this opens up a scenographic discourse situated firmly within the political realm and extends the reach of the field.

Notes

1 Funded by the Arts and Humanities Research Council, the PRISaC network was launched in January 2015, the core members of the UK team were:

> Dr Daniel Baker, a Romani Gypsy, artist, curator and theorist, holds a PhD on Gypsy aesthetics from the Royal College of Art, London. Recent publications include *We Roma: A Critical Reader in Contemporary Art* (2013) and *Ex Libris* (2009). Baker's work is exhibited internationally, including the Roma Pavilion at the Venice Biennale and he is a former Chair of the Gypsy Council (2006–2009).

> Delaine Le Bas is a performer, artist and activist working extensively in the UK where she runs educational programmes in a range of venues and arts spaces. Le Bas's artwork is also exhibited internationally and at a number of biennales, including the Roma Pavilion at Venice.

> Dr Pratap Rughani is an award-winning documentary filmmaker who has presented and written widely about the relationship between film, philosophy and the evolution of post-colonial thought. He is currently Course Director of the MA Documentary Film at the London College of Communication.

> The authors, Professor Ethel Brooks and Professor Jane Collins.

2 *Gadzhe*, *gadje* or *gorgio* are the terms for non-Roma in most Romani dialects. In the Spanish Romani language, Caló also use *payo* or *paya* to signify a non-Romani person.

3   See http://www.fagacv.es

4   As Michael Teichmann points out (2002: 1), the number of nomadic peripatetic Roma has always been below the number assumed by politicians and scientists. The majority of Romani communities are, in fact, sedentary.

5   All of these notions of freedom and outsider status are de-linked from Romani subjects and re-linked to the figure of the lone (white/*gadzho*) male subject. Even the female figures, from Carmen to Mimi and beyond, are products of this individualist white male fantasy.

6   La Voix des Rroms, cofounded by Saimir Mile and Pierre Chopinaud, was one of the first advocates for the recognition of 16 May and for education around the Roma Genocide, as well as in supporting survivors and their families. Created in 2005, the organization is at the forefront of Romani activism, both in France and internationally. La Voix des Rroms use writing, performance and the arts as a means for social change. See the organization's description on helloasso.com. See also their website, rroms.blogspot.com and the Insurrection Gitane website: insurrection-gitane.com. Available at: http://www.helloasso.com/associations/la-voix-des-rroms (accessed 1 October 2015).

7   Fanfare Ciocarlia (1999), The Esmeralda Flashmob was recorded and can be seen performing 'Asfalt Tango' on YouTube. Available at: https://www.youtube.com/watch?v=ImjYdG_Z9Tw (accessed 1 October 2015).

8   See Peter Brook's ([1968] 2008) discussion of the four aspects of theatre: deadly, holy, rough and immediate.

9   *Terne Roma* means 'young Roma' or 'Romani youth' in the Romani language, and is the name of a Romani youth collective based in Paris.

10   Reprinted courtesy of Pierre Chopinaud. We are grateful to La Voix des Rroms for sharing this material with us and allowing us to use it for this chapter.

11   The title comes from Tío Juan Fernández Gil, Secretary and Coordinator, Federación Asociado de Gitanos de Alicante (FAGA). Translated from the original Spanish, 'Cuando se acaba el petróleo, se necesitarán caballos', Alicante, Spain 2015. Translated by Ethel Brooks.

12   See, for example, the Hackney council website that features news of Gypsy Roma Traveller History Month. Available at: http://news.hackney.gov.uk/gypsy-roma-and-traveller-communities (accessed 1 October 2015).

13   See the Autograph-ABP website. Available at: http://autograph-abp.co.uk/who-we-are (accessed 1 October 2015).

14   The PRISaC team are grateful to Daniel Gould of Lyndwood Forestry who is the owner of 'Luna' and who brought her up to London from the Sussex coast for the performance.

15   The postcards are part of an ongoing series titled 'Altered States'. *Altered States: EU-R* presents a hybrid European Union/Roma flag. The new flags that form the Altered States series show the wheel from the Roma flag re-situated within the flags of various geographic territories. The series was part of an exhibition commissioned by The Roma Cultural and Arts Company with the financial assistance of the Arts Council of Wales. The ones used in the performance first appeared in Baker's solo exhibition 'Makeshifting: structures of mobility' at the Cardiff Story Museum, Cardiff in June 2015.

16   St Leonard's Church Shoreditch is of ancient origin and features in the famous line 'when I grow rich say the bells of Shoreditch', from the nursery rhyme 'Oranges and Lemons'.

17   The pegs were handcrafted by Chris Penfold Brown in West Sussex.

6

Scenographic Agency: A Showing-Doing and a Responsibility for Showing-Doing

Kathleen Irwin

According to British freelance-stage designer Simon Banham, the scenographer is the key agent in shaping what it is to be present and sharing an experience in 'the permeable border between maker and watcher' (Banham 2015). On the website of the Prague Quadrennial of Performance Design and Space (PQ) 2015, the largest international festival of theatre and performance design in the world, he writes that the choices a scenographer makes in directing the gaze – indeed scenography itself – can change 'our perception of space and how we inhabit it, it can teach us to look and allow us to see'.[1] With this statement, I believe, Banham sets up a new move in the consideration of scenographic practice as agential and the scenographer as shower, doer and agent operating within a broad social context. In 2002, summarizing, perhaps, a previous position on scenographic endeavour, Pamela Howard wrote, 'Scenography is the seamless synthesis of space, text, research, art, actors, directors and spectators' (2002: 130). The next wave, flagged by Banham, posits scenography as part of a complex network of creative actions and things within both a theatrical apparatus and a fluctuating and interdependent social context where meaning is anything but fixed and stable. This suggests the action, not merely of *observing* the world and manipulating its symbols as Howard suggests, but being *part of* the world in its ongoing inter- and 'intra-activity' (see Barad 2003: 828).

In this chapter, I suggest that the notion of agency, in regard to scenographers, has attained a level of consideration within the expanding and transforming field of scenography, the focus of which has alternated over the past fifty years between the conventional emblematic stage and the non-stage. Because of the oscillation, the remit of the discipline has dilated to embrace a profound consideration of the affective relation of space/spectator/social context as this triad makes meaning of the materiality of performance. The thickening of the term 'scenography', I argue, proposes ways in which the field manifests its essential role/responsibility to both show things and do things in the world.

Furthermore, as scenographers signal what is to be watched, there is a dialogue set in motion with the spectator who talks back, supplementing the stage event from a subjective body of knowledge, experience and cultural perspective. Through the exchange of intention and reception, the spectator constantly comprehends and augments the material aspects of performance in their representational density – 'made aware of the whole history, context and reverberations of its context in the contemporary world' (Aronson 2010: 146). Indeed, the theatre is exceptional in how it speaks about its own functioning and materiality as it simultaneously exceeds its own borders referencing matters beyond itself. Laura Gröndahl writes,

> it can make the spectator look at the act of looking, and even at the act of looking at himself looking … By perceiving the spatial structure of a performance we can perceive something fundamental about the ways in which social relationships are constructed through material conditions and human interactions in space. (Gröndahl 2012a: 7)

Considering the multiple ways scenography signals, reflects, shapes, illuminates and transforms who we are, I propose that scenography, its processes and materials, have come to be perceived, at the turn of the millennium, as demonstrably agential in engaging and affecting outcomes. This represents an amplification in the role of the scenographer from that of adjunct to a director, primarily concerned with filling and decorating the stage, to being an equal contributor in a collaborative artistic vision, to conceiving and realizing alternative genres of performance that engage with social issues in non-conventional spaces. This shift increasingly foregrounds the scenographic elements. In support of this claim, I point to three productions featured in two major, international performance festivals whose remit is to connect with the social and political in contemporary society. They exemplify the expanding role of scenography and recognize a scenographic agency that extends to the human and material elements of the stage and, importantly, reaches beyond it. In order to substantiate my claim, I will draw on current disciplinary discourse and then move further afield to consider physicist, philosopher and feminist Karen Barad's theory of 'agential realism'.[2] 'Objects do not precede their interaction, rather, "objects" emerge through particular intra-actions. Thus, apparatus, which produce phenomena are not assemblages of humans and nonhumans …, rather they are the condition of possibility of "humans" and "non-humans", not merely as ideational concepts, but in their materiality' (Wikipedia 2016). Following her formation of agency as a relationship rather than something one has, I link the term to scenography in order to open up a space of possibilities for scenographers not merely to show and do, but to demonstrate ethical consequences – thereby enacting agency or, to use Barad's terminology 'actioning' in an interdependent global network of people and things. Her work provides a way of understanding acts of observation and practices of knowledge, the goal of which is 'not simply to put the observer or knower back in the world but to understand and take account of the fact that we too [as artists] are part of the world's differential becoming' (Barad 1998: 91).

Through Joslin McKinney's cogent address to the actual constituents of performance, agency has already acquired a foothold in scenographic thinking. Responding to Jane Bennett's concern with human impact on the material world, McKinney counters the traditional definition of matter as inert or passive (Bennett 2010). She writes that 'trends in contemporary performance; multi-media, site-specific and immersive theatre, suggest that, more than ever, the materials of scenography …

play a central role in audience experience' (McKinney 2015: 1). Furthermore, she proposes (and exemplifies through her practice-based research) that scenography engages the vibrancy of materials, suggesting that exploring the agentive capacity of objects in the context of scenography reflects a redistribution of agency away from humans to whom it is traditionally ascribed (2015: 16). Broadening our understanding of how scenography operates, she focuses on 'thing power' (Bennett) and the ways that the creative intent of the scenographer may be superseded 'through the way the materials themselves behave'. Part of the delight of this, she writes, is to be found in the process of relinquishing mastery as the materials begin to work on the viewer (18). The redistribution of agency that McKinney suggests underscores, indeed, as I argue here, reveals the complexity and openness of representation and its potential for affect by recognizing that, while objects construe meaning beyond the intent of the scenographer, their agentive capacity is based on a propensity to operate in relation to other materials (human and non-human) in an ongoing and inter-determined relationship (2015: 9) that presupposes an ethical position-taking.

Furthermore, relationships operate in regard to materials and processes used, not just on the stage but also in the vicinity of the stage. As scenographers expand their practices into public space, reciprocity between the stage and not-the-stage leads to accounting for and responding to real-world circumstances on micro- and macro-levels. Recognition of such interrelations can be seen in many hands-on scenic applications: greening practices, recycling materials, procuring non-toxic supplies and reducing carbon footprints. Increasingly, technical processes and their impacts in relation to social, economic, biophysical environments and pressures are factored in and made transparent. An example of this was evident in the curatorial themes (Weather/Music/Politics) of the Prague Quadrennial 2015. The shift was readily apparent in many of the seventy-eight professional submissions exhibited in this signal arena of current scenographic practice. Engagement with these ideas was also evident in the fifty-seven student showcases in which one witnessed provocative and thoughtful actions and events that had little to do with the proscenium stage and very much to do with challenging social issues, digital technologies and public spaces.[3] This new focus, in the largest global forum of scenography, indicates the ongoing transformation of the practice to one, Gröndahl suggests, that conceives of scenography as 'event, experience, and action, rather than a set of physical elements, or representational or metaphoric images' (Gröndahl 2012b: 2).

While these directions were plainly apparent at PQ 2015, such ways of working are not entirely new. Since the 1960s, with the increasing deployment of found or adapted performance sites, scenographers have come to consider material locations as replete with meanings, histories and connections to be negotiated, where people, actions and things represent complexly, where temporal change, dynamics of use and social patterns determine how spaces are performed and read. Open and indeterminate, site itself performs as a confluence of human practice and memory, resisting absolute meaning and making sense only in relation to other bodies, materials and circumstances. Scenographer and theorist, Dorita Hannah, whose practice-based research (with choreographer Carol Brown) explores spatio-temporal qualities existing at the interface of architecture, theatre design and live dance performance, frequently demonstrates this way of responding to site. To apprehend how meaning is conveyed through performance in real, lived environments, she draws on Derrida's theory of language structure (Hannah 2014). For example, her call for proposals for *Spacing Performance, 2nd Annual Design Symposium 2014*, appealed to artists across diverse design practices to consider non-traditional sites of performance through differences and deferrals, the interplay of binaries such as presence and absence, distance and proximity – the range of doings and undoings that characterize social interaction.[4] The entreaty took up Derrida's concept of the 'becoming-time of space and the becoming-space of time' asking participants to consider a third transcendent space that exceeds binaries of temporalization and spatialization (Derrida 1982: 7–8; Taylor 1990: 78). Hannah's notion of *performance design*, a term she introduced to express a conceptually expanded form of scenography, operates across disciplines, extending beyond the arts into science, technology and global politics (Hannah and Harsløf 2008: 11). As an aesthetic practice, her work exemplifies how performance design reciprocates the dynamic forces of the lived world, as well as the participatory role of a co-creative audience, to provide a critical tool for reflecting, confronting and realigning worldviews (Collins 2009). The move that Hannah makes towards activating the 'spaces between' scenographic practice and real-world contingencies provides a point of entry into the reading of expanded scenography, and scenographic agency that I propose is exemplified in the following performances.

Scenographic agency illustrated: Three performances

I viewed each of these productions in significant international cultural festivals: the Holland Festival 2014 and 2015 and the Prague Quadrennial of Performance Design and Space, PQ 2015. In all of these events, I noted how curatorial statements framed creative work in expanded terms – extending their purview into social and political spheres. Ruth MacKenzie, Artistic Director of the Holland Festival 2015, asserts her role in furthering the festival's mandate to provide art that reflects the current global zeitgeist, bringing in work from all parts of the world that has 'a real impact on visiting audiences, staging life changing events and making art accessible to a new audiences' (MacKenzie 2015). Under MacKenzie, the festival's tradition of innovation is extended by opening the festival up to audiences by supplementing the ticketed programme with free performances, concerts and events in public spaces (2015). In her concept statement, Sodja Lotker, Artistic Director of the Prague Quadrennial 2015, writes that her aim for the event, certainly the most determining of the current state of scenography, was to rediscover the political powers and social responsibilities of scenography, within the shared space of live performance, that use and exceed the theatrical. The PQ website introduces *Politics*, one of the major themes, suggesting that the scenographer functions as

> a conductor who will establish interactions, promote actions, and provoke experiences of coexistence. Recognizing the critical role played by the designer in (re)defining a space; establishing a relationship between stage, audience, environment and society; creating a lively place formed by the overlapping of intertwining layers, building a plural identity, conflicts and narratives. (Lotker 2015)

Using the narrative of these major festivals as a marker, I propose that performance, in all the aspects and variants of its scenographic surface, which affects, responds to and promotes actions in the world – indeed, it's agency – is currently central to the interest and engagement of audiences in the international festival circuit.

I refer first to two productions seen in consecutive Holland Festivals – finely tuned commercial performances aimed at cosmopolitan international audiences. Secondly, I highlight one award-winning project exhibited at PQ 2015, where the audience is made up of a general public that is both native to Prague and embraces an international cohort of theatre professionals, students and academics. These productions are, I think, unique in how they address a range of presentational spaces and exhibit aspects of agential practices:

1 Holland Festival's production (2014) of Elfriede Jelinek's *Die Schutzbefohlenen,* directed and designed by Nicholas Stemann, performed at the Transformatorhuis Westergasfabriek, Amsterdam.

2 Holland Festival's *As Big as the Sky* (2015), an opera conceived and directed by Arnoud Nooregraaf, with Ai Weiwei as scenographer and filmographer, performed at Het Muziekgebouw aan't IJ, Amsterdam.

3 Theatre NO99's *Unified Estonia* (exhibited at PQ 2015), idea, concept and production by Tiit Ojasoo and Ene-Liis Semper, performed originally in Saku Hall, Tallinn in May 2010.

In their various guises, the productions exemplify how scenography may operate critically and responsibly by, as Barad writes, exploring the possibilities that exist for intervening in the world's becoming. I will further take up Barad's ideas and elaborate on her impact on my notion of scenographic agency in the conclusion of this piece of writing. In the meantime, let me introduce some concrete examples into this discussion. As I have neither interviewed nor read interviews with the artists behind the works, I relate my own response to the scenography, as well as a brief description of material elements augmented by programme notes and blogs and reviews. In a limited way, I also provide a succinct context for the events that, I believe, is important.

Die Schutzbefohlenen

The background to *Die Schutzbefohlenen* is as follows. In autumn 2012, Pakistani refugees occupied Vienna's Votivkirche; that summer most of them had been threatened with expulsion from Austria. Not much later, hundreds of Somali and Eritrean refugees drowned off the coast of Lampedusa, Italy, and survivors were sent to northern Europe by Italian authorities. In response, Elfriede Jelinek, the Austrian Nobel Laureate in Literature, wrote *Die Schutzbefohlenen* (The Supplicants). Her text, a reaction to the acute refugee problem in Europe, interlaces the modern tragedy of the asylum-seekers at the borders of the EU, the church occupation in Vienna and the catastrophe off the coast of Lampedusa with motifs from Aeschylus' play, *The Suppliants*. In it he recounts the myth of Danaus and his fifty daughters, the Danaides, who flee with their father in an attempt to escape a forced marriage to their Egyptian cousins and eventually find protection within the walls of Argos.[5] Combining this narrative with text from the Austrian government's brochure

Zusammenleben in Österreich (Living Together in Austria) and news reports in international media, Jelinek gives voice to the asylum seekers, confronting viewers with a Europe that has never fulfilled its promise as a protector of human rights.[6]

First staged in Germany in September 2013 (Thalia Theater, Hamburg), under the direction of Nicolas Stemann, it was remounted for the Holland Festival (10–12 June 2014) in the Transformatorhuis Westergasfabriek, Amsterdam. Stemann had originally staged a reading of the play at the St Pauli Church in Hamburg where eighty refugees had found sanctuary (Bohne 2013). Using actors from the Thalia Theatre, the impact of the modestly staged event was amplified by the immediacy of the refugees and the historic church itself, located in a working-class neighbourhood. Influenced by the original reading, the year following Stemann developed a fully staged version of the piece at the Holland Festival, finding, in the Westergasfabriek in Amsterdam, a building similarly situated in a working-class district. In 1904, it had originally housed a plant producing carburetted water gas; later the Amsterdam energy company used it as a transformer workshop. Remodelled now as a theatre, its narrow, high windows and wooden roof construction give the building an intimate, sacred atmosphere that exceeds its mundane past. In remounting the piece in Amsterdam, a city also coping with an influx of refugees, Stemann found, in the Transformatorhuis, the same feeling as the St Pauli Church provided. Notable in both situations was how each exemplifies the triad of space/spectator/social context that constitutes a potent agentic assemblage. The location of the sites, their past uses, their architectonic qualities – all these make up the latent action of scenography, which harnesses the potential of found site, adjacent populations and their interests.

How the event in Amsterdam differed from the Hamburg version was in the use of the members of a refugee group, Wij Zijn Hier (We Are Here), to supplement the professional actors on stage. Formed in 2012, the group's intent is to communicate the situation of asylum-seekers in Holland who, denied residency, may neither work nor make claims for food and shelter. Having exhausted all legal procedures, their aim is now advocacy. In June 2014, with the experience of several months in a tent camp and other temporary lodgings, the members of Wij Zijn Hier were surviving through the goodwill of Amsterdam churches, mosques, businesses and volunteers. At the time of Stemann's production, their situation was harrowing: the owner of the Refugee Mart, a temporary residence, had started eviction proceedings against them and the City had notified the residents of Port of Refuge (a former prison in Amsterdam South used to provide temporary shelter), that they were to be turned out into the street on 1 June 2014. Despite the production and many other efforts to resolve the tension, the situation in Amsterdam remains unresolved.[7]

How does the story of the current asylum seekers in Amsterdam play out against the backdrop of *Die Schutzbefohlenen*? The staging of the performance begins with actors in contemporary street dress chanting '*Illegalen!*' (illegals), a common epithet used to name refugees in Holland (see Plate 17). This scene reprised an actual eviction procedure a short time before. As the cacophony on stage grows more confusing, voices alternate between 'them', illegal immigrants and 'we', the actors who are also legal holders of the Dutch passport – the entry ticket that bestows universal human rights. 'We are here, but we are not here', repeat the actors (Ramaer 2014). The stage is almost bare, cut from left to right by a high barbed wire fence. A large display of digital numbers on the upstage wall counts unceasingly upwards, a discomfiting graphic indication of either time irrevocably running out or the growing number of *illegalen* in Holland (see Plate 18). Throughout the performance, actors with script in hand tell the story of the Danaides' flight to Argos – an overt comment on what it means to hold papers, the kind that many refugees can't get their hands on, that would make them legal. The text moves from the cries of the fugitives in Aeschylus' play to the pleas of the present illegal immigrants interspersed with the kind of offensive slur heard on the streets of any interracial city. This vacillation, as Gay McAuley (2000) suggests, picks up residual from the representational spaces that the performance facilitates – the real space of the theatre, the fictional space of ancient Greece and, by extension, the refugee situation unfolding all over Europe. At one point, actors playing the refugees receive a donation, an article of new clothing, which they excitedly pull on, strewing the stage with the empty boxes and tissue paper. However, the gifts are hoodies, the ubiquitous hooded sweatshirt, universal symbol of hip-hop culture, exclusion, menace and lawlessness. Despite the good intentions of this gesture, each individual is thus effectively criminalized. As the end nears, Stemann brings on stage the members of Wij Zijn Hier, who displace the actors as they move to the foreground. The impact of the actual *illegalen* crowding the stage en masse is profound. Each comes to the front to tell, in their own language or in English, who they are, where they come from, how long they have been homeless and what they need – in some cases simply some food, a warm jacket or a bed for the next few days. The actors respond, 'We can't help you – we're too busy playing you'. With this, it is clear how difficult it is to effectively help the refugees and how those who are legal sometimes build capital on the backs of those who are not. Despite (or because of) the dilemma presented, such questions are foremost in the production of *Die Schutzbefohlenen*, and they repeatedly bring the audience back to the central issues: what do we do when people in need arrive at our borders? Who can speak for whom here? How can this be acted, how can we come even close to grasping the whole scope of this problem's hideousness, never mind to solving it?.[8] Significantly, the present-day supplicants asked these questions themselves. Meeting the gaze of the audience members, they breech the fourth wall, delineated by the very palpable barbed wire barrier (see Plate 19), insisting that responsibility is inherent in watching as is, as Gröndahl notes, action and culpability. Furthermore, it is the scenographer that sets up the terms and circumstances of this potent bilateral viewing (Gröndahl 2012a: 7). That 'action' is an ethical response, as I read it, evoked through the palpable elements displayed – hoodies, barbwire, the site itself, the refugees themselves and what these matters and bodies evoke and set us to doing.

As Big as the Sky

The choice and placement of many of the material aspects of the opera *As Big as the Sky* (11–14 June 2015) also illustrates an agency through scenographic doing. In this particular case, however, it was also the relation between the absent and detained scenographer, dissident artist Ai Weiwei, and the staging of the production in the city of Amsterdam, historically a beacon of social liberalism. This tension profoundly underlined the agency inherent in the visual markers apparent through Ai's scenographic choices.

Conceived, composed and directed by Arnoud Noordegraaf, the production mixes traditional Kunqu opera with Wagnerian late romanticism. Adrian Hornsby's libretto evinces an exhausted Europe and a reinvigorated China, tradition and modernity, romance and reality. Intrigued by China's feverish energy, Noordegraaf wrote the work following a visit to view first-hand the construction for the 2008 Olympics. In real life, as in this opera, as cities subsume villages in the Chinese countryside, questionable land practices, inadequate regulation and accountability, shoddy construction and lack of due process in human rights and land ownership create an unambiguous backstory. Superbly sung and orchestrated, what makes the production noteworthy, within the context of this writing, is, in equal parts, the scenography and the identity of Ai, scenographer, activist and prolific blogger critical of the Chinese government on issues of democracy and human rights (Ambrozy 2011). As of 2015, the time of the production in Amsterdam, he remained under heavy surveillance and restricted movement. This production marked the first time he had worked in music theatre or indeed ventured onto the stage – accomplishing this via a Skype cameo in which he played the role of self-made millionaire Wu Cai. His face on the monitor was a canny reminder of the artist's primary method of communication though social media (see Plate 20). In the narrative, Wu Cai, raised up among the cows and rice paddies of a small village, returns to build an extraordinary domed structure over a traditional Chinese village – a monument to his own success and the rise of his country as superpower. Now, however, too shabby and rundown, the village he wants to enshrine must be remade in its own likeness: it is not authentic enough for the tourists who will flock to see it. Indeed, the tropes of authenticity, veracity and duplicity are referenced repeatedly in the material aspects of the production. For example, to signify the dome, Ai Weiwei hangs above the stage an immense, three-dimensional, geometric structure that revolves slowly to reveal an unsettling and ever-changing panorama of destruction and development (see Plate 21). With images of architectural plans, videoconferences, Twitter feeds, television news and documentary footage underscoring the rapidly changing Chinese media landscape, the scenography emphatically extends the artist's critique of China's economic and social policies.[9] Ai also fills the stage with polystyrene replicas of ancient Chinese ruins that double as projection surfaces. Shifting images transform these objects, as they effortlessly break apart to form the sleek office furniture of the architecture firm's head office. Nothing is what it seems, not least the central thrust of the piece, which is, simultaneously, the story of China's unprecedented building boom, a doomed romance and the designer's own record of dissident activity. Thus, the set aptly conveys and extends the critique Ai has persistently blogged and tweeted, the substance of which has been 'a steady stream of scathing social commentary, criticism of policy, thoughts on architecture, and autobiographical writings'.[10]

A notable footnote to this is Ai's personal demonstration, made concurrent with the creation of the opera, against his detainment in Beijing on suspicion of tax evasion. During this time, in an overt theatrical gesture, he filled the basket of his bicycle, locked outside his studio in the Caochangdi district of Beijing, with flowers each morning (Ramszy 2015). Not long after the production closed at the Holland Festival, I read that the artist had reported on Twitter and Instagram (22 July 2015) that, after six hundred days, his passport had been returned, after which he ceased the ritual of the bike and flowers. Reading this brought to mind the opening night curtain call in Amsterdam. In recognition of Ai's arrest, fellow artists had wheeled a bicycle on stage, its basket filled with tulips – affective symbols of the city of Amsterdam itself and the solidarity of everyone present on that occasion with the absent artist's predicament. Seeing this, the audience rose to its feet. The gestures described here connote the substance and potency of Ai's visual language, simultaneously evoking the artist himself, the plight of political objectors worldwide and creating an appreciable response in me (to, if nothing else, write this) as, I suspect, it did in other viewers.

Unified Estonia

I did not see the third production, *Unified Estonia* (*Ühtne Eesti*), in its original form as staged by NO99 Theatre in Tallinn, Estonia (May 2010). Notwithstanding, I am including it as a notable example of scenography that accomplishes 'a doing' through its highly affective citation of the strategies of political persuasion. While viewing documentation of the production, as I did, in the Estonian exhibit at PQ 2015 (and subsequently online[11]) is clearly different from experiencing it as it was initially conceived and produced, its effect was still palpable. The project was a performance event lasting forty-four days that looked like a political campaign: a fictional movement that became a political force. It culminated in a sold out election rally and launched a new political party attracting 25 per cent of votes in public opinion polls. As those who attended first-hand must have experienced, I was strongly compelled by the ambiguous, permeable and perplexing border between reality, theatre and political action that NO99 had created (Guha 2010). Awarded the Golden Triga for 'Best Exposition and for Innovative Approach to Performance Design', the success of *Unified Estonia* notably exemplifies the willingness of the PQ15 jury to celebrate non-traditional approaches that expand scenography's historical remit. Furthermore, the detailed context provided by the exhibit illustrates Gröndahl's assertion that 'the activity of making performance becomes almost as important as the performance itself, and it is often left visible to audiences'. The Estonian exhibit at the PQ, executed with particular attention to the architectural detail of the Topič Salon, represented the headquarters of *Unified Estonia* and the party strategy for building and marketing a seemingly viable political platform. Featuring a slick logo, posters of smiling candidates, glossy brochures and videos, the exhibit exposed the application of digital technology to political ends and parodied the cynicism of current politicians and voters alike. Daniel Vaarik writes that it was

> an interesting example of political theatre and a radical reinvention of the possible role of performing arts in contemporary democratic societies ... Within a short time span it managed to theatralise the whole society, exposing the hidden mechanisms of populist politics to a very wide audience. (Vaarik n.d.)

A virtual tour of the residual artefacts can be found on the PQ website[12] as well as all instructional videos.[13] *Unified Estonia*, the title of the performance and, for a time, the name of an actual political party, extended its impact by offering a franchise opportunity complete with guidelines and demonstrations of how to seek transformative political action. Again, I was left guessing whether this was an actual option or another blurring of lines between artifice and reality that NO99's original performance had clearly captured.

The claim for agency

If the three examples provided are insufficient to educe an understanding of agency in scenography, examining how the notion is taken up in analogous fields may help. For example, Linda Colness-Himes, writing about current practices in art education, provides a definition of what she terms art critical agency. She writes that, read through a contextualist or postmodern critique, critical agency expresses a shift towards the centrality of responsibility in art making. Agency in art practice, she argues, expresses a desire for integrity of thought and a level of confidence in influencing others (1999: 55). Mick Wilson, a key thinker in arts education policy, expresses new artistic agency as a strategy to counter a neoliberal tendency to reduce culture to exclusively economic terms by putting on the agenda conditions for understanding what it is that artists do in the world. At work here, he says, is the need for artists to better understand art practice within the social enterprise, 'to action ourselves to the world; to question our actions in the world; and to question the world we posit through our actions and our questions' (Wilson 2010: 24). He suggests that artists must rigorously self-evaluate, remaining firmly rooted in discrete art practices, traditions and self-understanding, but continuously initiating conversations outside habitual comfort zones in order to engage with the responsibilities of the world as creative agents and citizens (Wilson 2010). Both Colness-Himes and Wilson place the artist at the core of agential practice. Contrasting their model, I focus my argument for scenographic agency on the work of Karen Barad who refutes the centrality of the individual but calls for a shared service of duty. I find, in her challenge, ideas that bear on scenographic agency in interesting ways. Barad construes agency as a highly complex exchange or co-working. Key to her thinking is the aforementioned 'agential realism', in which interactive, or using her neologism, intra-active agency in organisms is at the heart of the matter. The scenographic process is, I propose, an apt example of Barad's idea of an organism – a whole with interdependent parts – a matrix of individuals, ideas and things. However, contrary to how one may have, historically, asserted single authorship in such creative practice (e.g. Colness-Himes 1999; Wilson 2010), the notion of intra-action troubles the premise of the originator. As per the three performances cited, scenography's affectiveness is not solely authored but is accomplished by means of the manifold and complex actions and planes of framing and reading bodies and material objects that manifest in no fixed hierarchy within the theatre's representational apparatus. It is in this that Barad's ideas shed light on the generative processes, materials and networks of scenography as put forward by McKinney. Barad argues for a posthumanist reading in which phenomena and events may be read as intra-active networks of links and relationships between bodies, things and ideas (Kleinman 2012).[14] However, rather than levelling or homogenizing their importance, bodies, things and ideas matter at different times resulting in exclusions – 'differential patterns of "mattering"' (2012: 77). An important condition of a given exclusion or 'cut' (to use Barad's nomenclature) is that what is excluded is, in fact, generative, constitutive, destabilizing and leads to productive inquiries into how differences and exclusions are made (2012). Indeed, in terms of scenographic practice, the sense of the cut (or absence) is not foreign to how meaning is made on stage. What is physically manifest readily points the spectator's focus to that which is excluded – making the spectator specifically aware of how and what reverberates in the contemporary world. Ai Weiwei's absence, for example, powerfully evinced the absent 'I' that vibrated at the centre of *As Big as the Sky.*

How the examples that I cite manifest scenographic agency may betray my own interest in space/spectator/social context. Nonetheless, I argue that the visual organization that supported the three productions was responsible for their profound impact – the scenography steered the focus outward and beyond, entangling that which was at the nub of the matter: (1) the sacrifice of a sustainable rural way of life and the abuse of human rights in China; (2) the forced displacement of and insufficient international support for Syrian, Libyan, Sudanese, Somali, Iraqi, Afghani and

Yemeni refugees; and (3) the near complete public distrust of and cynicism regarding systems and institutions of power in Estonia.

While densely theoretical, Barad's work, as she herself claims, may be readily applied to ways of understanding and actioning the world beyond the initial scope of her research around science studies, feminist technoscience and physics. At every moment, within the cut or exclusion, exist possibilities for acting and these 'possibilities entail a responsibility to intervene in the world's becoming, to contest and rework what matter is and what is excluded from mattering' (Barad 2003: 810). Her work is also pertinent to the idea of expanded scenography, understood as a complex network of creative actions and things, absences and presences, all simultaneously generating meaning and endlessly citing other things. It productively extends what scenography does, moving beyond the notion of theatrical mimesis, where something on the stage references something in the real world, into action (or intra-action) where something does something through a productive exchange of agencies. This is accomplished not by a single author synthesizing diverse points of view from an arm's length position but by sensing the variants and entanglements from within processes and, in doing so, 'putting oneself at risk, by troubling "oneself," one's ideas, one's dreams, all the different ways of touching and being in touch' (Kleinman 2012: 77). What is materialized through the idea of intra-activity is that responsibility is at the centre of it all: agential action is 'a matter of inviting, welcoming, and enabling the response of the Other ... what is at issue is response-ability – the ability to respond' (2012: 81). What makes this relevant to scenographic agency is the proposal that '"we" are not outside observers of the world. Nor are we simply located at particular places *in* the world; rather, we are part *of* the world in its ongoing intra-activity' (Barad 2007: 828).

Conclusion

Finally, scenographic agency expresses a showing-doing, and a responsibility for showing-doing. Within the terms of expanded scenography, the creative maker operates inside a burgeoning network of possibilities, interconnectivities and co-constituted intra-actions, working to make the most of the situation in relation to what is afforded by circumstances – negotiating limitations and opportunities accordingly and doing so with an obligation of care. Here agency designates how artists do and make do in relation to the materiality at hand (text, stage, found space etc.), and to the human networks within which scenographers maneuver. The examples I have provided serve, I hope, to illustrate an intra-action of elements in the vicinity of the stage that exceeds the stage: this 'doing' is co-constituted through multiply agential practices and is manifest by material objects poised in relation to the stage and the world.

Finally, platforms like the PQ and the Holland Festival are bellwethers of change: over time, they signal shifts in performative interactions. Referencing Howard's provocation in 2002, *What Is Scenography?*, of the forty-four designers who weighed in, no one applied an agential capacity to the term (2002: xiii–xvi). In 2008, in the introduction to *Performance Design*, Hannah and Harsløf took up Marvin Carlson's dismissal of agency attributable to the stage's visual trappings: 'even in the theatre we do not speak of how well the scenery or costumes performed' (Carlson 1996:

3). They refuted with: 'design artefacts ... are inextricably bound to performance ... within them stories are told, forces are harnessed and roles are played out' (Hannah and Harsløf 2008: 11).

We must now ask, not *What Is Scenography?*, but *What Does Scenography?* Looking once again to the Prague Quadrennial as the foremost determiner of new directions in scenographic practice, there is, made evident in the move in PQ 2015 out of theatres and into the buildings and streets of Prague a physical expansion of the remit of the discipline, a restructuring of spatial relationships and a rethinking of how scenographers work (following Gröndahl 2012a). In other words, there is an ongoing destabilizing of the terms of the discipline. Lotker's invitation to depart from conventional stages and become a part of everyday life in urban spaces and beyond[15] demonstrates that matter matters, that the materiality of site is performative and constitutive of agency. It kicks back, in incalculable ways, as the scenographer engages it. The dialogue thus set in motion – an interaction of space/spectator/social context – exemplifies the potential of agential scenography.[16]

Notes

1 Available at: http://www.pq.cz/en/program/intro/weather (accessed 21 March 2016).

2 Drawing on other science studies scholars (Bruno Latour, Donna Haraway, Andrew Pickering, Evelyn Fox Keller), physicist Neils Bohr and philosopher Judith Butler, Karen Barad puts forward the theory of 'agential realism', which holds importance for many academic fields, including science studies, STS (Science, Technology and Society), feminist technoscience, philosophy of science, feminist theory and physics.

3 A notable example of this was the Finnish student installation, which took the Gold Medal PQ 2015 for the Best Exposition in the Student Section, for a space bisected by an enormous sheet of rubber that visitors could press against from either side (and encounter the unknown 'other' by touch and pressure). *The Pittsburgh Tatler*. Available at: https://wendyarons.wordpress.com (accessed 6 August 2015).

4 Call for Proposals: *Spacing Performance*, 2nd Annual Performance Design Symposium, 7–13 January 2014 in Rome and Fara Sabina. In the CFP, Dorita Hannah writes, 'Spacing, like design, is both verb and noun: a doing and a thing done. Derrida emphasizes its spatiotemporal nature as "the becoming-space of time and the becoming-time of space." By provoking the event (social, political, aesthetic and affective), "spacing is both site and action, art and politics, subversive and enabling"'.

5 Available at: http://www.ancientliterature.com/greece_aeschylus_suppliants.html (accessed 25 July 2015).

6 Notes from the Holland Festival programme for *Die Schutzbefohlenen*, Available at: http://www .hollandfestival.nl/media/1453795/Die-Schutzbefohlenen-programma.pdf (accessed 7 August 2015).

7 'Gemeente Amsterdam Komt Belofte Niet Na'july', 30 June 2014. Available at: http://wijzijnhier .org/2015/07/ (accessed 31 July 2015).

8 Berliner Festspiele Program for Die Schutzbefohlenen (The Supplicants). Available at: http://www .berlinerfestspiele.de/en/aktuell/festivals/berlinerfestspiele/programm/programm_bfs /veranstaltungsdetail_bfs_123094.php (accessed 13 December 2015).

9 Notes from the Holland Festival programme for *As Big as the Sky*. Available at: http://www .hollandfestival.nl/en/program/2015/as-big-as-the-sky/ (accessed 15 July 2015).

10 Ambrozy (2011).

11 There are a number of excerpts on YouTube and Vimeo, for example https://movieo.me/movies /no75-unified-estonia-assembly-qptlwb

12 See http://www.pq.cz/en/program/estonia (accessed 13 August 2015).

13 'Uhtne-Estee'. Available at: http://www.eestieest.ee/eesti-eest/meedia (accessed 4 August 2015).

14 In an interview with A. Kleinman, Karen Barad explains intra-action: 'The usual notion of interaction assumes that there are individual independently existing entities or agents that preexist their acting upon one another. By contrast, the notion of "intra-action"' queers the familiar sense of causality (where one or more causal agents precede and produce an effect), and more generally unsettles the metaphysics of individualism (the belief that there are individually constituted agents or entities, as well as times and places). 'Intra-actions', *Mousse* 34. Available at: https://www.academia.edu/1857617/_Intraactions_Interview_of_Karen_Barad_by_Adam _Kleinmann_ (accessed 21 July 2015).

15 See http://www.pq.cz/en/press/2015/7/8/prague-quadrennial-reports-180000-entries-all-venues-over -course-11-days-three-times-more-2011 (accessed 6 August 2015).

16 The following authors argue for the performativity of site in a variety of art practices: Irwin (2007), Kwon (2002), Lippard (1998) and Massey (1994).

7

Thinking That Matters: Towards a Post-Anthropocentric Approach to Performance Design

Maaike Bleeker

'Designing is a process whereby the matter of the world becomes meaningful', observes Anne Balsamo (2011: 12). Objects, spaces and materials are not recipients of pre-conceived meanings that are imposed on them through the design process. Rather, objects, spaces, bodies and other materials participate in processes in which they come to matter in the double sense observed by Judith Butler (1993): their concrete materialization is inseparable from how they come to signify. Balsamo is not writing about scenography, yet her understanding of design is relevant for theatre and performance design because it proposes an understanding of design as process in which things and ideas come to matter together.

From the early 20th century, visionaries, such as Antonin Artaud, and theatre makers and designers, such as Edward Gordon Craig and Oscar Schlemmer, have foregrounded this inseparability of materiality and signification observed by Balsamo, Butler and others. Tadeusz Kantor, Robert Wilson, Heiner Goebbels, Jan Fabre, Romeo Castellucci, Kris Verdonck and many more have followed in their wake. In their work it is not drama that gives meaning to matter but design through which matter comes to matter. Their work foregrounds the role of scenography in the process of creating theatre. And also that this is not a merely supportive role of giving shape to what is (supposedly) already there – in the dramatic text, or in the mind of the director – but a practice of exploring ways of organizing and shaping materials of various kinds. Documentation of rehearsal processes shows how their creations take shape in and through explorations in which matter and meaning are inextricably intertwined. Wilson's sketchbooks, for example, show how what eventually will become worlds of objects, people and light on stage begins as explorations of shapes and colours on the page. Series of drawings become visual scores that are then developed into three-dimensional compositions unfolding in time. Although pre-existing narratives can be part of the materials that inform these explorations, the compositions that result are not illustrations of these narratives. They unfold according to their own, predominantly visual, logic. Some elements of these worlds are developed quite autonomously in workshops in which groups of performers use their specific expertise to investigate the potential of materials and ideas and create scenes that later on will be included in the performance. The detailed documentation of the creation process of Kris Verdonck's *End* (2008) in *Listen to the Bloody Machine* (2012) shows how this creation started from a small set of not very precisely defined first ideas and images like: 'the end of the world' and 'the theatre as a machinery'. These were, as dramaturge Marianne van Kerkhoven puts it, 'subjected to all kinds of tests' (Kerkhoven and Nuyens 2012: 57) to see if they endure. She describes how this involved 'filling' these first images and ideas with various kinds of materials like photographs, (parts of) films, documentaries, texts, events, sounds, news stories, ideas, metaphors, and questioning them in a process she describes as pounding them, turning them inside out and upside down, and confronting them with the world. From the description of the creation process of *End*, we may conclude this means exploring how the first ideas can be connected logically, associatively, or otherwise to materials of all kinds, and how these materials in their turn may provide inspiration for situations and images on stage. This first phase, Van Kerkhoven observes, could also be described as 'the cultivation, rearing, and growing of images, akin to how one nourishes a plant, tree or animal' (Kerkhoven and Nuyens 2012: 57). What will happen in the process is to a certain extent unpredictable. 'Some wither away, some snap during an unexpected hailstorm, some are afflicted by disease and die' (Kerkhoven and Nuyens 2012: 57). Those that survive and are sturdy enough are taken to a next phase of exploration in which images and ideas are further explored in tangible material forms. This is a trajectory of trial and error in collaboration with engineers, technicians and designers. After that, performers enter the process and begin to create their role in interaction with the framework developed in the previous phases of creation.

Creation processes like these can be understood as practices of material thinking in and through which performances come to matter in the double sense described by Butler above: how performances materialize on stage and how they make sense are two inseparable aspects of the outcome of thinking through matter. Accounting for how they come to matter requires a post-anthropocentric approach to performance design that acknowledges matter as active force in the creation process. I will elaborate such a post-anthropocentric approach in reference to Karen Barad's posthumanist performativity. Furthermore, the ways in which audiences engage with performances like these may equally be conceived as a practice of thinking through matter. Instead of representing a message or meaning to be interpreted, performances like the ones referred above take the audience along in compositions of materials of various kinds. They present what may be considered propositions incarnated in the heterogeneous components of the performance, the relations between these components, and between these components and what is not present on stage. Making sense of these performances requires enacting the logic of connections, composition and associations, which can be considered acts of thought in the sense described by Deleuze and Guattari (1994), and acts of thought embodied in the performance and reconstituted by an audience.

A significant number of theatre, dance and performance makers have claimed that their practice should be understood as a practice of thinking, and that such thinking is not a matter of representation of ideas, worlds or texts, by means of theatrical performance, but takes shape and proceeds through the means of the theatre. Their intuitions and observations gain increased actuality in the context of current interest in developing new approaches to thinking as a material practice. This is thinking that unfolds through embodied enactment in interaction with the environment rather than through mental representations inside the head of the Cartesian disembodied subject. In this context, creation processes like the ones mentioned above emerge as concrete manifestations of enacting thinking as a material and embodied practice. At the same time, enactive approaches to thinking prove useful to understand how work like that of the makers mentioned above (as well as that of many others moving beyond the idea of theatre as representation of a coherent dramatic world on stage) engages its audiences. Artaud, Kantor, Wilson, Goebbels, Castellucci and Fabre are all examples of what Hans-Thies Lehmann (2006) famously describes as the transformation from dramatic to postdramatic theatre. Their performances do not present coherent representations of dramatic worlds on stage. As a result, individual elements of their performances cannot be understood from how they represent elements of such a coherent dramatic representation. This does not mean the end to representation, as is sometimes suggested. Wilson's seminal *Einstein on the Beach* (1976), for example, includes many representations of Einstein. Yet, in *Einstein on the Beach*, the appearance of a performer dressed as Einstein and playing the violin is not part of a performance that can be understood as a representation of, for example, Einstein's life. The performer is one element in a larger combination of elements that resist being read in terms of such an interpretation. The performance presents a combination of a great number of elements and takes its audiences along in the unfolding of relationships between them. Furthermore, how this part of the performance is meaningful is not only a matter of how it represents Einstein (how it presents a kind of visual description of an absent referent). Also important are the visual, material and movement qualities of this representation, its role in compositions of heterogeneous elements on stage, and the ways in which this enactment of well-known images of Einstein resonates with other representations, associations, histories and ideas not present on stage.

Rather than inaugurating the end of representation, performances like *Einstein on the Beach* challenge the representationalist belief that words and other discursive practices have the power to represent things that exist independently from them. Such representationalist beliefs, Karen Barad (2003) observes, turn questions of signification into questions of correspondence and prevent us from taking matter seriously as active participant in the world's becoming. Taking matter seriously requires more than resisting representation in favour of the (assumed) presence of performance. Actually, such resistance risks reiterating the very binary thinking that opposes materiality to signification. What is required to take matter seriously as active participant in the world's becoming, Barad argues, is a posthumanist approach to performativity that not only acknowledges that bodies come to matter in performance (as Butler points out) but also acknowledges the agency of matter in this process. Such understanding calls into question the givenness of the difference between the categories of 'human' (associated with having agency) and 'nonhuman' (associated with not having agency) and examines how these differential boundaries are stabilized and destabilized.

Barad and Butler are not writing about theatrical performance but about performativity as perspective on the formation of all kinds of phenomena, from sexual identity (Butler) to the foundations of the universe (Barad). Barad shows how the ground breaking work by Butler – demonstrating how materiality and performativity are indistinguishable in how bodies come to matter – also has important implications for our understanding of how matter itself comes to matter. 'What is needed is a robust account of the materialization of all bodies – "human" and "nonhuman" – and the material-discursive practices by which their differential constitutions are marked' (2003: 810). To this end, Barad proposes a posthumanist approach to performativity that combines theories of performativity from the humanities with insights from science, in particular Niels Bohr's quantum physics. This brings her to a relational ontology that explains the emergence of phenomena from relationships or 'intra-actions'. Barad calls these 'intra-actions' and not 'inter-actions' because her point is that these intra-actions precede the existence of that what they relate and it is through these intra-actions they come to matter. What she means is that how relata (that what is related within a relationship) matter is not a matter of entities pre-existing the relationship but results from the relationship. If we translate this in terms of the theatre, we might say that the various elements that together are a performance on stage (people, objects, texts, movements, sounds etc.) matter as a result of the way in which the performance sets up relationships between them. Signification is not a matter of how these elements exist as things preceding the relationships. It is from the relationships between them that we can begin to understand their presence. How they matter is inseparable from how the performance materializes in the relationships that it enacts. Thus understood, performance design is not a practice of inscribing matter with meaning, nor of putting together independent entities, but proceeds through setting up intra-actions that allow matter its due in the performance's becoming.

In the following, I will show how the creation process of Verdonck's *End* presents an example of an approach to performance design that similarly acknowledges matter as active participant in the performance's becoming from intra-actions. Both the creation process and the performance that resulted from this process demonstrate what Barad describes as a posthumanist approach to performativity in how matter is acknowledged as an active agent. The documentation of the creation process and the performance show how this results in a destabilization of seemingly self-evident relationships and differences between humans and non-humans, as well as a decentring of human agency in the creative process. Humans did play an important role in the creative process that resulted in *End,* as well as in the performance, yet they performed their role (at least partly) in response to and in collaboration with non-human agents. In this respect, the creation of *End* points towards a post-anthropocentric approach to performance design. I will further elaborate such a post-anthropocentric approach through Barad's posthumanist performativity and Deleuze and Guattari's understanding of art, science and philosophy as creative practices of confronting chaos by making connections, grasping relations, and composing form. I will show that *End* demonstrates how the theatrical apparatus sets the stage for enacting such connecting, grasping and composing and presents a materialization of what Deleuze and Guattari describe as an image of thought, an image of what it means to find one's bearings in thought.

For my reflections on the creation process of *End*, I draw on the extensive documentation of this process compiled and edited by the late Marianne van Kerkhoven in collaboration with her younger colleague, theatre maker and dramaturge Anouk Nuyens. Together they documented in detail the entire process, including perspectives of all important collaborators of this project. Put together, these materials present a unique and detailed insight into the creation process, and show this process to be a complex collaboration between humans, objects and machines. The documentation is also instructive with regard to the shift, observed above, from drama as that what gives meaning to matter, to design as that through which matter comes to matter. Rather than designers taking over position of director, or directors taking control over design, the creation of *End* shows this shift to be part and parcel of more pervasive transformations in modes of creating and structuring performances. These transformations reflect a move away from the unitary world view and logocentrism characteristic of an approach to theatre as dramatic representation (as described by Lehmann in his *Postdramatic Theatre*) towards what Barad describes as a performative metaphysics (2003: 818). In this view, the world is an ongoing process of mattering in which phenomena come to matter in and through intra-actions. Discursive practices like the theatre do not 'get' their meaning through the thoughts or performances of individual agents but rather meaning is the result of how parts of the world become intelligible for other parts of the world in processes of enactment. From this perspective, creating theatre is organizing possibilities for enactment. *End* demonstrates how this is not a matter of creating representations of worlds, things and ideas, but of designing performance.

To begin with: *End*

I will start from the description of *End* that is included in the documentation.

Upon entering the room, the audience is confronted with a wide, empty, poorly lit stage. A large screen at the back shows thick, grey clouds moving slowly from stage right to stage left. A constant and indefinable sound fills the air. Black snow is falling incessantly from the start of the performance. There is an elevated strip placed right in front of the screen: a path or walkway.

After a little while, the first figure appears at stage right. A man, using a cable and a wide leather strap over his shoulder, pulls a heavy, invisible burden. Advancing requires visible effort. Eventually, we notice that whenever he takes a step forward, the projected clouds also make the same movement: the man, Stakhanov, drags along the set/the whole world. He completes his crossing from stage right to stage left, looking straight ahead, making no contact at all with the audience. He has almost disappeared when another figure appears on stage right, but further back than the first, and closer to the walkway. We hear his voice before we see the performer himself. This man 'carries a booth around him'; with its glass top, it rolls across the floor of the stage. He speaks unceasingly. Like the first, this man, the Messenger, looks straight ahead as he moves stage right to stage left, making no contact with the audience.

The other figures – the Birdman, the Musel-woman, the Woman with the Body Bag, the Engine (Dancer#2), the Choir, the Fire – also cross the stage, each within their own tracks, each in their own 'plan' onstage, each moving from stage right to stage left. The only exception is the Ludd, who enters by jumping and falling at the back of the stage left. He gets up, stands straight, and walks – on the elevated strip (the path, or walkway) – from stage left to stage right, so counter to the direction of the other characters.

Following each entrance, the figures exit behind the stage and return, invisible to the audience, to their respective starting points, from whence they'll cross the stage again. The timing for the appearance of the figures is not fixed. The only agreements are: Stakhanov opens the piece, and he is to be followed by the Messenger; moreover, the performers must make sure that there are never too many characters – three at the most – onstage simultaneously; for security reasons, the Engine generally traverses the stage alone.

About an hour later, a blackout concludes the performance. (Kerkhoven and Nuyens 2012: 15)

End lacks dramatic structure or narrative. Central to its structure is the continuous movement from right to left of all figures but one (the Ludd), as well as of the projection of the clouds on the back (see Plates 22 and 23). There is no development, only this continuous movement. It is unclear whether this is a movement towards something (what?) or away from something (what?) and why? Their actions and the unfolding of what happens on stage cannot be understood in terms of aims and goals and in function of a coherent interpretation, or what Lehmann describes as the teleological character of dramatic structure.[1] Instead, the composition on stage evokes associations of a post-apocalyptic world with people and other performers on a road to nowhere. The black snow, the texts spoken by the Messenger, the body bag, the man falling from the sky all seem to indicate disaster: disaster happening and disaster having happened already.

End confronts its audiences with a view of the world that is not only post-apocalyptic but also post-anthropocentric. The human figures on stage do not show emotions or motivations. Their behaviour does not invite the audience to empathize with them or to look at the world on stage as if from their perspective. They can hardly be called characters. They have only a very limited set of characteristics and exist in what they look like and how they perform their movements across the stage, or fall from above on the stage. They are elements of the landscape on stage rather than the landscape being the backdrop to their actions and stories, and they perform at equal footing with engines (the performer referred to as Engine is a real engine), amplifiers (the performer referred to as Choir is a set of amplifiers hanging on a rope) and fire (the performer referred to as Fire is a real fire crossing the stage). Johan Leysen (the actor performing the Messenger) describes:

> My relation to the Engine or the Choir isn't that dissimilar to my relation to the other characters. In the end, we've all been asked to do the same thing: to cross the stage while moving and making noise. I don't feel any struggle with the others; it's more a kind of concentration induced by technology. It's odd and outdated to divide the characters in two kinds: the discrepancy between what technology does and what the actors do doesn't exist. (Kerkhoven and Nuyens 2012: 148)

With this post-anthropocentric landscape, *End* presents an extreme example of what Elinor Fuchs (1996) describes as the death of character: the decentring and sometimes even disappearance of character as structuring element of theatrical representation. She traces the origins of this disappearance to the final decade of the 19th century, where what she describes as 'a certain de-individualizing impulse' can be observed in the work of, among others, Mallarme, Maeterlinck and Jarry. This impulse manifests itself in new modes of writing for the theatre, in different ways of constructing plays, and in plays in which characters no longer provide us with a point of entry to the imaginary world. In some cases these changes are reflected upon within these plays themselves, like in Chekhov's *The Seagull* when Nina complains to Treplev that 'It is difficult to act in your play. There are no real living characters in it' (Chekhov [1895] 1951: 126).

These changes on stage also result in a different address to the audience and require a different engagement from the audience. Lacking 'real living characters' standing in for them in the world on stage, the audience has to find a different way of 'entering' what they find themselves confronted with. Without human character as central focal point around which time and space are organized, spectators find themselves confronted with situations that require different ways of relating. Fuchs mentions allegory, meta-theatre and Brecht's critical dialectics as three different methods of redirecting the focus from the character to the relationship between different layers of the dramaturgy. She also refers to Gertrude Stein's notion of the landscape play as a way of conceiving of theatre that is not about characters taking us along in a linear narrative but about a situation we are invited to dwell in, imaginary wander through, contemplate.

Similarly *End* presents its audiences with a landscape to dwell in and contemplate. The composition that is the performance proposes connections between elements, shows transformations, evokes feelings and invites interpretations and associations. Understanding how performances like this one come to mean requires a shift from questions of correspondence between the performance and a world represented by it, towards performance as a performative practice of making sense and how audiences are involved in this practice. This involvement I propose to understand in terms of thinking as conceptualized by Deleuze and Guattari.

Listening to the machine

In *What Is Philosophy?* Deleuze and Guattari describe philosophy, art and science as three forms of thought. 'What defines thought in its three great forms ... is always confronting chaos, laying out a plane, throwing a plane over chaos' (1994: 197). Art, science and philosophy do so in different ways. Philosophy creates concepts, science defines states of affairs and functions, and art confronts chaos by means of composition. Art does not put an end to chaos but renders (part of it) sensory 'in order to bring forth a vision that illuminates it for an instant, a Sensation' (1994: 204). Art does so by laying out a plane of composition that sets the stage for sensations and aesthetic figures. Aesthetic figures 'are sensations: percepts and affects, landscapes and faces, visions and becomings' (1994: 177). They are not characters represented on a theatre stage, or the figures in *End*. Rather, they are the 'I's' that are the agents of the distinctions and relations proposed by the composition. They are the subjective positions implied within the logic of the composition, the position in relation to which elements are brought together. In this sense they are closer to what in narratology is called a focalizor: the 'I' implied within the vision presented by something said or shown. These 'Is' Deleuze and Guattari observe have to be reconstituted by a reader, viewer or listener, and this happens in the grasping of the compositional logic suggested by a work of art as a result of which sensations happen.

In Deleuze and Guattari's understanding of thinking there is no fundamental difference between the production and the sharing of thoughts. They do not explain the sharing of philosophical, artistic or scientific thoughts from how philosophical or scientific texts or works of art represent philosophical, scientific or artistic ideas but from how these texts and works of art engage their readers and audiences in thinking. Making sense of a composition like, for example, *End* is not a matter of decoding representations but enacting the logic proposed by the composition. In grasping this logic, aesthetic figures are reconstituted when a spectator grasps the logic of composition as a result of which sensation happens.

Deleuze and Guattari thus present an understanding of thinking in which relations also precede relata and in which the subject and object of thought emerge from intra-actions. Such thinking happens in the world, in intra-action with the world rather than in the head of the autonomous subject. Thinking, thus understood, is something we participate in by engaging with a work of art. In engaging with, for example, *End*, and grasping the logic of its composition, we participate in the thinking embodied in the composition that is the performance.

The documentation of the creation of *End* shows how not only the ways in which the audience engages with the performance but also creating *End* can be understood as a process of thinking through matter in which the creators participated and from which the creation emerged. The documentation of *End* presents an image of creation not as expression or externalization of ideas but as responding to material in exploratory interactions. A recurring observation in the documentation is that creating as well as performing *End* required learning that what would also become the title of the book about the creation process, namely to *Listen to the Bloody Machine*. Performers had to literally learn to listen to the machines they were performing with. Marc Iglesias who performs Stakhanov writes:

I first met my machine in the Kaaitheaterstudio's. It was a fight. No, not a fight: more of a checking of the limits. I pulled and the machine resisted. I had to find out how hard I could pull. Felix was there making the connection between me and the machine interactive. He had to figure out the range of my pulling; he had to know my minimum and maximum.... Me and the machine we had to get to know each other.... The machine restricts me, but at a certain moment it is no longer a restriction: rather it turns into something that triggers the state which creates or elaborates a character, namely Stakhanov. (Kerkhoven and Nuyens 2012: 152–153)

The character of Stakhanov was not created beforehand by a writer as part of a dramatic play or by the actor and the director and then represented on stage by the performer, but emerges from how Iglesias learned to interact with the machine that produces the effect of him pulling the world behind him.

Performers also had to learn to listen to the performance itself as machine. From the documentation of the creation process we learn that the performance was from the very beginning conceived of as a machine, a system in a never-ending perpetual motion (Kerkhoven and Nuyens 2012: 39). That is, even before there was a performance, creation was described in these terms. This makes the creation process such an interesting image of an understanding of thinking through matter in which relations precede relata. The machine that is the performance emerged from listening to it and in response to the materials from which it would emerge. Furthermore, as performance *End* exists only in how time and again it emerges from how everyone involved listens to the bloody machine. The performance is not a fixed set of interrelations between elements (re) presented on stage but emerges from how everybody involved listens and responds to the bloody machine as it unfolds in action. The Ludd, for example, can decide himself when exactly to fall in response to what the Messenger is saying, which in its turn will affect the composition and thus how this text can be experienced by the audience. Evelyn van Bauwel (the Musel-Woman) describes how as a result of the cables and counterweights that make her cross the stage in a state of semi-weightlessness she is unable to accelerate. This forces her to listen in a different way:

I am always the slow one, though I do have the choice to enter the stage more often or less often, or stand still and do nothing. Sometimes I try to pay a lot of attention to such things as: how many people are on stage? Can I enter now or would it be better later? What about the rhythm right now, can I blend in? Should I get into its flow or move against it? (2012: 170)

The description of the performance quoted above also explains that the timing for the appearance of the figures is not fixed. They make their own decisions in response to the machine that is the performance and in turn their decisions are co-constitutive of this very machine. Johan Leysen observes: 'We do have a shared responsibility: everyone influences the whole, even though we don't know what that entity is' (2012: 151).

Leysen's observation is interesting for how it points to the fact that conceiving of the performance as a machine to which they listen and respond does not mean a denial of their responsibility or agency. His observation shows that the performance as a machine is not conceived of from a unitary point of view but as something that emerges from the combination of individual creative responses. Kris Verdonck makes a similar observation when comparing *End* to a musical composition:

there is a basso continuo, there is someone who occasionally strikes the kettle drums, someone whose voice continues, as well as a number of 'refinements': other rhythms, counter rhythms, very musical. If you talk to the actors in the piece, it is always about rhythm and counter rhythm. What the various characters do, exactly, doesn't matter in the end: they are free to do what they want. The piece functions almost abstractly as music does: creating lines and curves, sometimes bringing out the basso continuo, then making the sound lower and slower to make the timpani stand out. If you talk with the actors, it's mainly about that. (2012: 44)

End thus presents an image of creation as something one participates in. Creation is not a matter of externalizing ideas conceived by autonomous creators but the result of engaging with and listening to the materials one works with and involves acknowledging the agency of these materials and of the others involved. The performers, designers and technicians listen to the machines and materials and other performers they are working with. Kris Verdonck listens to the machine in which they are all participating. Furthermore, creating does not happen from a position outside but from enacting the potential of the material. Such creating I argue can be conceived of as thinking in Deleuze and Guattari's terms outlined above.

New modes of thinking to come

Deleuze and Guattari conceive of art, science and philosophy as three different forms of thinking. Each of them proceeds in its own way. Yet, they also observe that sometimes modes of thinking of philosophy or science and of art become indistinguishable, for example when 'we speak of the intrinsic beauty of a geometrical figure, an operation, or a demonstration' (Deleuze and Guattari 1994: 217) in which case the logic of the way in which they confront chaos is evaluated in terms of aesthetic sensation and composition. Or in the case of Zarathustra in Nietzsche's philosophy, mediating in modes of thinking in which philosophical concepts become thinkable as or through aesthetic sensations evoked by composition. These instances, or these interferences, as Deleuze and Guattari call them, herald new modes of thinking to come.

I propose to conceive of *End* as such instance of interference in which the plane of composition of art becomes an image of thinking through concepts that are physical arrangements. As pointed out above, Deleuze and Guattari describe art, science and philosophy as different ways of casting planes over chaos. In philosophy this happens by means of concepts. A concept they define as 'a set of inseparable variations that is produced or constructed on a plane of immanence' (Deleuze and Guattari 1994: 208). The plane of immanence, Deleuze and Guattari state, is not a concept that can be thought but rather 'the image of thought, the image thought gives itself of what it means to think, to make use of thought, to find one's bearings in thought' (1994: 37).

The creation process of *End*, one might argue, also presents an image of what it means to find one's bearings in thought. Yet here it is not the plane of immanence of philosophy that presents such an image, but the theatrical apparatus. With apparatus I am not referring only to the actual stage and machinery around it but to the totality of elements that the makers of *End* refer to as 'the bloody machine'. The bloody machine sets the stage for thinking that does not proceed through philosophical concepts but through composition. The observations by Johan Leysen, Marc Iglesias, Evelyne van Bauwel and Kris Verdonck show how they find their bearings in a process of thinking through matter in which they participate and how this involves acknowledging the agency of the materials with which they interact.

Deleuze and Guattari describe the plane cast over chaos by thinking through composition in art not as the image of thought, or an image of what it means to find one's bearings in thought, but as 'an image of a Universe (phenomenon)' (1994: 65). In *End*, finding one's bearings in thought literally produces an image of a universe. Finding one's bearings in thought here results in a composition of materials that presents an image of a post-apocalyptic universe and a universe that is post-anthropocentric in that this image no longer centralizes a human perspective. This post-apocalyptic and post-anthropocentric universe takes shape in a composition of materials, yet this composition is also conceptual in the sense that it embodies a concept of what the universe is and how it can be thought. *End* thus presents an image of what it means to find one's bearings in thought in which the plane of immanence of philosophy and the plane of composition of art interfere in ways that point towards Bohr's observation (discussed by Barad) 'that theoretical concepts ... are not ideational in character but rather *are specific physical arrangements*' (Barad 2003: 814). Concepts, Bohr points out, do not exist independently from the material world, nor are they inherent attributes of the material world. They come to matter in specific material arrangements and through practices embodied in material configurations. Barad gives the example of the notion of 'position'. This notion 'cannot be presumed to be a well-defined abstract concept, nor can it be presumed to be an inherent attribute of independently existing objects' (2003: 814). Position gets its meaning only when an apparatus of measurement is used and from how an apparatus of measurement affords things to be measured. Furthermore, this measurement 'cannot be attributed to some abstract independently existing "object" but rather is a property of the *phenomenon* – the inseparability of "observed object" and "agencies of observation"' (2003: 814).

The creation process of *End* shows finding one's bearings in thought to be a process of thinking through matter in which an image of the universe takes shape as a result of how physical arrangements are composed and material configurations are enacted. The result is an image of a universe whose characteristics are not properties of independently existing objects but properties of this universe as a phenomenon that takes shape as a result of the intra-actions for which the theatrical apparatus sets the stage. In *End*, the theatrical apparatus as a materialization of the inseparability of 'observed objects' and 'agencies of observation' modes of enactment in which thinking through concepts and thinking through composition begin to interfere with each other and with the modes of thinking of science as explicated by Barat after Bohr. These interferences point to new, posthumanist modes of thinking as well as to theatre and performance design as embodiment of such thinking.

Note

1 I am referring here to Lehmann's observations (in *Postdramatic Theatre*) that dramatic theatre is structured in such a way that the various elements that constitute the performance can be understood as part of a coherent world that unfolds according to a logic that works towards a goal or endpoint that provides closure.

PART FOUR

Audiences

8

Audience Immersion, Mindfulness and the Experience of Scenography

David Shearing

Over the past decade there has been a rise in immersive design-led experiences in theatre and art contexts that are inviting new modes of embodied engagement. With the proliferation of experiential artworks and performances, audiences are invited to move, touch, listen and interact; there is now a need to examine the nature of audience experience away from traditional 'end-on' modes of spectatorship. This chapter examines audience engagement in environmental theatre and focuses on how audiences might become aware of their own individual shifting requirements as a participant in relation to the scenographic space.

'Environmental theatre' is a broad term that describes the active usage of space(s), people and production elements to create and sustain performative actions. Developed by Richard Schechner (1994), environmental theatre offers a spatial frame presented through a series of 'transactions and exchanges' (1994: x). The environment is what surrounds, sustains, envelops, contains and nests these theatrical exchanges (1994: x). In the environmental tradition, the production elements no longer need to support a performance, nor are they to be subordinated to a theatrical text, and can, in some situations, be more important than the performers (1994: xxv). This marks environmental theatre as inherently scenographic and offers the contextual frame in which to position this chapter.

While there has been a rise in immersive practices that often utilize an environmental frame to 'surround' and 'contain' performative and scenographic actions, theoretical perspectives on the shifting participant/space and participant/design relationships have remained largely underdeveloped. Art experiences are blurring different types of physical, sensory, cognitive and reflective modes of engagement. Throughout this chapter, I draw upon my own artistic project *The Weather Machine* (2015), a fifty-minute immersive performance designed for a black box theatre, which had no live human performers except the presence of an audience within the space. I articulate how the design materials in *The Weather Machine* can be seen to perform for an audience, but also how an audience can become bound up with the scenographic elements, forming an immersive, relational encounter between body and environment. Through my practice I identify how self-reflection and self-awareness forms part of a participant's encounter with scenography and I offer a model for understanding participant engagement in immersive experiences as a form of mindfulness encounter. I examine audience immersion by proposing how 'mindfulness/awareness' developed by Varela et al. (1991) might help build relational encounters with design material. Mindfulness is the alignment of cognitive and sensory modalities in the here-and-now and can be applied to the emerging field of immersive theatre and art installation. Varela et al. use 'mindfulness/awareness' as a term and method to draw together cognitive science and human experience. Their approach is based upon Buddhist meditative practice and embodiment through Merleau-Ponty – situating 'mindfulness/awareness' within a Western context. Mindfulness is a path through which to examine and embrace groundlessness with the ultimate intention of developing compassion:

> [m]indfulness means that the mind is present in embodied everyday experience; mindfulness techniques are designed to lead the mind back from its theories and reoccupation, back from the abstract attitude, to the situation of one's experience itself. (Varela et al. 1991: 22)

My intention and use of 'mindfulness/awareness' is to offer an alternative perspective as to how we might articulate audience engagement away from traditional binaries of active and passive spectatorship. In a 'mindfulness/awareness' encounter, participants in scenographic environments might become aware of their thoughts, actions and sensory capacities within the experience, thus reflection becomes a particular mode of participation. I shall first map the rise in immersive events (in art installation and performance) and identify some characteristics in order to help define audience immersion within an expanded scenographic field.

Immersion in art

There is a close correlation between contemporary immersive performance and the type of encounters offered in art galleries and installation contexts. First, I shall explore how since the turn of the millennium there has been a marked shift in the use of design material to fill whole spaces and eschew conventional modes of spectatorship.

London's Tate Modern has been instrumental in curating large-scale events that have afforded artists the opportunity to present their practice in an environmental context. The Unilever Series (2000–2012) invited artists to respond to the Turbine Hall's cavernous space.[1] Perhaps as a by-product of the vast nature of the space, the artworks produced engaged audiences in a physical negotiation of the work, often drawing attention to an audience's own sense of scale in relation to the surrounding environment. Olafur Eliasson's *The Weather Project* (2003) saw the creation of a giant sun, constructed of mono-frequency lights that bathed the space in a brilliant yellow colour. The haze-filled room provided a unifying atmosphere in which participants engaged in acts of social play initiated via their mirrored reflections on the ceiling. What materialized in the experience was a relational encounter between bodies and a stimulation of the audience's senses through light and haze. *The Weather Project* operated at a junction between individual perceptual processes and social play. More recently, in the same space, Tino Sehgal's *These Associations* (2012) introduced performers who were choreographed into action, movement and conversation both with each other and also directly with members of the public. The line between performer, participant and audience became deliberately blurred in the offer to accept the invitation to participate and engage with the performers, or to remain as spectators having a distant and reflective position on the work. Sehgal's project straddled a threshold where action might become an immersion *in* an encounter with the work.

In the collective exhibition *Psycho Buildings* presented at Southbank Centre in 2008, artists were invited to transform the Hayward Gallery spaces. Mike Nelson, in his installation *To the memory of H. P. Lovecraft* (2008), violently hacked at the walls of the gallery providing the impression of a space ravaged by a rabid beast. The impression for me, as an attendant to the work, was both a physical and psychological positioning inside Cthulhu's lair (a fictional deity in Lovecraft's writing). The result was an unnerving experience as I became entwined with the world that Nelson had created; the psychic operation (of becoming the subject of the space) and the physical objects and architecture were all brought into relation. This experience was not a heightened mode of participation with other bodies, nor was it interactive, but was both a sensory and cognitive immersion in the relational encounters that it fostered. In Nelson's work, the audience's embodied position activates the art experience.

Immersion in performance

In performance, audiences have increasingly been brought into close proximity with performers and scenographic materials. In contrast to installation art, performance emphasizes dramaturgical and narrative concerns, which might draw upon additional modes of cognitive and sensory engagement through the performance text. Narratives, stories, characters and other performing bodies might further enable connections between audience and performance. Josephine Machon offers a useful taxonomy of immersive theatre and suggests that immersive experiences 'combine the act of immersion – being submerged in an alternative medium where all the senses are engaged and manipulated – with a deep involvement in the activity within that medium' (2013: 21–22).

Punchdrunk, one of the UK's most dominant performance companies working in this form, explore the use of designed spaces *as* performance alongside narrative and highly physical movement sequences to convey meaning. Punchdrunk frequently use classic texts as inspiration for their epic free-to-roam performances that take place in totally transformed and found spaces. In *The Drowned Man: A Hollywood Fable* (2013), the audience, wearing masks, are left to wander the four floors of an old post office depot packed full of intricately designed sets that represent multiple hyper-real worlds. As the audience journey through the space, they piece together elements of the text through isolated scenes, dances, and for the chosen few, one-on-one encounters. The fragmented nature of the performance and the need to navigate the space leads to a multiplicity of subjective experiences of the performance. The audience actively construct narratives through their individual journeys, which is a distinct trope of theatrical immersion.

Punchdrunk's use of space provides the audience with an 'alternative medium' through the construction of a performance world. While Punchdrunk are not the first theatre-makers to choose to work in this way, there are an increasing number of other companies reconfiguring spatial and sensory modes of engagement. These include ZU-UK dreamthinkspeak, WildWorks, Fuerza Bruta, Shunt, Sound & Fury and practitioners such as David Rosenberg and Janet Cardiff, all of whom have been referred to under the ever-expanding label 'immersive'. These companies and artists, to varying degrees, position the audience as central to the theatrical exchange, involve multisensory engagement and allow a freedom to navigate the performance space. Embodied modes of engagement are encouraged, such as journeying, fostering intimacy and activating attentive listening strategies. Not all performance companies aim to create the distinct theatricalized worlds as Punchdrunk do: many artists working within an immersive context prioritize the use of pervasive technologies to augment sensory experience. The application of wireless headphones in Janet Cardiff's and David Rosenberg's work provides the possibility of instant transportation to different aural environments. In these headphone-based experiences, the scenography enables the possibility of multiple spatial shifts through the layering of experience. It is helpful to consider audience immersion as a plural concept that accounts for multiple subjective immersions in an aesthetic experience.

Immersive practice might best be described as a range of art events that are constituted upon (and at times exploitative of) the participants' spatial relationship with the design materials of performance. Immersion need not be considered a goal or destination, but as a process that might materialize in the relational encounters between participant and scenographic environment. My interest lies in understanding the nature of this encounter as a triangulation of body, mind and space in events that invite a specific type of engagement that is neither interactive nor distinctly participatory.

Relational aesthetics

Debates surrounding relational encounters in artistic practice have been developed through Nicolas Bourriaud's *Relational Aesthetics* (2002). Bourriaud articulates an evolution of artistic practice that no longer wishes to form 'imaginary and utopian realties' but to be 'actual ways of living and models of action within the existing real' (2002: 13). In this context, the artwork operates as a relational device, 'taking as its theoretical horizon the realm of human interactions and its social context, rather than the assertion of an independent and private symbolic space' (2002: 14). From Bourriaud's perspective, a relational artwork establishes 'intersubjective encounters', where meaning can be formed collectively rather than individually. The relational encounter is important, as the audience becomes the central locus of meaning-making and forms part of the art experience; immersion in this sense might be thought of as a specific type of encounter.

Analysis surrounding relational artwork has been predominantly concerned with notions of participation. Claire Bishop (2012) expands upon Bourriaud's realm of intersubjective encounters by exploring the politics of participation. Bishop similarly acknowledges a trend, developing from the 1990s, of an artistic orientation towards the social with a 'shared set of desires to overturn the traditional relationship between the art object, the artist and the audience' (2012: 2). However, Bishop is critical of Bourriaud, suggesting that his concept of relational aesthetics is more concerned with structure than with subject matter (2004: 64), and she proposes her own theory of the 'social turn' (2012). Bishop chooses to question the quality of relational encounters. She proposes that the next logical question for the theory of relational aesthetics is to ask 'what *type* of relations are being produced, for whom, and why?' (Bishop 2004: 65, emphasis in original).

Jen Harvie (2013) extends Bishop's concern with the social, but seeks to pay attention to the conditions of participation, such as class and wealth (2013: 10). Her aim is to consider the broader social and material contexts, to question not just the qualitative experiences, but how those opportunities of participation are 'affected by the practices' social and material context' (2013: 10). As the focus for Harvie is on the social forms of participation in cultural events, she alternates between art practice and theatre, expanding the field of the immersive events to including theatrical encounters, such as Kate Bond and Morgan Lloyd's *You Me Bum Bum Train*.[2] Relational aesthetics, for Harvie, provides a link between art practice and immersion in theatre experience:

> [v]isual, sculptural and aural art that immerses its audience in similar ways is generally installation art that sometimes produces relational aesthetics. Installation art is not simply composed of an object or objects but produces an environment which, as in immersive theatre, surrounds and contextualizes the audience. (Harvie 2013: 31–32)

The relational encounters fostered in the works cited above such as those created by Eliasson, Nelson and Punchdrunk encourage different encounters with scenography, including in the construction of performance worlds, sensory augmentation and social play. Immersion in this chapter is understood within a relational field, where the environment for performance contextualizes the audience and is central to critical sense-making of the audience experience.

The problems of immersion

Participation and a multisensory engagement with performance are not new, but the recent rise in immersive practice has demonstrated distinct modes of embodied engagement. Any understanding of immersion in performance needs to take into account the relationship between the body and its environment. The body is not an isolated object and is always understood against a background or structure; as phenomenological philosopher Dermot Moran notes, 'stimuli are always perceived and interpreted in a rich and complex environment' (2000: 393). In being in the world we are bound up with it, as Merleau-Ponty insists: '[t]he world is not an object such that I have in my possession the law of its making; it is the natural setting of, and field for, all my thoughts and all my explicit perception' (2002: xi–xii).

The term 'immersive' has the danger of presenting the idea of a homogenous medium in which a body is saturated or engrossed; however, it would be better to consider immersion as a heterogeneous concept (Ingold 2014). The sensation of feeling when immersed in the rain, for example, would depend on the fluctuating forces of the wind, the size of the raindrops and the temperature of the air and water; it is their distance, force and speed that give way to particular feelings and emotions. A heterogeneous immersion is the subjective experience of a set of specific conditions. What is needed in current discourse on immersive practice is a more nuanced understanding of how a participant body is situated and bound up within a 'rich and complex [scenographic] environment' (Moran 2000: 393).

In an aural context, the term 'immersion' shows itself to be a contradictory concept. Ross Brown (2010a,b) details the complex sonic environments in which we hear and highlights a paradigm shift in the promotion of immersion in theatre sound. Brown cites semiotician Theo van Leeuwen who states that the 'aural perspective … had been challenged … by new forms and new technologies of listening which aim at immersion and participation rather than at concentrated listening and imaginary identification' (2010b: 1). Van Leeuwen's critique is that there has been a distinct focus *towards* the subject, rather than through concentrated or attentive listening *from* the subject *to* the sound. Brown's argument is that the notion of immersion, in aural experience, is something of a cliché, seeking to drown out external noise (such as traffic or ambient sound in the auditorium) and thereby positioning noise as an unwanted problem of the theatre space. The development of an all-encompassing immersion in surround sound, according to Brown, can be seen as just another version of the same ideological notion of silence in the theatrical auditorium (2010b: 1). The 'demonising of noise', as Brown puts it, 'seemed … to stultify theatre with its nervousness that any extraneousness – including that of any overt theatricality – might distract the audience from purer, abstract, intellectual edification' (2011: 10). Brown suggests that the 'negotiation of noise is part of the process of establishing meaning in sound (or of any signal perceived in an immersive aural field)' (2010a: 132). He puts forward the notion that there is an active engagement on behalf of the participant to focus, select and make sense of sound through continual background noise. Immersion in an aural sense needs to consider the dialectic between attention and distraction – between noise and meaningful agitation – as an active part of our being-in-the-world. It is more useful to consider 'audience immersion', rather than 'immersive performance', as this places an emphasis on an active multisensory and imaginative negotiation between the body and the performance environment.

In the following analysis I propose that 'mindfulness/awareness' might foster and lead to the sustaining of relational encounters with performance as a form of audience immersion. Through audience 'mindfulness/awareness' I want to articulate how a participant might encounter scenography and become bound up with the overall scenographic orchestration of the event. I want to evaluate to what extent design-materials, environment and body relate as an expanded conception of scenographic reception.

The Weather Machine

The Weather Machine (2015) was designed as a landscape constructed of wooden pallets and real grass (see Plate 24). Spread throughout the space were objects that related specifically to different sections of the performance, such as glass jars, radios, photographs and bird wings. In the centre of the space and above the audience's heads were twelve hanging cymbals that were activated at specific moments of the performance by water falling on to them, like rain (see Plate

25). The audience, at times wearing headphones, were guided through a series of atmospheric conditions; light, cloud, wind and rain, each lasting twelve minutes. As each section unfolded, the audience were invited to engage, connect and reflect upon their place within the environment and their relationship with others in the space. Designed for twenty audience members at a time, the piece operated without the physical presence of actors. The space was animated through light, video projection, voice over and a multichannel sound design composed by James Bulley. Musical sound was heard through sixteen speakers located within and surrounding the landscape, which remained audible throughout the performance because semi-porous, 'open' headphones were used to convey the spoken narratives. The headphones and speaker setup sought to bring about an attentive and active listening strategy in the audience, so rather than being saturated with sound they were encouraged to listen outwards into the environment. Using light and voice the audience were taken on a journey that unfolded both around them and through their embodied engagement with the design. The performance was structured so that each section aimed to build a physical and cognitive relationship between the individual and the environment using the affective potential of design to bring about a state of self-awareness.

As a scenographer I am drawn to explore the rather illusive and intangible aspects of design that are often classified as part of the 'atmosphere' of performance. I define the atmosphere of performance as the elements that fill space such as the air, light and sound that are often given little attention as embodied experiences. The weather offers a metaphorical and affective frame in which to consider how the audience body and design might come to be incorporated together, where the design elements can be experienced as an atmospheric phenomenon which is acted upon and within the body (Welton 2012: 131). Each section of *The Weather Machine* (light, cloud, wind and rain) sought to explore the affective potential of design. The light wall for example (see Plate 25) not only aimed to provide the suggestion of the sun, it also produced heat that could be felt upon the skin. The cloud section (see Plates 26 and 27) used three different haze effects to slowly surround the audience, encouraging participants to move and touch the fog as the mist rose upward from underneath and around the audience. During the cloud section, the audience, wearing headphones at this point, were invited to picture the image of a dead bird and to contemplate death, absence and the impermanence of life. The intention here was to offer a psychophysical activity that folded within it the transient and ephemeral nature of the physical mist and fog. In the wind section, the audience were plunged into darkness as they heard a vivid description of an abandoned house. As the description progressed, the wind began to howl both in the story and was simultaneously experienced physically in the space. In the final section, rain water fell upon the cymbals overhead, with each cymbal connected to a contact microphone (see Plates 28 and 29). Audience members stood below and felt the 'raindrops'; as they fell, their sound could be heard directly and also amplified through the speakers surrounding the audience.

The Weather Machine sought to explore the elemental aspects of our daily environment and to consider their aesthetic potential in performance. The grass had an earthy smell, which after the rain and the warm heat of the 'sun' made the air moist and damp. The breath was continuously referenced in the text and the wind was made present in the space. The water, soil, warmth, wind and mist all drew attention to the medium of air as central to the design conception. My intention was to bring about a multisensory commingling of image, touch and sound – a cycling of scenographic materials, body and environment.

An ecological approach to perception

In day-to-day life, the perception of light, sound and odour are not objects of perception; we perceive in and through them and this guides and controls action. Anthropologist Tim Ingold outlines this in his ongoing investigation into how individuals engage with their environment. Ingold develops an ecological approach to perception of the environment by considering human existence as part of a 'weather-world' (2011: 115–139). He articulates an entwined connection between the air and body and suggests that in open space the body and medium (air) mingle:

> [t]o feel the air and walk on the ground is not to make external, tactile contact with our surroundings but to mingle with them. In this mingling, as we live and breathe, the wind, light and moisture of the sky bind with the substances of the earth in the continual forging of a way through the tangle of lifelines that comprise the land. (2011: 115)

Ingold's observations offer a profound way to consider audience experience in environmental theatre as well as in other performances that employ expanded notions of scenography (such as those detailed in this volume). Ingold presents a subject bound up in the material elements of the air, light, wind, moisture and breath. He observes a multisensory immersion in a weather-world that is both the 'essence of perception and the essence of what is perceived' (2011: 117). The experience of weather, he says,

> is just as much auditory, haptic and olfactory as it is visual; indeed in most practical circumstances these sensory modalities cooperate so closely that it is impossible to disentangle their respective contributions. (Ingold 2005: 97)

Depending on the phenomena in question – the temperature of the room, the wind brushing against the skin, or the sound of rain at night – we can attune to these various conditions, which activates self-awareness, drawing attention to our immersion in the world. The design elements in *The Weather Machine* were used to encourage a multisensory engagement with the performance, where the elements themselves were not distant objects of perception, but through the active use of the air as medium (haze, wind, light, warmth, smell and sound), the participant became bound up in design elements.

In immersive experiences, conceptualizing the participant as bound up with the elements of scenography, rather than saturated by the scenography, enables us to consider the degree to which audiences might become sustained in a relational encounter with the environment. As I have reflected above, the condition of scenography to produce an affective experience provides a cyclical relationship between participant and environment, as Welton discusses,

> [i]n noticing a change in the weather, we notice also a corresponding change in ourselves: it has grown colder, because I have grown colder. Sensing (rather than instrumentally measuring) it to be thus is neither to make a wholly objective judgement, nor an entirely subjective claim; rather, it falls somewhere in between the two as a feeling of a change (a movement) in the atmosphere.
> (Welton 2012: 150)

Rather than being an immersion via a form of sensory saturation, it is more useful to consider our engagement as a process of self-reflection or self-awareness where we are not lost in the experience, but become aware of our bodies as we participate in the art experience. In order to articulate this experience, I propose 'mindfulness/awareness' as a frame in which to understand the cycling of body, mind and environment. 'Mindfulness/awareness', I argue, offers a method or mode of engagement that is distinct from notions of active spectatorship as outlined by Jacques Rancière (2009), and accounts for an embodied mode of engagement with design.

'Mindfulness/awareness'

The main thrust of mindfulness – in meditative practice – is not to become absorbed, but to render the mind able to be present with itself long enough to gain an insight into its own functioning (Varela et al. 1991: 24). When becoming mindful, we are often reminded of how 'disconnected humans normally are from their very experience' (1991: 25). Meditation as a practice offers a method to interrupt our habitual flow:

> [t]he dissociation of mind and body, of awareness from experience, is the result of habit, and these habits can be broken. As the meditator again and again interrupts the flow of discursive thought and returns to be present with his breath or daily activity, there is a gradual taming of the mind's restlessness. (1991: 25–26)

An example of this, in performance, is where a participant might be made aware of his or her habitual behaviour, therefore activating a contemplative self-awareness. Encouraging processes of self-reflection in performance gives rise to the following questions: how might self-awareness operate in relation to scenography, and how might we place mindfulness within the realm of theatre attendance, away from skilled meditative practice?

In applying mindfulness to audience experience, I am not suggesting that the participant needs to shut out external stimuli by, for example, completely and attentively focusing on the breath. Instead, we might consider mindfulness in terms of audience experience as an embracing of the scenographic material. This can be achieved through processes of self-reflection and an awareness of habitual behaviour and cognitive modes of engagement that disrupt normative modes of participation.

Attention, for example, is a conditioned and normative mode of theatrical engagement that could be displaced by mindful participation. Jonathan Crary asserts that

> what stands out is how attention continues to be posed as a normative and implicitly natural function whose impairment produces a range of symptoms and behaviours that variously disrupt social cohesion. (Crary 2001: 35)

Inattention is considered socially disruptive; attention therefore becomes a normative mode of spectatorship. Normative modes of engagement in theatrical experience are institutionally, socially and spatially constructed towards audience productivity. Richard Wagner (1813–1883) epitomized this approach. For him, deeply attentive or 'higher' forms of attention were favoured over 'lower' distracted forms of listening and viewing; the former, for Wagner, was a pure, ethically questionable, superior mode of perceptual engagement (2001: 249). Wagner's assertion extended to his own theatre design and architecture for the Festspielhaus in Bayreuth. Here, Wagner's control over the attentiveness of the audience was in effect to subordinate them to the will of the artist and to 'generate a collective state of reception worthy of an art with such social aspirations' (2001: 250). For Wagner, it was the architectural design of the auditorium, with the audience in the darkness and the orchestra pit hidden (Palmer 2013: 79) that aided most in conditioning the audience – rather than the stage design. In environmental theatre, the audience have free bodily movement and are surrounded by multiple possible distractions that might disrupt normative modes of attention by encouraging audiences to explore, use their bodies and seek out performance material. Therefore, disruption of normative modes of theatre attendance, such as conditioned attention, can encourage the participant to become aware or mindful of the ways they are being invited to encounter the experience.

Ellen Langer (1989) offers the most significant insight into mindfulness in Western psychology, which she considers in relation to its apparent opposite, 'mindlessness'. Langer observes that '[i]n daily life we do not notice what we are doing unless there is a problem' (1989: 43). For Langer, a disruption of automatic behaviour (mindlessness), for example, can bring about a reflective modality. It is this reflective process (mindfulness) of awareness of automatic behaviour, in contrast to attentive modes of engagement such as those advocated by Wagner, that I believe encourages deeper associations between individuals and scenography in environmental contexts. Inspired by Langer's writing, I have identified the following headings to form a taxonomy of audience mindfulness:

1. Awareness of Bodily Sensations (Via the deficient body)
2. Unlearning of Normative Cognitive Modes of Engagement (Suspending desire to seek out meaning)
3. Cutting Across Automatic Behaviour (Mindlessness and self-questioning)
4. Possibility (Forming new categories and multiple possibilities of experience)

In the following section, I outline these concepts in more detail drawing upon *The Weather Machine* and wider practice to illustrate my thinking. It is hoped this will be useful in considering how audiences might become immersed in scenographic environments.

1. Awareness of bodily sensations via the deficient body

Throughout *The Weather Machine* I used haze effects as part of the design composition. Haze can be seen as part of an overall construction of mood, rhythm and pace that might aid in the conditioning of audience experience. Haze does not only provide a substance to the air, it helps draw attention to light by creating three-dimensionality as light is reflected by the mist particles. The experience of haze is therefore a multisensory engagement of vision and touch. The haze deployed in *The Weather Machine* was used in different sections of the production, as one might with any other scenographic element, to create perceptual shifts in clarity and to obscure visual perception of the space in the moments of discovery. Haze makes the air and light active as conjoined elements. In experiencing haze, we come to move it, taste it and smell it, which makes us mindful of our bodies in the space. More than just giving light a materiality, haze draws attention towards the medium of air, that medium in which we inhabit and experience the performance. Haze also invites bodily action – it helped to facilitate subtle interactions in Eliasson's *The Weather Project* and in Antony Gormley's *Blind Light* (2007) exhibit, where the whole body was mobilized as participants reached out in trepidation as they entered a room full of brilliant white mist. Through dense fog and lack of vision, participants might reach out to guide their way, or attempt to grab the haze as it swirled past them. In some artistic experiences, the materialization of light beams in haze often encourages participants to reach out to touch the light. In these performance moments participants become aware of their presence as they become alert to sensations they are having. Drew Leder articulates how 'actions are motivated and organized by outer-directed concern' (1990: 19), and that in action the body recedes. However, in some situations attention can 'shift so as to reside within the body here-and-now' (1990: 19), such as meditative attention towards the breath or when feeling one's way through haze. This engagement becomes what Martin Heidegger terms as a 'deficient' mode in relation to our usual concern with the world (1990: 19). This deficiency, as Anna Fenemore notes, 'implies not a hierarchy, but an extra-ordinary mode of embodiment such that absence is the norm and presence the "deficiency" from that norm' (Fenemore 2001: 78–79). In response to *The Weather Machine*, participants described their experience as akin to the sensation of floating. The act of being immersed in water or floating is often used metaphorically by participants to describe their experience feeling 'immersed' and is indicative of an 'extra-ordinary mode of embodiment' (2001: 78–79). These sensations express a body in full saturation, not a loss of awareness of the body, but where an all-encompassing sensory stimulation actually draws attention towards the body in the here-and-now moment.

2. Unlearning of normative cognitive modes of engagement

Mindfulness tactics can encourage audiences to unlearn normative cognitive processes. As a scenographer I am interested in offering participants multiple ways in which to experience an installation. For *The Weather Machine*, participants were offered a field guide that detailed the different sections of the performance. No direct instructions were given to participants in how to use the guide. Some audience members sat and read the book in detail, others flicked through as the different sections arose, and some decided to reject using the book altogether. Not forcing participants to respond in prescribed ways offers up instead an invitation to engage in a selective process to determine how each individual might want to connect with the performance. In previous research (Shearing 2015), participants commonly considered their experience on a continuum between active and passive modes of engagement. The binary of activity and passivity in spectatorship is one Rancière contests. For him, spectatorship is not passivity that must be turned into activity. It is our normal situation. We learn and teach, we act and know, as spectators who link what they see with what they have seen and told, done and dreamed. (2007: 277)

Although Rancière calls for the emancipation of the audience in theoretical terms, through 'the blurring of the boundary between those who act and those who look; between individuals and members of a collective body' (2009: 19), participants often consider their experiences in binary terms of being active and passive. 'Mindfulness/awareness' offers an alternative perspective in understanding audience engagement as it embraces a perceived passivity as a conscious decision undertaken by the participant. Active engagement is often connected with the sense of being physically engaged, and passivity, on the other hand, is often expressed as non-physical engagement, such as sitting back and relaxing (Shearing 2015: 107). The decision to become passive is a conscious one, where participants feel as though they have a choice over their engagement. The awareness of choice can be regarded as a mindful process that offers agency to the participant. The participant experiences a level of perceived, if not actual, control over their chosen mode of cognitive engagement.

'Mindfulness/awareness' does not merely mean a skilled process of meditation, which would otherwise be problematic for a time-limited non-skilled audience, but rather 'mindfulness/ awareness' can be considered within the realm of the quotidian – in daily processes in which we notice, or at moments where we are consciously brought out of habit. For example, the simple action of watering a plant (Langer 1989: 81) might aid in our awareness of self and environment by providing purpose to actions. Links can be made here to simple actions or tasks that audiences complete in attending to scenography. In *The Weather Machine*, cognitive processes, such as questioning the nature of where and when to move, sit, reflect and engage, all challenge audiences to let go of usual habits of theatre consumption. According to Varela et al., mindfulness is best described 'as a letting go of habits of mindlessness, as an *un*learning rather than learning' (1991: 29). As the individual takes control of the meaning-making process, they conduct a process of *un*learning, working against normative modes of attentive engagement.

In post-show feedback, one participant attending *The Weather Machine* noted how they 'settled into it'. Over time, the participant allowed their self to be more open to how the performance was making them respond, rather than seeking out meaning. This comment suggests a tuning into the different possible modes of engagement, a process in which the audience member selects the appropriate tools and strategies to best make sense of the work, in this case an *un*learning through time. This sense of tuning, according to Richard Coyne 'connects to the lived experience of temporal and spatial adjustment' (2010: xvi). The participant settles into a mode of reception where an attentive strategy of seeking out meaning is replaced with what I call a 'sampling' or 'filtering' of the performance material. A sampling of material is a process that allows scenographic material to 'wash' or 'pass over' the participant. Through a process of sensory and cognitive filtering the participant rejects stimuli that they regard as less significant, allowing them to select the elements that grab their attention, opening up possible subjective associations of scenographic materials. This is an important observation as it suggests that not all performance material will be experienced as significant. Participants might reject performance moments, design elements and images that are not of interest or significance to them personally. The process of mindfulness in this case is more akin to tuning an instrument than playing it (Varela et al. 1991: 29). While a participant might have chosen a strategy in which they feel they are being passive, that might hint at a disinterest, or that shows a lack of attention, the experience of selecting material that is personally significant can be a liberating one for the participant.

3. *Cutting across automatic behaviour*

The notion of cutting cross 'automatic behaviour' (Langer 1989: 12) expands upon the process of the *un*learning of cognitive engagement and considers this in relation to automatic bodily and behavioural processes. Automatic behaviours are learnt by habit (1989: 16) and can lead to mindless behaviour; an example of this in daily life might be attempting to use the office keys to open the front door at home. When in this mode, 'we take in limited signals from the world' (1989: 12), basing our experience on repetition. Scenographic environments have the potential to challenge habitual processes, enabling the audience to question their automatic engagements.

In *The Weather Machine* audiences were invited to explore the space as they entered the environment. Rather than taking a seated position, participants could move through the space and around the landscape of wooden pallets. The intention here was to act as a decompression period, to allow time for participants to adjust to their new environment. Similar staggered entrances and multiple beginning techniques can be found in other design-led performances such as *You Me Bum Bum Train* (2012), a solo experience in which audience members are individually guided through a series of life-like situations and are cast as the protagonists in each scene. In the 2012 iteration, participants were led through a series of small waiting rooms before being guided into the experience by a 'medical officer'. The impact for the participant is they begin to feel prepared for their experience; this might be a calming process or in this case an increasing feeling of suspense and anticipation. In Shunt's production of *The Architects* (2012), staged within The Biscuit Factory in Bermondsey, London, participants needed to navigate a series of twisting and repetitive corridors before finally arriving at the centre of the performance space, a fictional cruise ship which would become the audiences' home for the duration of the piece. The twisting corridors led us to the psychological heart of the experience, like a labyrinth leading to the Minotaur, where the audience become physically and psychologically entwined in the experience. These acts of transition and decompression confront the audience to question their engagement through physical participation. The use of the foyers, dressing rooms, box office and transition spaces into the performance are distinct troupes of environmental theatre, where '*all the elements or parts* making up the performance are recognized as alive' (Schechner 1994: x, emphasis in original). The physical transitions disrupt normal habitual processes, the audience become aware of the shift into the performance medium. Drawing attention to automatic behaviour might foster a 'mindfulness/awareness', indicating that mindfulness is not, therefore, a skill to be mastered, but a process experienced as a lived reflection upon action.

4. *Possibility*

Possibility is the process of forming multiple imaginative interpretations of events, things and situations. Campbell Edinborough (2011) applies mindfulness and possibility to a performance context by asserting mindfulness as a method in which to help develop decision-making skills in performer training. Edinborough's adoption of mindfulness in performer training seeks to bring about awareness of automatic behaviour and to open up the performer to new and multiple possibilities of action. Edinborough summarizes Langer's (1989) approach to mindfulness by suggesting that 'mindfulness is the ability to attend to the nature of a process before committing to a specific outcome. It is the ability to develop new categories and new ways of seeing' (Edinborough 2011: 22). Edinborough notes of the actor: '[t]he mindful individual is able to relate her decision-making to the changing nature of her presence within varying environments' (2011: 23). As opposed to the de-categorization of objects and materials (as with some Eastern traditions), mindfulness in Langer's approach opens up objects, experiences and situations to the realm of possibility, multiple perspectives and new and numerous clarifications:

> [j]ust as mindlessness is the rigid reliance on old categories, mindfulness means the continual creation of new ones. Categorizing and recategorizing, labelling and relabeling as one masters the world are processes natural to children. (Langer 1989: 63)

Central to Langer's argument is the playful and explorative nature of labelling and re-categorizing the world about us. As a scenographer I select and use objects and materials for their expressive and communicative potential but I am open to allow them to have a flexibility and fluidity to their interpretation and experience. In *The Weather Machine* the grass landscape aimed to provide a space to sit and explore and an invitation to lie back and listen as the sounds surrounded them. The aim here was to offer a form of transportation, to be somewhere familiar but with no set location. One participant commented that they felt 'transported inside myself, refreshed + emptied'.[3] The atmospheric conditions in the light sequence (see Plate 25) produced a heat that was felt upon the skin of the audience that aimed to offer a feeling of being inside a memory; using light as a material to connect us with the past. Rather than offering a direct location, this moment allows for multiple possible readerships and impressions. Through letting go of the specific significance of material, the audience were free to reclassify and reinterpret their experience through an embodied engagement that was part physical (laying down or feeling the heat upon the skin) and part imaginative conception (a personal subjective memory). The participant below captures this sensory/cognitive experience:

> The whole space took me into an imaginative state where the way I perceived things became detached and my body only needed as a method of touching and sensing. My mind floated above thinking!
>
> (Participant response to *The Weather Machine*)

Imaginative possibility works in tandem with physical engagement. Langer identifies how the mind provides the context for the body and mental projection situates the body in that context:

'[w]hen the "mind" is in a context, the "body" is necessarily also in that context' (Langer 1989: 177). The participant above demonstrates a psychosomatic experience of mental projection and bodily sensation forged through an openness of the potentials of scenographic material. The imaginative mind in the example above is providing the context for the body, and the body then the context for the mind. This process is fluid and changeable, with the participant accepting and embracing multiple possibilities of place and feeling. Often participants described their experiences as affording multiple impression of place and time with comments suggesting that it felt like 'spring, summer, autumn and winter' or 'being in a dream'. These participants are open to the fluidity of the theatrical experience itself, choosing to value their experience as a particular feeling, rather than understanding it within an existing paradigm of 'coherent' theatre. Rather than closing down meaning, mindfulness possibility affords the potential for audiences to continuously classify and reclassify their experience that ultimately might lead to a deeper, more compassionate relational encounter.

Summary

'Mindfulness/awareness' offers a distinct mode of embodied reflection that brings the mindful participant into a conscious self-awareness with scenography. The scenographic orchestration of *The Weather Machine* aided in drawing attention to automatic behaviour, offering agency to the sense-making process and by orchestrating materials to offer multiple possibilities of categorization. Furthermore, 'mindfulness/awareness' not only acts as an explicit tactic of engagement but it can also be considered as part of the experience. Varela et al. assert that:

> What this formulation intends to convey is that reflection is not just *on* experience, but reflection *is* a form of experience itself – and that reflective form of experience can be performed within mindfulness/awareness. When reflection is done in that way, it can cut the chain of habitual thought patterns and preconceptions such that it can be an open-ended reflection, open to possibilities other than those contained in one's current representations of the life space. We call this form of reflection, *mindful, open-ended reflection*. (Varela et al. 1991: 27, emphasis in original)

What is important here is that mindfulness is a dissolving of mindlessness, rather than the acquiring of a practical skill. Mindfulness makes the participant aware of their experience; 'mindfulness/ awareness' aligns bodily and imaginative processes through reflection, creating an open-ended space of possibility. 'Mindfulness/awareness' formulates an integrated picture of the self within the environment – an embodied process of thought, emotion, body and mind (Edinborough 2011: 23). Expanded notions of scenography acknowledge the importance of these inter-relationships and how materials inspire multiple possibilities of interpretation and impressions. It is difficult to attribute mindful responses to specific scenographic materials from audience comments. However, approaching the design through an ecological cycling of environment and body offers up the possibility of multiple subjective impressions where the audience body is integrated into the environmental image. Scenographic materials can be orchestrated through the performance event to bring about mindfulness/awareness activities that help to create profound experiences through establishing deeper and more meaningful *relations* between the participant and their environment.

Notes

1   For further details, see http://www.tate.org.uk/whats-on/tate-modern/exhibition/unilever-series.

2   This extraordinary experience for individual audience members was originally created in 2004 and has been re-imagined periodically in disused buildings in London in 2010, 2012 and 2015–2016.

3   Audience responses were collected after the experience of *The Weather Machine*. Participants were invited to offer written reflections as to what it felt like to be part of the experience.

9

Cognitive Approaches to Performance Design, or How the Dead Materialize and Other Spectacular Design Solutions

Stephen Di Benedetto

Magical material objects are not durable or tangible. As Theodor Adorno theorizes, objects are more than the sum of their parts and they may be what we perceive them to be, or what we expect them to be (1997: 100). Historically, on the stage, solid objects seen from a distance were represented by paint, muslin and illuminated light and became percepts of monuments of stone. This worked because audiences expect stone to behave as we know stone to behave and accept that which looks like stone is solid. Magical design creates a fluid context for the materials of composition to make objects appear to be and then also quickly cease to be. Conjuring uses deception techniques to build for an audience an experience of illusion. The conscious effort audience members exert to follow and figure out the way an illusion is created is intrinsic to the successful performance of an illusion. The act of trying to understand an illusion directs our focus and attention to the designed distractions from the mechanics of the effect. Our cognitive habits are used against us (misdirecting our attention) for us (stimulating wonder) to create an experience of amazement, or of magical experience. Audiences enter an event with the implicit expectation for the magician to fool us. For the performer or designer of the event, as the Amazing Randi declares: 'it is a grand sort of trickery, a skilled imposture that fascinates, puzzles, and entertains by confounding the sensory system in a delicious and titillating fashion. Conjuring is a specialized acting, a performing art, an entertainment. It is inherently honest, though it deceives' (1992: xii).

Magical design foregrounds the processes of using scenographic techniques to structure environments within which performers create illusions. While this does not differ considerably to traditional theatrical design, magical design relies on the audience's engagement to convey the experience of the act. In other words, theatrical design creates an environment meant to signify as material representations of the natural world while in magical design that which seems material through acts of transmogrification becomes immaterial and then material again signifying as supernatural. Randi explains: 'Magic is a comprehensive, scientific performance. Magicians us their knowledge of science, specialized equipment and considerable skill in order to "openly deceive" their audiences' (1992: xi). He goes on to describe that this entertainment is crafted as an interactive match guiding the audience's experience of the shape of the magician's story. Theatrical illusion emerged out of the development of the perspective scene as a deliberate attempt to deceive the eye of the audience into a 'suspension of disbelief'. Magical illusion is a logical extension of this principle using the audiences' expectation that what they see they are to believe, as a means of directing attention away from the mechanics of creating the illusion.

From a phenomenological standpoint, objects are the raw material of the context of the lived experience. Our physiology guides us in everyday life how to relate to the things that surround us. In each situation that we find ourselves, our sensations define the environment and seek ways to actively engage and respond. Objects are at once what they appear to be and carry with them what the culture and society endow them to be. Magic illusion is related to contemporary scenography from the perspective of the integrated role of the conjurer in the conception of the illusion design and the pre-eminence of the intertwined processes in the creation of an overall experience for an audience. As Jim Steinmeyer explains, 'The art of the magician is not found in simple deception, but in what surrounds it, the construction of a reality which supports the illusion' (2006: 8); an intrinsically scenographic impulse. A study of the way magic illusion works (its design, objects and the cognitive response of audience to its performance) broadens our conception of the ways in which scenography is both the mechanical creation of an environment and a structural dramaturgy for the event experienced by audiences. Its function is more than embellishment but rather mechanics for triggering responses to the acts unfolding during the performances. By describing recent research into the neurobiology of magic and the design of magic acts descended from the history of illusion that harness technologies to create illusions that exploit our psychological responses to the world, this chapter suggests that the objects harnessed in design, structure physiological attendant response.

Performing objects

There is a basic acting exercise where a performer is given an object and asked to find as many uses for it as possible. The actor picks up the object, feels it, weighs it in the hand and begins to play with it. Not only does the actor explore what the object is but also what potentials it invites. This sensual exploration of 'objectness' is not simply one of utility, but also one of demonstrating to those watching what something is and its utility. The performer teaches the audience a relational context through his or her experiences with it giving life to a thing. As Tim Ingold argues, objects are revealed through perceptual analysis of their qualities, but things are given life through use (2010a: 6). This relationship between thing, performer and audience is tied together through shared experience. The object holds action potential (Noë 2004). These objects invite a range of behaviours from the actor and engage the audience's sense of what actions and uses are plausible; they are what Robin Bernstein has termed 'scriptive things' (2009: 67). She analyses objects as items of material culture that prompt physiological responses from those who interact with them. Reading historical objects as performative scripts, she suggests objects invite certain manners of use without absolutely demanding them; they are potential narratives. We need not interpret these objects in any particular way, but discover how they are used. Objects imply a choreography of use – their form was created to be used a particular way or in a range of ways that can be discovered using the objects and playing with applications. Understanding how the mechanisms of illusion work is more than knowing what the mechanism is, but the actions necessary to bring the illusion to life. The performer needs to discover its choreography of movement. Not only are the props and devices important in order to facilitate illusions, but they are also conduits to understand blocking, tempo and conventions used to achieve the effects.

Magic acts estrange us from patterns of sensation through the disruption of illusion. That is, by creating illusions that consistently mislead us, magicians call into question our faith in our perception of the world. This shared experience between performer and audience, and between the individuals comprising the audience, is a shared experience of a deception or what Stephen Macknik and Susana Martinez-Conde describe as 'sleights of mind' (Macknik et al. 2010). Magic works because our biology has hardwired processes of perception that respond to the material world that surrounds us. In that way the design of magic can mislead our body and brain's inherent processes of attention. Optical and other technological devices and illusions of stage lighting such as Pepper's Ghost can create objects that are not material but are perceived as material to our minds. That which is not there is there and we believe it to be real even when we know it is not.

Magicians are tricky. They misdirect. While they borrow, steal or purchase each other's illusions, they also reinvent age-old ones. They will blacklist one of their own for revealing how illusions work, even though the basic concepts and methods of magic design are widely known, described and illustrated. Their power is derived from this obfuscation. For example, Penn & Teller will demonstrate and 'reveal' how a concept works, yet still manage to mask the mechanics of the illusion from audiences. Their television programme, *Fool Us* (2011 to date) pits their own extensive knowledge against magicians who compete to win a spot on the Vegas Penn & Teller stage. The magician performs and then Penn & Teller deliberate with great aplomb revealing part of the trick or feigning ignorance. Most of the object manipulations shown are readily known; however, it is the way that the magic is finessed that makes the illusion. If it is all known, then why does is still work? Another level of deception is at play that relies on the rule that the same illusion can be achieved in multiple ways, thereby a conjurer seldom uses the same method of creating the illusion repeatedly. It is in our human nature to try and discover and understand that which defies expectation; magic exercises our perceptual abilities by obscuring the process of creation.

Harnessing objects: Performance design

An aesthetic background in art-making treats the notion of materiality as that which is formed from the raw material, the stuff that artists work with, in line with modernist concepts of material; however, as Andrew Sofer points out in 'Spectral Readings', analysis is not so straightforward or simple as Marxist, new historicist or other theoretical models would have it (2012: 325). Objects do not only exist in the here and now, they retain the traces of the history of what they were once, or for that matter what they may become in the future. A phenomenological reading conceiving how the matter of theatre affects the consciousness and emotional responses of attendants becomes a foundation, rather than transumption, to aid in the analysis of these acts as signs, commodities or social life. While an analysis of a magical illusion drawn from aesthetic theory, where unity, integrity and harmony are the qualities of a work of art can be made, the magic act displays Adorno's challenge that a work of art is as much an event as it is an object; that is, it is something whose mode of existence is fluid, dynamic and irreducible to the thing-like condition it takes on as an aesthetic object. An illusion is created by a host of unaesthetic parts that come together in a unified illusory object such as an avatar, a dematerialized corporal being or disappearing candelabra. The crisis of semblance is made manifest in the dissolution of the magic act.

At the heart of our interactions with designed objects is our bodies' sensual processing of their textures, shapes, sounds and smells. Furthermore, objects do not exist in a vacuum. They are housed in a spatial context. Objects in context hint at use and guide our interactions with them. Magic is an extension of the manipulations inherent in stage design, which is a deliberate process constructed to drive audience reception by predicting how they will react, based on biological habits and processing system assumptions combined with the objects' pregnant semiotic meanings. Magicians, in particular, are able to exploit expectations of what we think should transpire onstage so that we see something that might not be there while they prepare to provide something different. In other words, they lead us to sleights of mind; misdirection of all the senses leading us to false assumptions. Thus theatre is a medium that sets out to craft sleights of mind to use the audience's sensations to create a world that is not material. A growing number of neuroscientists are using magic as a means to show what it reveals about our everyday perception. Our perception of objects is an interaction between those objects and the individual experience of the perceiver.

The fabrication of the magician's illusions is a form of performance design that considers the role of design as a collaborator actively structuring a kinetic spatio-temporal event. The fabrication of a performative exchange is a conspicuous blending of conception, performance and reception. From the perspective of performance design, the conception and realization of a magician's performance, whether performed as close-up magic on the street or performed in a nightclub or traditional theatre, the designer is aware of the ways that design elements trigger visceral responses in spite of their fictive presence. It is the creation of a context where the audience expects the action potential of the present objects. While biologically this means that the attendant's neurons are ready to fire based on a range of probable outcomes, in the world we scan the environment to see what choices we have to act upon. Magicians exploit these predictable human characteristics of scanning for predictable cues. While we are all aware that duplicity is at stake, we are taken in by the challenge of uncovering the close at hand illusion. That attention to spotting the deception distracts us from the moves to carry off that illusion. While we have the semblance of choice we are forced to proceed in controlled patterns as delineated by our biological processes.

Conjuring something out of nothing

'Black Art' illusions became popular in the 19th century and were used by stars such as Alexander Herrman and Harry Kellar. In that period all that was needed was a stage space hung with black velvet, a ceiling of black velvet and a floor of black felt. These acts that rely on masking and lighting effects were possible even with limited lighting technology. The edges of the black box were lined on the perimeter of the floor and up the sides with open gas jets, and the house lights were extinguished or dimmed. Audiences could only discern the light from the flickering gas on the perimeter. These techniques were consistent with a vogue for different types of spectacular reveals in melodramatic performances with design innovations such as the vampire trap where a figure could step through a slit in the flat and mysteriously appear on stage before the audience.

The infamous 1901 book *Magic: Stage Illusions and Scientific Diversions, Including Trick Photography* exposed the mechanics of 19th-century magic. It describes an act where a magician in white appears and materializes a series of common objects out of the blackness only to dematerialize them a moment later. Vases, orange seeds, oranges and watches appear and vanish as a skeleton is dismembered and dances before re-articulation. It describes:

> While the stage is draped in black everything that appears is painted white and the magician is dressed in white. There is an assistant on the stage all through the act but as he is dressed in black with gloves on his hands and a hood over his head made of black velvet he is not seen by the spectators whose sight is somewhat dazzled by the open gas jets. The tables are on the stage but covered with pieces of black velvet rendering them invisible…. The … assistant removes the piece of velvet and causes a table to appear at the magician's command. The vases are also sitting on the stage but covered with pieces of black velvet. By picking up the covered vases the assistant can cause them to appear by removing the velvet, one on the table and the other on the performer's hand. (Hopkins 1901: 64)

Combining the elements of the colour mixture, lighting intensity, black masking and the props with the choreography of performance, the magician is able to create an image that is perceived as miraculous. Substance and form are transformed wilfully as objects are rendered invisible and visible by manipulating the visible properties of light reflection upon materials.

'Omar Pasha' is an act by Michelle and Ernest Ostrowsky with their son Louis-Oliver. They harness the intrinsic physical properties of stage materials, such as the light absorbing characteristics of black fabric, the phosphorescent qualities of Vaseline, paint surfaces and paper. Audiences expect to be able to see what is onstage, counting on their experience of the world and of natural light – that they are able to see the visible spectrum. However, the conjurer manipulates what we can see by adding light to the stage picture, blinding parts of our ocular receptors to parts of the spectrum, or by rendering invisible the changes that take place. He counts on afterimages within our visual processing system. It works on the same principle of how sunlight renders the stars above us invisible to our eyes during the day. The conjuror's act deliberately misguides our attention to overwhelm our sensory processing system for aesthetic effect.

When the curtain rises, the audience sees a Pasha costumed in a white turban covered in brocade, pure white silk tunic, pantaloons accented with a red sash and cape, and Arabesque slippers curled at the toes. The décor is black – from the floor to the walls and to the side curtains. Black Light, or ultraviolet light, illuminates him. Through the deft manipulation of black curtains, costumes and props made of phosphorescing materials, Pasha is able to make people and objects appear and disappear at will. With the wave of a brush, a candelabrum appears and disappears a few minutes later. The objects in themselves are incidental. We are fascinated with the irrational appearance of objects that defy probability. The act focuses the audiences' responses because it makes use of our basic cognitive behaviours for noticing stimuli that capture attention. We look where the magician wants us to because we cannot help ourselves and discount stimuli that are not expected within the context of the environment established frame of the performance.

Playing with our ability to process different wavelengths of light to delight our expectations of what should be possible in a three-dimensional volume allows us to marvel at how the two-dimensional becomes three-dimensional and back again. What I really want to focus on here is our tendency to try and see how and where the magician is trying to fool us. By so doing, we, perhaps, miss the obvious. The magician has already prepared the illusion before we think to look for the moves necessary to carry out the illusion. Christopher Chabris and Daniel Simons study selective attention and demonstrate that in order to accomplish a task efficiently our processing systems have the tendency to blind us to information that is not relevant to the task at hand (2010). They have published a study where subjects are assigned the task to count how many times basketball players, dressed in white, pass the ball back and forth (Chabris and Simons 2011). Two groups, one costumed in black and the other in white, toss a basketball around. In the middle, a large gorilla walks to the middle and pounds on its chest. The better the respondents were at counting the sixteen passes, the worse they were for noticing the gorilla. Observers concentrate on looking for white movement so they disregard black movement. Focused attention necessarily omits stimuli to complete the task at hand. Players in two groups of players move and the ball moves. To count the passes one must watch the movement of the ball. All other information is irrelevant. The path of the object becomes the actor and scripts our response if we are attentive.

In another version of the study, a student stops a professor on campus and pulls out a map to ask directions (Simons and Levin 1998). As the professor responds to the student, two men walk between them with a door and the student switches places with another student. Most professors continued as if nothing had changed. The door masks the movement of the student and the task distracts the professor. General costume similarities fill in the details remembered from the first encounter. Why would someone have switched places with the student? It is improbable. The professor continues on in a predictable manner despite the interruption of the door. When we are engaged in another task we attend to it and exclude other relevant information. In close up magic, the magician uses more of your senses to misdirect your attention away from the action. Even objects touching our body can disappear. Apollo Robins demonstrates that by touching various points on the body, the respondent will not notice a watch or wallet go missing (Robbins 2011). He touches a pressure point on the wrist that fools our processing system into feeling our watch until we forget about it. This is called accommodation. When we put on a watch or a shirt we feel the weight and the texture, but our processing systems put the percepts on the back burner, monitoring instead when change occurs. We note change more than constant stimulation. Robins distracts the perceiver with a touch so that the brain does not pay attention to the change in the weight of the watch or the movement of the band across the skin. By the time the brain is paying attention, again it has accommodated to the new state. Thus objects can disappear in the cracks. Our perception of the world is being crafted by the shared experience of a moment. The interchange sets up the rules of the exchange even as it is violated. In looking for patterns we are fooled by variation and what neuroscientist describe as change blindness, when a change in visual stimulus is introduced and the observer does not notice it.

We are led by our by our brains to see the paths that our experience predicts and assumes to be correct. In that way, we are misled/deceived by our own brains. Our control over what we think that we see is immense; we see what we think that we ought to see. Gustav Kuhn and Michael Land have been studying magic tricks as a means to understand how the mind perceives illusion. They argue that magicians have an ability to distort our perceptions to get us to perceive things that never happened. They chart a sleight-of-hand trick called the 'vanishing ball', where a ball apparently disappears in mid-air. While we scan the environment, we have an impression that what we see is what is. However, what Kuhn and Land demonstrate is that the way we see the world is more strongly dominated by how we perceive it to be rather than what it actually is; their results show that an observer's percept was driven by the magician's cueing (Kuhn and Land 2006: 950). Even though the ball never left the hand of the magician, observers believed they saw it leave the hand. This is a result of our expectation that the ball would leave the hand. Our beliefs about what should happen override actual visual input. Even though attendants did not see an object, they perceived one because the cues from where they were watching suggested that an object would be visible. Kuhn and Land found that observers spend a lot of time looking at the magician's face even though they claim that they are looking at his hand. He looked up, so did we. This is called joint attention. Social cues influence how we perceive – while our eye movements were not fooled by where the ball was, our perception was. Not only do the eyes detect the raw stimulus of the object's movement but they also interpret the data according to social experience.

We have an intuitive sense that we have free will and our conscious choices of what to pay attention to convince us that our automatic unconscious brain functions are not an influence. However, our brain's sensory receptors make all sorts of decisions for us as it takes in all sorts of information and pays attention to, or shines a spotlight of attention upon one task at hand. As adults we are pretty good on focusing only at the task at hand. However, the brain has already made a prediction of what it needs in the moment and has disregarded other bits of stimuli. This autopilot is what helps us find interest in performances or magic acts where even though we know what will happen, we do not know what to look for. We see what the artist has crafted for us. We are so intent of seeing what they do that we disregard seemingly innocent behaviour.

Pepper's Ghost returns to the 21st-century stage

In the spring of 2012 at The Coachella Valley Music and Arts Festival, the rapper Tupac Shakur walked across the stage and gave a 'shout-out' and performed, singing, dancing and later sharing a duet with Snoop Dogg. This was the same Tupac who had been murdered in a drive-by shooting in 1996. The Coachella audience went wild. Tupac's materialization – a virtual thing – triggered a crowd of people (and later those watching footage on social media) to tremble with excitement and weep for joy. While anecdotal evidence is rife on the Internet of the experience of the Tupac hologram, what attendants experienced was an updated version of a Pepper's Ghost effect. They perceived a three-dimensional human figure, yet actually witnessed the reflected two-dimensional image of Tupac's avatar.

Pepper's Ghost is an illusion dating from 1862. Originally conceived by Henry Dirks who brought the invention then called the 'Dircksian Phantasmagoria' to John Henry Pepper to be performed as a scientific demonstration, the illusion created transparent figures on the stage by way of lighting and clear glass. Jim Steinmeyer (2003) describes the generation of this idea from Baptista Porta's *Natural Magic* (1558) to a provisional French patent by Pierre Seguin for a child's toy, to Dirks and then to Pepper. The concept is straightforward. It is as if you are looking through a window into darkness and you see both your hazy image reflected in the glass and superimposed on the setting outside. The transparent glass is also a reflective surface. Aileen Robinson has discussed the illusion and its technical attributes in detail, recounting the uses and limitations of the technology (Robinson 2014: 135–148). Directors used this device to showcase moments of great spectacle, such as in any number of melodramas where a child's spirit ascended to heaven, while magicians used it to startle audiences with sudden reveals and vanishes. Pepper's patent documents explain how this works:

> The arrangement of the theatre requires in addition to the ordinary stage a second stage at a lower level than the ordinary one, hidden from the audience as far as direct vision is concerned. A large glass screen is placed on the ordinary stage in front of the hidden one. (Newton 1863: 64)

It takes an army of stagehands to move the image and to prepare for the fleeting effect. The actor playing the ghost would have to be placed against the angled glass. Stagehands pushed and pulled him across the glass to imitate movement. They used brightly burning lamps to illuminate the figure enough to get it to appear on stage – the heat generated in the pit from the lights gave the effect's pit the nickname of 'the oven'. Magicians saw this invention as full of possibilities and began a new range of practices called 'optical conjuring'. Disembodied heads could float in mid-air, a figure could vanish and appear somewhere else on stage, or a single object could manifest itself as many.

Perceptually we have to learn through experience how these relationships between bodies, space and objects work. My daughter practices in the mirror trying to figure out what is being reflected back – where is the object? She tries to grasp something that is not there. This playfulness is what instigated Pierre Seguin's children's toy that created figures in a box that children would try and grab. This optical trick impelled the children to try and respond and react to the stimulus of that which was not there – an attempt to grasp a material object that was immaterial. It was an object that was perceived that guided a response and then entertained the player. Performance design harnesses that impulse in the crafting of an object within a context to create an effect that will lead to responses from those who become engaged with the illusion.

Coachella attracts thousands of music aficionados to listen to some of the world's most famous musicians, as well as see art installations for two weekends of partying and concerts in April each year. The acts play on five main stages. Alongside the advertised bands are unannounced visitors who will perform at the end of a set. Unexpected appearances are a part of the attraction of the event and often entice listeners to stay put until the end of a performance rather than wander off to another stage for a new act. Audiences are primed to expect treats during the course of the day and it is not surprising that they would go wild when an unannounced celebrity suddenly appears on stage.

In Tupac's spectacular digital resurrection, however, Pepper's Ghost thrilled a new generation of audience. The contemporary illusion is a result of emerging technologies sold by the British company Musion. Their Musion EyeLiner is a reimagining of the technique using a three-dimensional holographic projector.[1] They then combine it with lighting to mask the apparatus and stage dressing, and the result is a living phantasm. A high-definition projector above the stage casts the moving image onto a fully reflective surface on the stage floor. The reflection then bounces onto a long sheet of semi-reflective metalized foil stretched under high tension which is angled at 45 degrees over the floor. This foil replaces the mirror that is commonly used to achieve the illusion. To an audience, the projected three-dimensional volumetric image appearing on the invisible film seems to be standing on stage. Movement adds credibility to the liveness of the manifestation.

To complete the illusion of the virtual being, sensors are placed on the face of the stand-in to generate contact points to overlay the animation of the visage of the figure. They then combine this actual human movement with the computer-generated images to create seamless physical movements and a facial expression that is then paired with a voice over. Rather than stick to clips of audio to recreate a voice where the inflections would be stilted, as they are with computer voice software, an actor mimics the idiosyncratic vocal details of the subject. They harvest images and sounds from recorded footage to generate plausible sounds and movements for the avatar. It is possible to have a living stand-in come to life through telepresence if they are filmed against a plain background and illuminated with LED lights. These presences invite attendant reception using similar interactive skills as to a live being.

In the case of Tupac's return, the designers needed to control the space of the performance. To achieve the effect, the stage had to turn into a dark cavern, and Snoop kept his distance so as to not interfere in the illusion. The narrative of Tupac's death and resurrection is familiar to his fans and his materialization was a logical extension of myths surrounding his lyrics which suggest he might return from the dead. This apparition fulfils a long-standing fantasy, so crowds were to some extent primed for his re-appearance. Later YouTube responses were ecstatic also because fans then had the chance to build their own enhanced narratives, fans showed their trembling hands as they were electrified by the appearance and performance of their long-dead hero.

In the context of the experience of Coachella, a digital materialization is apt as many other experiences of the festival also make use of technological installations and projected and amplified musical experiences. Production designers conceived of a performance that made use of the technologies available at the event crafting a dream performance, like a fantasy match-up between Muhammed Ali and Evander Holyfield, designed to create an ecstatic response from the audience. The story of Tupac's return unfolds as a part of a larger sensory experience tied to standing in desert sun listening to forty-eight hours of music amidst throngs of partying people moving like nomads between performances satisfying their need to see and hear their favourite artists. Coachella is known for its fashion scene, its west coast vibe and its desire to be an experience greater than the infamous 1969 Woodstock music festival. How else to surpass that experience but to materialize the dead and create a performance that no one could forget? The overall conception of the performance design of the act is a careful consideration of the shape of the experience and the elements that will coalesce to achieve the desired response and memory of the illusions presented. As a popular magic teacher recounts to his novices:

> if you think about it, every interaction you have with the public is an experience – a show of sorts – which you can craft to suit your needs, intentions…. These are choices others around you will experience whether you make them consciously or not, and if you don't make them consciously, the ones made accidently may not convey the message you want them to- or lead to the result you desire. (Beckwith 2014: 197)

Production techniques have become more sophisticated since Pepper first thrilled audiences with his illusion. AV Concepts responsible for the holographic projection use a Mylar foil rather than glass to project onto which when combined with more intense lights allows them to create live two-dimensional images that appear to be three-dimensional. Ed Ulburuch, working for the company, describes the illusion as 'a brand new computer generated-Pac performance … using splices of old appearances and tours' to create a synthetic human being (Greenfield 2012). By placing the virtual in the proximity of other live performers, the virtual became more alive. The shared experience of the performers gave credence to the Tupac embodiment. Similar to the Black Art manifestations of objects, explained above, lighting and context also invited the audience to perceive in a habitual manner. Performance conventions such as choreography, costume and presentational acting helped to divert attention away from cues that would distract from the 'invisible' choreography. Just because an object is not visible, it does not mean it is not there, and in turn simply because it is visible does not make it present. We can experience the immaterial as material on stage depending on our focus and attention.

Videographers, lighting technicians and sound engineers interacted with live performers to create Tupac's materialization and provided the audience with the semblance of live interaction. Since we perceive this mirage as three-dimensional and alive, is it not alive? The thing dances with us allowing us to see and hear a material body. It baits our neurological system to perceive life where there is an immaterial object. It is both sensational and unreal. We sense that which is not as real. It is the playful relationship that endows the feeling with substance. How the illusions must be executed, limits the ways in which the performers on stage behave, their movements, tempos and cadences. Like an actor standing on a raked perspective stage, the performer must be conscious of the fiction so as to not destroy the illusion. It is the task of the performer to distract where necessary and to not take attention away when necessary. We can wilfully ignore qualities of material objects so that they seem to be something else in entirety. That is the fun of performing with the inanimate. The live plays with the object to play with the live presence in the audience. Magic is both fantasy and reality because by its nature it is unreal but perceived as real. It is that paradox that makes it appealing and allows us to ask crucial questions about the nature of perception and the future possibilities for scenography.

What memories audiences walk away with of a magical illusion is often embellished or differs in detail from what was presented. Even descriptions by skilled practitioners can deviate from the content of the experience, Randi points out that the magician P.C. Sorcar's accounts of the Indian

Rope trick failed to note that witnesses of the illusion were either seeing different performances or that they were not capable of describing what they actually saw.

> It is vital to point out that observers of conjuring tricks very often misreport what occurred, not necessarily because they are witless or are lying, but more-often simply because they have been misdirected so effectively that they do not have an accurate memory of the event, and unconsciously fill in the details that were not there. It is a common failing. (Randi 1992: 13)

Audience memories become enhanced by their emotional and cognitive responses to what they experience as a part of the total performance event, blurring together their feelings about the day, their mood or their feelings about the other audience members they are with. A network of stimuli coalesces in memory rich with detail, edited by subjective and selective habitual cognitive patterns. Performance design not only aids in the integration of the material of performance within the experience of the event, from the place, space and the content of the performance to the choreography of presentation prepared to be seen, but also felt in relation to the live interaction of the audience in the space of performance.

Magic acts are a continual recapitalization of a range of scenographic techniques. Hints, outlines, artefacts pass from one magician to the next. Under the cloak of secrecy the past is preserved for the initiated. But the illusions are not the thing. The craft of the magician is one of making the illusion work and work within the context of an act conceived by a distinctly different individual with a different style for a different audience. Its objects invite use, invite scrutiny and will guide the way. To make an illusion work is to walk in the choreography of the past making manifest that which is gone. As audience attuned to the sensations of the event as a whole, we cannot believe what our senses tell us is true. We cannot conceive of that which we cannot see. At the end of the Coachella performance, Tupac dematerialized in front of the audience exploding into pixels of light. We marvel at the seeming impossibility of dematerialization. Similarly we can also marvel at the recovery of a scenographic technique obscured in its description by the magician's code used a century before, come to life again and then disappear. The magician and his team has defied what we believe to be the action potential of reality and transformed the material into nothing. Amazed by what has happened the conscious mind takes over to consider the possibilities of how it may have happened.

Objects as perceptual roadmaps

The neuro-scientific study of attention has made it possible for performance theory to blur the multidisciplinary boundaries between cultural studies and performance design. Instead of decoding aesthetic responses related to beauty related to compositional arrangement, an approach-focused study of attention is a means to looking at design coupled with a *thing-centric* focus highlighting how performance studies can question the role of the technologies of performance as a co-creator of experience. By understanding the centrality of the object in the role of creating the scene since the 19th century, we can begin to trace how all the materials of performance, from the stage setting, the actors' bodies to the utterances and sounds of performance, are virtual experiences that are 'part of a continuing process of production, exchange, usage, and meaning' (Edwards and Hart 2004: 4). Scenography is as much a collaborative actor in performance as the audience. This expanded notion of scenography is pregnant with possibility suggesting that scenographic performances are more than the visible, constructed elements on stage; scenography also is constructed as a part of the audience's embodied experience. A scenographer not only creates a stage design but stimulates a experiential journey. The materials of performance are a collaborative exchange between the conceptions of the co-creators, the performers and the perceptions of the attendants. Understanding how the matter of theatre constructs environments and affects the consciousness and emotional responses of attendants can serve to generate innovative practices that integrate advances in technology and challenge assumptions of how we experience the world.

By creating an unexpected apparition alongside live actors, designers were able to titillate attendants providing substance to otherwise unremarkable material. Apparitions on stage created emotional responses from spectators who knew it was not possible for ghosts to appear; they knew the immaterial was appearing on their stage as if it were tangible alongside living beings. Technological spectacle seen intimately in proximity to a live actor may produce a deep visceral response by manipulating our perceptual faculties to fill in the details subconsciously of the three-dimensional qualities of the object in our minds; as the mind seeks to reconcile what it sees with what it predicts it should see. In this way, Tupac can sing with Snoop Dogg without a problem. It is ultimately the audience's collective live response to an animated special effect making perceivable an impossible illusion that allows for visceral reaction to swell in the crowd. Our joint-attention synchronizes and we respond to the sounds of laughter or derision of those who share in this experience. Design practice ties the audience to the performance by creating situational awareness defining the elements of the visceral interaction. As scenographers constantly find solutions to using new technologies as a mode of storytelling that conveys emotion and engages audiences, we will better be able to re-conceive the potentials of what live theatre's deliberate harnessing of the cognitive abilities of the brain to respond to stimuli can make possible to depict on stage. By capturing the spotlight attention of working brains, conscious thoughts and perceptions can be directed to the misdirection, masking the elements that conjure the illusions. Scenography both creates and supports the illusions and through encouraging engagement instigates a range of unanticipated visceral responses.

Note

1   For further information on this technology, see http://www.musion.co.uk

PART FIVE

Materials

10

The Matter of Water: Bodily Experience of Scenography in Contemporary Spectacle

Nebojša Tabački

Contemporary aquatic theatres that combine visual spectacle with the materiality of water challenge us to think through the nature of extravagant scenographies and the ways in which different senses are engaged. These purpose-built spaces that enable large audiences to witness thrilling visual displays of water intertwined with human performers are now developing participatory and immersive opportunities for some privileged audience members. In a wider theatrical context, the term 'immersion' is used to describe involvement of the audience in a number of ways – most notably for the exploration of performance space by spectators during the play, usually by walking in it but also through the senses of touch or smell (White 2012: 221). In contemporary aquatic spectacle, a literal immersion in water is now a possibility. Along with its unique characteristics, water as a scenographic element offers new opportunities beyond the visual perception of the viewers. It immerses them physically in a sensual bodily experience, adding haptic and kinaesthetic sensations to heighten their overall experience. In discussing the bodily experience of scenography in this specific environment, I will be looking at three contemporary aquatic spectacles in detail – *The House of Dancing Water* (City of Dreams, Macao),[1] *Le Rêve* (Wynn, Las Vegas)[2] and *The Han Show* (The Han Show Theatre, Wuhan).[3]

In contrast to their origins as staged naval battles (*naumachia*) in the early Roman Empire, contemporary aquatic shows combine circus, acrobatics, theatre and dance in a form of commercial entertainment. *The House of Dancing Water, Le Rêve* and *The Han Show* are used in this case study because they deploy the latest technologies to encourage physical immersion and a range of different strategies. All three of these aquatic shows make sure that water splashes from the pool stage and that water from the jets occasionally spray the first rows of the audience. These moments provide a palpable connection between the viewers and the action on the stage. If the experience of getting splashed is insufficiently exciting for some viewers, *Le Rêve* at Wynn offers an additional opportunity for spectators to expand their theatrical experience by joining the divers in the pool stage tank and watching the show from the other side of the water surface. Pushing the boundaries even further, *The Han Show*'s aquatic spectacle in Wuhan offers movable audience galleries above the pool stage that rotate and move horizontally or vertically during the show, crossing the line between theatre and fairground ride.

Performance spaces for these spectacles are purpose-built for each show. They include state-of-the-art technologies for stage automation, pneumatics, water pumps, air conditioning, rigging, light, projection and sound. A focus on the engineering of water spectacles reveals scenographic strategy as the creation and management of the 'machine'.[4] Supported by the latest technology, a formless liquid such as water can assume different shapes during the show: switching between open and enclosed spaces, water can be quickly adjusted to the requirements of the scenes. Moreover, water as a scenographic medium can also contribute to our understanding of the dynamics of communication between performers and viewers.

Taking into consideration the technical difficulties of working with huge amounts of water on the stage and the financial demands of realizing such projects, this chapter will explore the significance of water's materiality in the perception of scenography. Despite the commercial success of aquatic shows, the materiality of water as a scenographic medium has been given little consideration. However, research from fields as diverse as bioengineering, neurophysiology and the phenomenology of scuba diving may shed more light on this. By looking closely into the spectator's bodily exposure to scenographic environments in aquatic theatres, I intend to explore the capacity of water to engage senses beyond vision and to discuss, more generally, the way materiality modifies our understanding of scenographic perception.

Origins of aquatic spectacles

The origins of contemporary aquatic spectacles can be traced back to the Roman Empire. The first ancient *naumachiae* (46–44 BCE) were staged on existing or specially excavated lakes outside of the city of Rome (Beacham 1999: 79). By the time Nero became emperor (54–68 CE), aquatic spectacles were being presented in enclosed spaces such as wooden amphitheatres and later even in the Coliseum. The engineering systems that were used to supply and drain the water in amphitheatres is not documented, so we rely on the records of Cassius Dio, who mentions the flooding and draining of the amphitheatre for spectacles based on historical naval battles as integral part of the event (1867: LXI, 9). Staging naval battles required considerable adjustments to the building's architecture and infrastructure. The transformation of the arena stage from dry surface to a pool added an impressive dimension to the spectacle and established engineering prowess as an inseparable component of aquatic spectacle in ancient times.

Naumachiae were revived in Italy during the mid-16th century and have reached the peak of their popularity in the early 18th century as part of baroque courtly theatre (Conan 2007: 172). The events took place in existing natural surroundings and were less extravagantly realized than those during the Roman Republic. However, even if their settings had changed, the purpose of aquatic theatre stayed the same presenting historical naval battles that aimed to impress the audience and to display the political and economical strength of their sponsors. One of the most notable of these spectacles mimicked the battle between a French and a Portuguese ship and took place in Rouen in 1550 on the River Seine as part of the Royal Entry Festival for Henry II (*L'Entrée de Henri II á Rouen*) (Wintroub 1998: 469). Until the mid-18th century, lakes in gardens and parks on the premises of imperial villas and palaces served as temporary stages that were appropriated for patriotic *naumachia* as part of court entertainment for the elite in Italy and England (Conan 2007: 171). These sites were rarely designed for the performance and were mostly used in their natural state.

Although during the 17th century some existing theatres such as Teatro Farnese in Parma were occasionally flooded in order to stage naval battles (Conan 2007: 172), conditions for reviving the aquatic spectacle within enclosed spaces were created with the advent of the industrial revolution. Production possibilities in mechanical engineering, the rapid rise of urban populations and a need to create original entertainment venues brought these spectacles back into the built spatial environment. Special theatres for aquatic melodramas and spectacle emerged in England and the United States during the first half of the 19th century. Venues such as Sadler's Wells Theatre in London and the Bowery Theatre in New York became very popular through their specific art of staging aquatic drama (Wilmeth and Bigsby 1998: 155; Brockett et al. 2010: 179). In 1804, theatre manager Charles Dibdin installed a water tank within the stage of Sadler's Wells Theatre that was briefly advertised as 'Aquatic Theatre' and staged elaborate full-scale naval battles such as *The Siege of Gibraltar* (Trussler 1994: 198).

Water displays in urban spaces

The issues of privilege and wealth have always been closely connected to aquatic spectacle. The extravagance of using so much water for entertainment signifies the power and financial superiority of those who staged the performances. Throughout history extravagant water displays symbolized prosperity, especially in places where the climate is dry and natural water sources rare. In the desert landscape of 16th-century Marrakesh, Sultan Ahmas al Mansur (1549–1603) commissioned an impressive courtyard for the El Badi palace. The reception space that opened on three sides towards the lavish garden with five water basins and fountains was intended to impress visitors and strengthen the Sultan's influence in the region. Fountains in our western urban spaces were originally meant to provide drinking and bathing water, operating through gravity and the slope of the terrain, but their decorative role came to be viewed as their primary function. As a fixture of urban public squares, fountains often served as a background image for plays and processions. David Wiles mentions that in Lucerne in 1583, the Easter Passion Play was staged in front of the fountain in the public square (2003: 106).

Use of the latest technologies for water display is still a privilege of economically strong communities. The record for the highest fountain is currently held by Saudi Arabia, one of the wealthiest countries in the world, which also covers a territory that is 95 per cent desert. The constant improvement of fountain and water jet technology, especially in the last decades of the 20th century, resulted in the increasing heights of water jets, allowing greater options for display, especially in combination with developments in water projection technology. This progression led towards spectacular fountain shows in public spaces that have become particularly fashionable since the end of the 1990s. They aimed to amaze the audience with skilfully arranged water streams that were catapulted up to 150 metres in the air, featuring choreographed movements to music and high-quality images projected onto the surface of fine droplets of water. This type of water technology started being integrated into open spaces in cities with new-found wealth – the Bellagio Fountains in Las Vegas, the fountains at Khalifa Tower in Dubai, and both *Wonder Full,* at Marina Bay Sands and *Wings of Time,* on Sentosa Island in Singapore (see Plate 30). These fountain shows are often incorporated into hotel complexes, amusement parks or shopping mall areas to attract visitors and boost the income of surrounding businesses. To ensure an adequate water supply, fountain shows are positioned in natural water surroundings (e.g. Singapore Bay) or even more prestigiously, in specially constructed artificial lakes within a desert environment (e.g. Las Vegas, Dubai). Though visitors may experience the touch of occasional water droplets and splashes, the fountain displays and projections on sprayed water usually aspire towards a visual impact in the same way that *naumachiae* and aquatic melodramas once did. Any tactile physical experience for the audience is normally the result of changes in wind direction or the effect of ionized air that is commonly experienced near waterfalls. Fountain shows present visually stunning images that are designed to entertain from a safe distance. Spectators' bodily reaction to this type of show is rooted in previous experiences that involve other senses beyond the visual (McKinney and Butterworth 2009: 178). We all carry embodied memories of how water feels on the skin. However, the sense of distance that audience experience when watching fountain shows became a more immersive, tactile experiences when the same technology was implemented and adjusted to indoor water spectacles.

The stage-machine

Rooted in the contemporary circus (*nouveau cirque*), the aquatic spectacles that I consider here combine diverse circus acts – predominantly floor and aerial acrobatics with dance, high diving and synchronized swimming routines. Each show has its unique attractions such as motorcycle or flyboard acrobatics.[5] While *The House of Dancing Water* presents a clear dramaturgical connection between the scenes in an effort to tell a love story, *Le Rêve* presents a more loosely structured entertainment held together by the main theme – a collection of the leading character's dreams. *The Han Show* is based on individual and group acts that signify time travel through Chinese history. The show pays homage to the Han Dynasty and its golden age of Chinese culture.

In contrast to previously mentioned examples of theatres that used water tanks as a setting for staging different naval melodramas, these contemporary aquatic theatres were built for one specific spectacle. Due to very particular requirements and safety issues, theatre architecture and scenography for these custom-made contemporary spaces are mutually dependent and simultaneously developed to fit the needs of the show. The clear separation between building and the show, or engineering and scenography disappeared, merging these historically independent entities into one body. Theatre in the round was adopted as the spatial concept for both *The House of Dancing Water* and *Le Rêve*, with a pool stage in the centre. The Han Show Theatre could be described as proscenium theatre that by means of movable audience galleries changes to a thrust stage configuration during the performance. All three theatres have 8-metre-deep pool stages and auditorium areas to host up to 2,000 visitors.[6] Each theatre has its own combination of specific technical features. Entrances and exits to the stage, underwater canals, movable stage platforms and the fountain systems vary significantly from one aquatic theatre to another. The artistic merging of visually stunning large-scale displays of acrobatics combined with breath-taking circus stunts incorporates the action in and around the pool stage into an overall experience and strives towards a holistic approach to contemporary spectacle.

At the forefront of these developments stands the Canadian global enterprise Cirque du Soleil and director Franco Dragone, who revived a trend for aquatic spectacles with the show *O* (Bellagio, Las Vegas). Since 1998 when the O Theatre opened, the range and technical complexity of aquatic theatres has risen steadily and become more extravagant with every new aquatic stage. The pool stage of *The House of Dancing Water* which opened in 2010, only twelve years later, contains two and a half times more water than the O Theatre with almost twice as many stage lifts and 258 water jets.[7] By 2014, when *The Han Show* had its premiere in Wuhan, the technical features and efficiency of aquatic theatre were pushed even further. The stage of the Han Show Theatre reached 44 metres in width and the number of stage lifts increased to sixteen.[8] For the same show, the German engineering company Siemens also developed three gigantic robotic arms, each capable of holding a 10-metre-wide LED screen and able to move them up to 28 metres across the stage within a few seconds (Müller 2014) (see Plate 31).

The technical details above serve to underline how the effect of spectacle seems to rely on a display of technology that places it on an equal footing with the human performers. This rapid enlargement of technical and technological infrastructure in aquatic theatres has involved teams of engineers and architects that had to deal with a wide range of environmental factors: different humidity levels, temperature sensors, filtering and draining pool water, multiple air conditioning systems and powerful electrical and mechanical distribution equipment (Tabački 2015: 64–68). In addition to making a profound impact on the spatial and technological possibilities of aquatic performance,[9] the introduction of pool stages in large-scale spectacles has also created the preconditions for active audience involvement. For seated spectators in the general audience, the spatial and technological developments enhance their active viewing capacity. Seating disposition in the round, size of the stage and rigging options that enable use of the space outside the stage area, also stimulate peripheral vision and its capacity to sense the motion in the unfocused field of vision.[10] Along with a sense of collectivity the audience additionally bond with performers through dynamic empathy.[11]

Sensing the wetness

The developers of this new genre of spectacle have fostered a close relationship with up-to-date technological developments in the field of mechanical engineering, hydraulics, robotics, water pumps and rigging equipment in their mission to gain a commercial edge in the market and outdo the competition.[12] But the audience experience is also a way in which aquatic performances can claim distinctiveness.

The pool stage has enabled an approach to scenography that focuses on tactile and kinaesthetic experience, involving spectators with the action on the stage as much as possible. For the audience in the first rows of *The House of Dancing Water*, *Le Rêve* and *The Han Show* spectacles, a real sense of immersion comes in the form of water droplets splashed from the pool stage and fountains to provide further excitement for spectators. On the seating plan that customers view when they purchase their tickets, the splash area is marked so that they can decide in advance on the scale of their involvement in the show. For those who want to take part without leaving their seats, towels and raincoats are provided. For others who want to get very wet, there is another option: the purchase of a 'VIP' ticket gives access to complete bodily immersion.[13] The 'Diver's Dream Package' for *Le Rêve* at Wynn in Las Vegas offers customers the opportunity to dive into the stage pool and be among the performers themselves. In this production, the scenographic use of water is not simply a distant visual spectacle but an instrument of communication through direct bodily contact: it redefines notions of perception beyond visual impact or semiotic symbolism. To understand how this process works we shall take a closer look at phenomenological studies of scuba diving, which explain how the materiality of water influences our sensory experience.

With the 'Diver's Dream Package', *Le Rêve* opened its backstage doors to audience members who are certified divers, allowing these special ticket-holders to join technical staff in the pool stage tank and extend their experience of the show by watching the action from beneath the water. According to research on the perception and performance of scuba divers in seawater, visual perception changes the most in the transition from a dry to a wet environment (Adolfson and Berhage 1974: 12). This research revealed that a diver's view in the water is restricted up to 50 per cent in the lateral field, caused by the rubber part of the mask, refraction of light and the occasional effect of a 'fogged up' mask (Adolfson and Berhage 1974: 60). A subtle blurred effect that occurs in the stage pool and a different depth of focus also reduces spectators' view when underwater.[14] This condition is experienced in addition to the temporary disturbance of vision that is caused by splashes and water bubbles from high dives, water jumps and swimming routines. Furthermore, when people are submerged in water and seeing through the lens of a mask, nearby objects appear to be closer and bigger while objects at 12 metres or more distance give an impression of being much further away (Adolfson and Berhage 1974: 97). As the surface of water and objects in the water refract light differently than objects in a dry environment, colour intensity changes. Water selectively absorbs colours, primarily red and yellow light as well as green and violet to a certain extent, so that light blue prevails as the least absorbed colour. The quality of light also changes, given the softer and more pastel spectrum in the water, in contrast to its intense counterpart of coloured haze witnessed above the water surface (Tabački 2015: 71).

In addition to the impact on visual perception, the auditory experience is fundamentally changed in underwater conditions. As noted by Adolfson and Berhage, who followed the research of Reysenbach de Haan (1957), the sound pressure in seawater needs to be sixty times stronger under water to achieve the same intensity as in the air (Adolfson and Berhage 1974: 115). As the atmospheric pressure under water rises, hearing ability declines. The capacity to localize the source of sound also decreases, although this is less evident for low frequencies and broadband noise (1974: 134). Instead of the middle-ear mechanism that we do not use under water, we rely upon the medium of bone conduction (1974: 133). Regarding spatial orientation, it is interesting to note that differences in pressure on the middle or inner ear and the surrounding area causes difficulties in attaining a vertical body position.

PLATE 16 Delaine Le Bas, St Leonard's Church, Shoreditch, London, June 2015 (Alice Clark).

PLATE 17 *Die Schutzbefohlenen*, Holland Festival, 2014 (Janiek Dam).

PLATE 18 *Die Schutzbefohlenen*, Holland Festival, 2014 (Janiek Dam).

PLATE 19 *Die Schutzbefohlenen*, Holland Festival, 2014 (Janiek Dam).

PLATE 20 *As Big as the Sky*, Holland Festival, 2015 (Ada Nieuwendijk).

PLATE 21 *As Big as the Sky*, Holland Festival, 2015 (Ada Nieuwendijk).

PLATE 22 Evelyn van Bauwel as the Musel-Woman in *End* by Kris Verdonck (Reinout Hiel).

PLATE 23 Johan Leysen as the Messenger and Marc Iglesias as Stakhanov in *End* by Kris Verdonck (Reinout Hiel).

PLATE 24 *The Weather Machine*, landscape of wooden pallets, grass, projection screen and hanging cymbals (Tom Joy).

PLATE 25 *The Weather Machine*, light wall illuminated above grass (Tom Joy).

PLATE 26 *The Weather Machine*, audience member reads the 'Field Guide' while immersed in haze/cloud (Tom Joy).

PLATE 27 *The Weather Machine*, one of eight radios that emit sound and voice (David Shearing).

PLATE 28 *The Weather Machine*, audience members stand underneath cymbals during rain sequence (Tom Joy).

PLATE 29 *The Weather Machine*, raindrops fall on cymbals (Tom Joy).

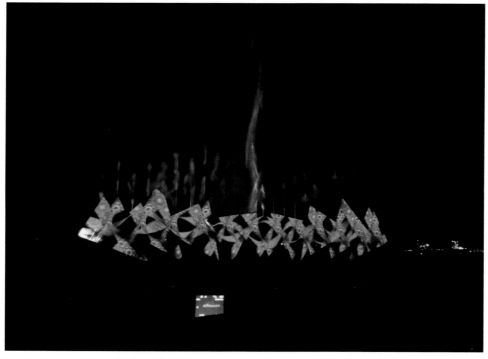

PLATE 30 *Wings of Time*, Sentosa Island, Singapore (Nebojša Tabački).

PLATE 31 Screens with robotic arms. *The Han Show*, Wuhan, 2014 (courtesy of Siemens AG).

PLATE 32 *Le Réve*, Wynn, Las Vegas (courtesy of Wynn Resort Ltd).

PLATE 33 *The Han Show*, Wuhan, 2014 (courtesy of Siemens AG).

PLATE 34 A child meets Foxy in the Forest environment (Nicola Shaughnessy).

Needless to say, these sensory alterations are not the only change to the spectator-divers' experience. A whole new world of visual references that are usually hidden from the regular spectator – such as the supporting constructions for scenography, the team of professional divers, pool infrastructure and the complex logistics that keep the show running – are now visible and provide a very different scenographic landscape from that which most viewers will see. The audience who are in the pool are able to see how professional divers build and dismantle scenographic constructions: how they position the fire ring, erect a giant tree and move properties such as loaded fishing nets that are lifted out of the pool and used as trapeze swings. Their role demands a high degree of technical expertise which can be experienced as a performance by the audience who are in the pool with them. These privileged audience members are also able to witness how performers are provided with airlines (breathing apparatus) and are guided into and out of the pool. In view of restricted hearing in the pool tank, a system of fifteen speakers allows performers, professional divers and spectator-divers to hear the stage cues as well as become aware of audience reactions above the water (Brown 2008). Additionally the diving masks of professional divers are equipped with intercom devices. Hidden from the audience above the water surface, professional divers take on a leading role in this underwater spectacle. Unlike the precise and controlled motion of dance, swimming or acrobatic routines above the water surface, spectator-divers see chaotic action in the stage tank (Lucht 2014). They have a chance to admire the movements of the performers that are not choreographed and as such very different from the movements seated spectators experience (see Plate 32). When viewed from an underwater perspective, the pool's architecture and infrastructure, which was originally intended to be a strictly functional setting, becomes a scenographic environment for the spectator-diver.

Whereas the experience of most of the viewers will be shaped by simple narrative and dramaturgical frames that can be accounted for in terms of semiotic analysis, the experience of watching the show from underwater draws much more on the subjective experience of the participant. Here the experience is centred on emotional input derived primarily from the spectator's 'bodily movements, anticipation and surprise' (Tabački 2015: 72). Instead of an attempt to draw us into the dramatic action on the stage or engage with the inner world of leading characters, immersive strategies in aquatic shows focus on sensory experience. At a depth of 6 metres below the water surface, spectator-divers are guided by professional divers for the best view of certain scenes (Lucht 2014). By activating almost all muscle groups underwater, spectators are constantly moving. They experience a similar sensation as audiences watching promenade performances or immersive theatre productions that require them to pass through the performance space during the show. However, here their involvement is more intense, due to perceptive, haptic, audio, kinaesthetic and breathing restrictions.

Materiality of water

The phenomenology of scuba diving offers a profound understanding of water's impact on our senses and on the body when it is submerged. Although it enables us to grasp the difference in the perception of scenographic elements in the transition to a wet environment, it does not explain its materiality. According to Gerald H. Pollack, scientific interest in water has shifted in the second half of the 20th century towards specialization in molecular research (Pollack 2014: 37). In his book *The Fourth Phase of Water* (2014), Pollack examines the formation of a crystalline entity that appears in the molecular structure of water on surfaces of hydrophilic materials which are immersed. This 'exclusion zone', as the phenomenon was named, is commonly negatively charged (Pollack 2014: 136). The water surrounding it in contrast is positively charged. It is assumed that the energy needed to divide water zones into these two oppositely charged parts comes from radiation sources such as natural or artificial light (Pollack 2014: 137). Comparing this phenomenon to photosynthesis, Pollack suggested that water as a battery could return some of the energy and put it in use for chemical, optical, electrical, mechanical or other forms of energy or action (Pollack 2014: 137). Seeing water as an energy transformer challenges the established approach in scenography where water predominantly displays its unique visual and interactive potential. Might this notion of water as an active agent be relevant for its more diverse application in aquatic theatres regarding design or audience perception?

To shed further light on this it helps to consider hydrophilic materials used in aquatic theatres. For example, concrete which is commonly used for building of a swimming pool basin or pool shell allows water to spread across its surface maximizing contact and is therefore considered to be hydrophilic (Zhang 2011: 14). Pollack's results suggest that an exclusion zone forms when hydrophilic materials interact with water (2014: 52–54), indirectly implicating concrete as a hydrophilic material that could cause the same molecular reaction in the water tank of aquatic theatre. Powerful lighting above the pool stage and in the water tank is facilitated through 3,500 amps of power and 450 lighting fixtures in the pool (Brown 2008). This infrastructure should be more than sufficient to provide the power capacity and conditions for an exclusion zone to form, but the evidence to support this claim is still not proven. So far it has been confirmed that only soft hydrophilic materials such as gels and many polymers almost always create exclusion zones, but there is no available information about their toxic characteristics. Therefore, it is hard to tell if any of the tested hydrophilic materials could in any form find application in architectural or scenographic surfaces in the pool stage of aquatic theatres. It is also doubtful that the molecular reaction that causes an exclusion zone to form would lose its relevance on a bigger scale, especially in a pool with 4 million litres of water. While it is not possible to judge this phenomenon's precise relevance in the scenographic context at the moment, it is unlikely that this phenomenon will have any impact on sensory experiences of the spectator-diver in the pool tank. Nevertheless, its potential could possibly be put to use for creating self-supported energy transformation systems and point the way for a more ecological approach to scenography. If we want to explore the full potential of applied materials in scenography and architecture of aquatic theatres, further studies are required regarding behavioural characteristics of non-toxic hydrophilic materials in water.

Neurophysiological point of view

There is also something to be considered in relation to our tactile experience of water's materiality. There is a sustained belief that our skin is not provided with specific receptors that register wetness (Filingeri et al. 2014). This research assumes that our senses 'learn' the sensation of wetness from previous experiences such as contact with wet surfaces or sweat on our skin. Although it is still poorly understood how our nervous system connects central and peripheral tactile and thermal stimuli, sensory tests performed on the skin of the forearm and index finger show that warm or neutral wet stimuli create significantly less wetness sensation than cold wet stimuli (2014). Even though tested stimuli, such as a wet piece of fabric, had an equal level of physical wetness, its perception increased with lower temperature during a static contact. However, dynamic interaction increases the wetness sensation, irrespective of the temperature of the stimuli.

Taking into account the usual water temperature in the aquatic stage pool tank of 31–32°C, which is just a few degrees lower than the average temperature of the skin (37°C), it is hard to estimate whether the connection between coldness as tactile stimulus and wetness perception could have any significance to seated spectators' tactile response. Concerning the spectator-diver's tactile stimuli, the closest information on the topic is provided by Bowen (1968), who has conducted experiments on tactile sensitivity with divers in cold water, and reported a reduction in tactile sensitivity of 23 per cent when the subject is submerged in relatively warm water at 21°C (Adolfson and Berhage 1974: 173). The fact that the spectator-diver wears a diving suit that leaves only small body parts directly exposed and senses a slight decrease in tactile sensitivity in water that is colder than skin temperature suggests that diver-spectators do not have a deeper tactile sensation of wetness then the audience seating around the pool. Actually the dynamic nature of haptic stimuli, the moment that the water touches the skin, could prove more relevant for seated spectators' tactile experience of wetness at aquatic shows, considering the dynamic interaction caused by water splashes and fountain water droplets. Widening the scope of this interaction and developing further spraying options that create dynamic tactile stimuli for more than just the front rows of seated spectators might be the way in which it would be possible to increase the effect of aquatic scenography. This would maximize sensory experience of the audience sitting further away from the stage and deepen their immersion in the spectacle.

Interconnection of senses

Based on narratives about water from neurophysiology, it could be argued that tactile awareness of water as a scenographic element could be either perceived in the moment or presupposed from a memory. Nevertheless the wetness perception still relies predominantly on its visual aspect. As phenomenological studies noted above show, vision undergoes the most profound changes by moving from dry to wet surroundings. This is not much of a surprise, taking into account the traditional and dominant focus on sight in Western society as a way to acquire knowledge or pass judgement (Ingold 2000: 283; Paterson 2007: 6). Although it enables us to collect valuable results through observation, scientific knowledge cannot be understood alone without reference to cultural and social contexts (Fleck cited in Aronowitz 1988: 287). As Tim Ingold reminds us, visual perception is culturally and socially conditioned. According to David Howes, it is a skill like any other that needs to be practised and cultivated and therefore 'can vary from one individual to another, even within a single society' (Ingold 2000: 283 cited in Howes 1991: 3–21). However, perceptual change that happens under water, as in the case of Le Rêve, offers a different way of seeing and experiencing spectacle for everyone involved regardless of difference in cultural or social background. In comparison to previously discussed issues of wealth, power and social hierarchy that were closely linked to aquatic spectacles in the past, this new approach to perception in scenography shows potential to change cultural conditioning in aquatic theatres. The absence of deliberate communication with the audience through semiotic meanings puts priority on the phenomenological approach and creates a space for pure visual, tactile and kinaesthetic involvement. At the same time, this extravagant way to witness the performance from underwater is not accessible to everyone. The diving certificate requirement and the high cost of the VIP experience that comes with the 'Diver's Dream Package' keep the visual spectacle in aquatic theatres partially exclusive and for an elite audience.

Furthermore, 'the active character of visual attention' (Berthoz 2000: 87) does not necessarily mean direct involvement in the spectacle. Even though performers acknowledge spectators' presence in the pool by waving or giving hand signs, seeing has a connotation of distance (Paterson 2007: 6). It is more likely that a spectator-diver will feel overwhelmed by the complexity of the show's logistics than experiencing actual involvement (Tabački 2015: 72). In opposition to seeing, hearing is the sense that connects us with the world, penetrating consciousness. As a result, our consciousness penetrates the world to create 'a two-way flow of sensory traffic', which makes hearing a more participatory sense then seeing (Ingold 2000: 266 cited in Zucherkandl 1956: 336, 368–369). As Ingold states: 'The space of vision is one from which you, the viewer, are excluded, a space where things are but you are not (2000: 266). Alfonso and Berhage's data on audition under water, which explains the decrease of hearing ability with the rise of atmospheric pressure and an inability to localize the source of the sound under water, shows why spectator-divers in the tank have to rely on a speaker system (Adolfson and Berhage 1974: 133, 164). This sensory deprivation could additionally reduce the overall sense of participation. Additionally, when we look at the assumption that our skin does not have specific receptors for feeling wetness but reacts with a combination of thermal and mechanical sensory impulses (Filingeri et al. 2014), this suggests that it is not the wetness of water in aquatic theatres that heightens our sensory experience but its temperature and the dynamic of its touch. Previous knowledge of how water feels on the skin, supplemented by the visual sense, presumably plays a more important role in the sensation of wetness than its materiality. In the context of tactile audience immersion, it is evident that the 'tactile field has never the fullness of the visual, that the tactile object is never wholly present in each of its parts as it is the case with the visual object' (Merleau-Ponty 1962: 224).

Ingold also notes that 'perception is not an "inside-the-head" operation, performed upon the raw material of sensation, but takes place in circuits that cross-cut the boundaries between brain, body and world' (2000: 244). When we put the spectator's body into motion, it diminishes the body's nature as an object in the world and transforms it into a means of our communication with it (Merleau-Ponty 1962: 106). Whether this happens with the movement of seated audience galleries above the pool stage in *The Han Show* (see Plate 33) or through the physical submersion of spectator-divers in the pool tank of *Le Rêve,* involving the spectator's body kinaesthetically in aquatic theatre, affects multiple changes of perspective and view towards the stage and backstage areas. By conquering theatrical space, the audience is physically integrated into the spectacle. When viewers are shifted through the space as if they are on a funfair ride, demands are made on their visual, proprioceptive and vestibular senses above the pool stage. Diving in particular calls for movement of almost all body muscles in addition to haptic sensations which change our visual, auditory and motor experience underwater profoundly. Concerning this matter, Rob Spruijt explains that the excitement that comes with a roller-coaster ride form of interaction is triggered by our physical engagement rather than visual observation, leaving us without the distance necessary for an aesthetic response (2013: 73). While giving us joy through interaction with the world, physical immersion in the spectacle restricts the possibility of an active visual response to our surroundings in order to identify objects (Spruijt 2013: 73). According to Spruijt, 'the aesthetic experience becomes possible when we abstain from interaction, even in environmental art' (2013: 75). This transformation in consciousness and perception caused by stage technology (Aronson 2005: 74) aim to push the boundaries of human physical and perceptual abilities in contemporary spectacles as far as possible, no matter the extent of the financial cost. Throughout theatre history this ambition always risked the danger of overshadowing the performers with technology – as in the case of three gigantic LED screens in *The Han Show* – or overwhelming the spectators through an immersion process that lacks any safe distance for reflection, aesthetic response or a critique of ideology as in the experience offered by *Le Rêve*.

Conclusion

With regard to the materiality of water, the field of bioengineering does not currently offer enough data on the specific behavioural characteristics of hydrophilic materials in water that could be applied in architecture and scenography. The idea of creating a self-contained power system that gives back some of the energy it uses in the way Pollack's experiment results suggest is still open to question, but it certainly inspires us to think of more ecological approaches to scenography regarding options for reusing energy. For now, in scenography as in art: 'Everything depends upon the way in which material is used when it operates as medium' (Dewey 1980: 66). Water as scenography in aquatic theatres has shown so far a wide scope in its presentation and possible meanings. Supported by the latest technology it changes its metaphorical appearance fluently as it mimics sea, river, rain or waterfall and creates numerous variations of open and enclosed spaces. The uniqueness of water as a material and its transformative quality as a scenographic element has the potential to penetrate all our senses, making water an ideal material for the creation of *psycho-plastic space*. This concept, suggested by Josef Svoboda (Baugh 2005: 87), is an ideal scenographic space which changes and modifies itself according to the dramatic action and so reflects life itself.

To conclude, the reflection on aquatic narratives regarding vision, touch and kinaesthesia reveals the different properties of our senses – both their advantages and disadvantages. The experience of wetness in the aquatic theatre reminds us of their mutual interdependence in our experience of the world. In the contact between our body and the world, 'we shall also rediscover ourself, since perceiving as we do with our body, the body is a natural self, as it were, the subject of perception' (Merleau-Ponty 1962: 206). If being in the world means to be able to see and to exist in the sight of the others (Ingold 2000: 277), does it really matter if this happens through the process of previously learned experiences or through the immediacy of perception in the moment such as experienced with a splash of water? For as long we are able to see how water touches our skin we are reminded of our presence in the world, even if it means we are looking back upon ourselves and we are only feeling the touch of our own memories.

Notes

1 *The House of Dancing Water* (City of Dreams, Macao): Created by Franco Dragone. Stage designer: Michel Crête. Architect: Li Chung Pei. Costume designer: Suzy Benzinger. Lighting designer: Luc Lafortune. Choreographer: Giuliano Peparini. Date of premiere: 15 September 2010.

2 *Le Rêve* (Wynn, Las Vegas): Created by Franco Dragone. Stage designer: Michel Crête. Theatre designer: Claude Santerre. Costume designer: Claude Renard. Lighting designer: Koert Vermeule. Choreographer: Giuliano Peparini. Date of premiere: 6 May 2005.

3 *The Han Show* (The Han Theatre, Wuhan): Created by Franco Dragone. Performance space designer: Mark Fisher.

4 Anne Robb, a general stage manager for *The House of Dancing Water*, referred in an interview with Catherine Prosser to stage management as 'to manage the machine' (Prosser and Robb 2014).

5 Motorcycle acrobatics are facilitated through a system of concave ramps that catapult the motorcycle drivers up in the air, giving them time to do different figures before they land. Flyboard is a way of surfing on a board through the air above the water. The board is connected to water pressure jets that enable a person to float in the air up to 15 metre above the water surface.

6 The theatre-in-the-round of *Le Rêve* has a pool stage of 20-metre diameter by 8-metre depth. The stage contains centre, 'donut' and three VOM lifts. There are 42 water jets in the stage floor. Available online: http://preview.thenewsmarket.com/Previews/WYNN/DocumentAssets/316552.pdf. The purpose-built theatre for *The House of Dancing Water* show is a 270-degree theatre-in-the-round with a pool stage in the middle (20 metres in diameter by 8-metre depth). Stage contains of 11 stage lifts and 258 dancing fountains. Available online: http://theatreprojects.com /files/pdf/ pubs_houseofdancingwater-lsi.pdf. As of March 2015, technical data regarding the infrastructure of *The Han Show* was only given partially in a documentary for the Arte TV channel. Available online: http://www.arte.tv/magazine/futuremag/de/.

7 Stage lifts are custom-made mechanical systems built into the stage floor that offer different vertical stage configurations.

8 Source for given technical data was documentary film available online: http://www.arte.tv/ magazine/futuremag/de/.

9 The positioning of technical infrastructure followed the aesthetic vision of theatrical space: 'The air ducts and terminal boxes in the O Theatre for instance are positioned under the seating area, which leaves the ceiling free for technical requirements of design' (Tabački 2015: 65).

10 The idea that biological motion can be as accurately perceived in peripheral as in central vision is explained in *Peripheral vision: Good for biological motion, bad for signal noise segregation?* (Thompson et al. 2007).

11 As suggested by David Wiles: 'The circularity of the Roundhouse is the basis of its power to create a feeling of collectivity, when spectators contemplate each other as equals, and feel that theatre has the activity of circus, with embodied human beings risking something of themselves in what they present' (2003: 205). In *Semiotics of the Circus*, Paul Bouissac refers to the discovery of mirror neurons in our brain in an attempt to explain why we react intensively when we witness extreme actions within a circus (2010: 178).

12 The designer responsible for *Le Rêve* and *The House of Dancing Water* was Michael Crête. Each project had different architectural firms, which also designed the theatres. The Han Show Theatre was designed by Mark Fisher. Stage designer was François Séguin.

13 As of 2015, the Diver's Dream Package 'includes a two-night stay in a Wynn Deluxe Resort room or an Encore Resort Suite, a VIP Indulgence ticket to the show, a private backstage tour, a SDI certified scuba training session with the *Le Rêve – The Dream* diving team and the opportunity to watch a live show while diving the 1.1 million gallon aqua theatre' according to the website, and 'starts at $1,750 for one diver and $2,450 for two'. Available online: http://www.wynnlasvegas .com/Entertainment/LeReve/DreamDivePackage.

14 In an interview for *Stagebitz*, general stage manager of *The House of Dancing Water* Anna Robb reported on reduced visibility in the stage pool (Prosser and Robb 2014). Available online: http:// stagebitz.com/2014/05/backstage-house-of-dancing-water/.

11

Ecologies of Autism: Vibrant Space in *Imagining Autism*

Melissa Trimingham

This chapter demonstrates how scenography may be 'expanded' into therapeutic applications. The focus is the affective space of scenography within *Imagining Autism: Drama, Performance and Intermediality as Interventions for Autistic Spectrum Conditions* (2011–2014), a project run at the University of Kent, UK.[1] This potential for 'applied' scenography within real-world contexts has been little understood, identified or exploited within education or artistic practice. In *Imagining Autism* drama specialists and psychologists undertook an interdisciplinary approach to testing the impact of immersive drama on autistic children, which centred on adapting different scenographic spaces to the difficulties and differences in autistic perception. As co-investigator my responsibility was as a scenography specialist working with the team to design, build and deliver the environments, the puppets, masks, props and costumes.

Autistic children lack skills in communication, social imagination and empathy (the so-called triad of impairments[2]) which has a devastating effect upon their ability to function socially, even if only mildly affected. Because we do not know what causes autism, and have so far discovered no biological basis for the condition[3] (though it may be inherited), we are forced to address the behaviours it presents: no drug is yet available to ameliorate the symptoms of autism. Skills-based approaches try to compensate for the deficits, and underlie much of our current education system for autistic children. If parents can afford both money and time, skills begin with intensive Applied Behaviour Analysis early in life where, based on a reward system, the child may learn to respond appropriately, if somewhat inflexibly, to people and situations. Alternative methods concentrate on a more fundamentally embodied approach to autists' learning. This approach includes traditional therapies using the arts and art education, such as music, drama and dance, and may be used in complementary ways alongside skills training within mainstream education.[4] In my experience, most parents would prefer to address their child's problems using a multi-pronged approach, but parents are rarely offered a sustained or radical supplement to the skills learning, simply because no alternative is widely available. Hobson and Hobson go so far as to suggest that '"emotion recognition" or "interpersonal skills"' are not abilities that can be 'taught or trained (even by computer)' and suggest instead that we 'seek ways to foster development in intersubjective engagement ... to help children with autism shift to a more fruitful development trajectory' (Hobson and Hobson 2008: 85–86).

Imagining Autism, as I will demonstrate, provides exactly this sustained intersubjective engagement through the medium of scenography. The drama work takes place within an affective three-dimensional scenographic space where children can begin to develop what Jordan Zlatev and others called 'The Shared Mind' (Zlatev et al. 2008).

Cultural theory, anthropology and the humanities as well as performance studies have shown a gradual increasing emphasis and interest in materiality and the material object, both of which traditionally define scenographic space.[5] This shift in emphasis includes widespread acknowledgement of the new perspectives that phenomenological analysis can bring, the growth of embodied approaches, particularly situated cognition within cognitive science, and discourse around so-called 'New Materialism' whose ecology does not privilege human subject over material object. Parallel to this and key to *Imagining Autism* is, within theatre studies, the deep change in perceptions of what scenography is or might be.[6] Cognitive approaches to scenographic reception, particularly embodied and enactive theory, have recently extended the philosophical insights of phenomenology into close analysis of the relationship of body, brain and matter in cognition (Trimingham 2011, 2012; McKinney 2013: Chapter 7). Linked to these cognitive and embodied understandings of scenography are Dorita Hannah's large-scale environments and installations. Hannah's *HEART OF PQ: A Performance Landscape for the Senses* (Prague 2003) (see Hannah 2011; Zupanc Lotker 2015: 9–10) introduced us to scenography as a fluid and responsive medium, now often called the 'new' scenography. Even in more conventional theatre design processes 'new' scenography is usually deeply implicated in the rehearsal and/or devising process, acknowledging that scenography is the 'principle dramaturgy' in contemporary performance making (Baugh cited in McKinney 2015: 79). Drawing on these two paradigm shifts, that is, a renewed interest in materiality particularly in cognitive studies, and the changed function of scenography, I here offer a context where affective embodied scenography offers a powerful, vibrant and even explosive learning medium.

Imagining Autism involved three schools over ten weeks of a school term, in vivid and richly sensorial built environments: the Forest, Outer Space, Underwater, the Arctic and Under the City. Typically the children involved were between the ages of eight and eleven. Because many of the children were on the severe end of the autistic spectrum, with extreme difficulties in communicating, empathizing and playing, the ratio of practitioners to children was always at least one to one. Our hypothesis was that a 'drama triad', that is, principles of communication, empathy and imagination, might address the triad of autistic deficit. The psychologists on the project employed a range of quantitative and qualitative measures to test this. Given the different sensory basis of much autistic perception, the project relied upon scenography in the broadest sense – in this case, the total multi-sensory environment, the props and puppets, masks and costumes, the lights, sound and projections.[7] Autistic children may be hyper (over) or hypo (under) sensitive to stimuli – visual, auditory or tactile; their physical difficulties are often hidden and go some way to explaining their often challenging behaviour and frequent distress (Bogdashina 2003). No two autistic children's perceptual difficulties are the same: we would do better to talk of autistic perceptions rather than autistic perception, and even on a day-to-day basis children's physical sensitivities can vary. But all autistic children, even the apparently very verbally able, share the difficulties in communication, social imagination and empathy. There is also a wide spectrum of ability, and between 2011 and 2014 we worked with the full range, including children with no speech at all. The project demonstrated that children are capable of strong imaginative engagement: but this is differently inflected depending on where they are on the autistic spectrum.[8]

The 'pod' in which the drama took place and the scenarios were built was a stand-alone collapsible structure three metres by four metres and two and a half metres high with a floor covering, detachable lights, laptop computer, sound system, projection and live feed. Each environment was designed to be immersive although the way out was always clear: for example, the Forest, into which the children entered guided by a Forest Ranger, surrounded the child with leaf cover and branches, they crunched fragrant leaves on the floor, and enjoyed the soft, dappled light; it was populated at various times by a chatty Woodpecker puppet, a tall masked Fox (see Plate 34) and a cuddly masked black furry Mole, who variously appeared as the loose narrative developed, and whose length of stay and actions depended largely on the children's responses. Similarly sensory and all enveloping, as well as fluid and loose, was the softly changing Underwater environment with a water soundscape, blue/green light and wavering shadows, sometimes with children seeing projections of swimming fish and dolphins, and sometimes live UV puppetry: here the children were guided by a sailor who sometimes with children on the severer end of the spectrum never even spoke, as children delighted in the sensuous feel of the rocking boat or the brush of the wind over their faces (a light-weight plastic film rising and falling gently over them). Loose 'poor theatre' objects such as cardboard tubes were as much part of the play as the rustling leaves in the forest, the sand underfoot and underwater, the paper snow in the Arctic and rubbish under the city. In each scenario there was a simple narrative that could be elaborated by the performer/practitioners (depending on the children's responses) or even dropped all together. For example, in the Forest, with the more verbal children, Foxy kept trying to steal the Woodpecker's eggs; the children had to decide what to do, perhaps hiding them from Foxy, chasing him off, even deciding on a suitable punishment. There were prefixed 'scripted' events within the loose narrative structure, such as a crisis or climax (for example, a storm at sea in Underwater), though never at a fixed time, but dependent on the judgement of a team member. As Erin Manning suggests: 'For a work to be successful, enabling constraints must be embedded within its conceptual design, and these constraints must to some degree direct the work toward its unfolding. But these constraints must also remain flexible enough to refrain from the preposturing of the work (touch it, but get it right!)' (Manning 2011: 42).

Because of the need to respond to the children's cues, as well as needing to sense when *not* to do anything, practitioners were strong ensemble players, with experience in devised work and drama with special needs groups. Their role as 'facilitators' was played out either in costume as a character (sometimes masked, sometimes not) or simply accompanying the children in their experience. An ability to improvise was key, accepting and developing whatever the children offered and responding to the unexpected. One of the hardest skills to learn was simply to 'be', that is, do nothing, be silent, wait. Gauging the children's responses, the company added or removed props, new characters and scenic elements between or even within shows. These 'loose' elements included clocks, camp fires, cocoa, scientists, snowmen, trampolines, treasure and tents. Sound and light were fluid elements that the technician (also a trained performer/practitioner) changed, moderated or intensified; the children, moreover, could easily access the technical desk in the corner of the environment and change the lighting, sound and projections themselves, and often did so. The pod was placed in a reassuring and familiar setting within the school, usually the hall, ideally with ample 'space' around it,[9] so that children were free to go in and out. When getting used to the pod, children sometimes chose to play outside it for the first session or even longer. Characters came out to play with them and before long they entered (and left) the pod freely.

I suggest that the project demonstrates the new methods of devising that Hannah's 'new' scenography (2011) demands. Traditional methods of production in the theatre mean that stage designers, frequently designing alone, are required to adopt linear, goal-based thinking rather than a process-based, embodied engagement by a team, working in an iterative cycle with materials, space and performers. They may for example use a model box visually presenting a three-dimensional version of the set in advance for consideration by the director and team and the scenography is largely set by the first night opening. *Imagining Autism* in contrast developed its scenography in iterative patterns of discovery, a process that continued after it was 'stood up' and performed within. To begin with, the rudiments of the *Imagining Autism* scenarios, necessarily built before we went into the schools, were the result of a practical collaborative process. The bare bones of the environments were even at this stage fleshed out by reworking ideas from an earlier pilot project:[10] creating the Forest itself as a new environment; adding a greedy Penguin to the Arctic; or creating a spaceship for Outer Space. However, competence and skill in improvising with these characters and puppets was hard-won through trial and error in performance with the children; an iterative rather than linear process, that involved practitioners in a steep learning curve gradually letting go of our intentions to follow the pre-arranged storyboard, and abandoning trying too hard to get a 'result' from the child, that is, a response. We had to be careful not to impose what *we* wanted or what we thought *ought* to happen on the children but allow events and actions – such as slap-stick humour – to repeat, sometimes over and over, which autistic children found reassuring and pleasurable. Characters such as two clowning snowmen or a mischievous husky dog who stole the warm blankets were added as we progressed, and as obvious gaps and opportunities arose.

I have highlighted the importance of practitioners' presence not purpose, and this sense of live presence, being in the moment, is vital to Hans-Thies Lehmann's contemporary performance stages. Indeed the performances in the schools drew heavily on aspects of postdramatic contemporary performance paradigms as articulated by Lehmann- 'shared energies instead of transmitted signs' (Lehmann 2006: 150) with practitioners and children sharing a 'level of commonality' (cited by Shaughnessy 2013b: 326). In this way *Imagining Autism* questions key terms that are commonly used to describe this kind of work, such as 'applied', 'immersive' and 'interactive' theatre. 'Applied theatre', increasingly critiqued in the literature of socially engaged theatre (see Adebayo 2015: 123–130) implies that practitioners do something *to* the children losing the sense of shared action between participant and performer. 'Immersive' theatre is perhaps even more problematic, again not stressing sufficiently the agency of the participating individual. The term hints at passivity (especially when 'immersing' autistic children who tend to 'stim' anyway, that is they repeat actions or are transfixed by an object, to the exclusion of all else). 'Immersive' also reminds us of sensory rooms that are used in almost every special school to calm a distressed (autistic) child or simply provide sensory enjoyment. 'Interactive' theatre is misleading in that it implies a binary to-and-fro exchange between child and the material world encountered, as well as between practitioner and child instead of a richly emergent experience.[11] In order to stress the iterative cycle of emergent meaning in the *Imagining Autism* pod, 'interactive' as well as 'applied' and 'immersive' are here deliberately avoided. Karen Barad's term '*intra*-active' (Dolphijn and Tuin 2012: 14)[12] seems better suited to the 'worldings', to use Manning's inspired term (Manning 2011: 44) that the pod produces. Barad's intra-action is 'the action *between* (and not *in*-between) that matters' (Dolphijn and Tuin 2012: 14, emphasis in the original). Barad also originated the term 'diffraction' (2012: 52) in connection with intra-active experience, which allows study of both the nature of the apparatus and the object. This touches on ethics and responsibility, which in considering the potentially powerful 'affect' of responsive scenography we would do well to note: 'Diffraction … is not just a matter of interference but of entanglement … Objectivity, instead of being about offering an undistorted mirror image of the world, is about accountability to marks on bodies, and responsibility to the entanglements of which we are a part' (2012).

Barad sees agency as an 'enactment' (2012: 53) and not something we possess: that is, agency is seen as more of a verb than a noun, just as Manning turns 'world' into 'worlding'. Barad and Manning take us away (as Barad puts it) from 'choice in any liberal humanist sense' (2012). In other words, the humanist tradition of the superiority and power of human agency and control is put into question. As Hobson and Hobson put it: 'Sharing experience with someone else is not merely like having one's own experience of the world then adding something' (2008: 77) but is a qualitatively new and often unpredictable experience. I shall return to Barad at the end of this article in connection with this unpredictability and the weight of ethical responsibility it places upon us.

Within the cognitive turn in performance studies, materiality is important (Tribble 2011; Paavolainen 2012): but within cognitive science itself, the external world within which the subject cognizes has in general received less attention from neuro-scientists than what is happening inside the head. This is unfortunate since 'The surround – the immediate physical and social resources outside the person – participates in cognition, not just as a source of input and a receiver of output, but as a vehicle of thought' (Tribble 2011: 139). With the exception of Hutchins's work on material anchors for cognitive blends (Hutchins 2012), Sinha's work on affordances (Sinha 2005, 2009)[13] and to some extent the work of extended cognition theorists such as Andy Clark (2008), attention is more often focused on interior processing *of* the material world.[14] Situated cognition, a less extreme form of extended cognition, opposes the Artificial Intelligence model of the brain which sees the brain as a centralizing 'computer' dealing with disembodied representations of the outer world. Situated cognition theories turn for the most part upon the more or less 'common sense' position (Clark 2012: 275–276) that the mind is a great deal more than the brain (Varela et al. 1991): in other words, cognition is dependent upon a situated body within an environment, interacting with others (Thompson 2001; Spivey 2007; Zlatev et al. 2008). The brain is seen as 'co-dependent on bodily process' and 'co-dependent on extra bodily processes' (Stephan et al. 2014: 69). This is also called 'intercranialism'. As a theatre practitioner who is used to team work, somatic communication in rehearsal and performance, handling objects and puppets on stage to communicate meaning, and thinking creatively through materials and being inspired by them, intercranialism seems to me absolutely indisputable. Surprisingly, however, it remains somewhat outside mainstream cognitive science: Clark may call it 'common sense' but it is far from widely accepted.[15] My experience of *Imagining Autism* pushes me towards an even more radical claim within situated cognition, which may be described as a fusion of the environment into cognition itself, closer to what Wilson and Clark describe as 'spectacularly transformative mixes of organismic and extra organismic resources' (2009: 73). This is *intra*cranialism or 'extended' cognition which is '*co-constituted* by extra-bodily processes' (Stephan et al. 2014: 69) (italics in the original). I claim that Wilson and Clark's controversial and dynamic mix of 'organismic and extra-organismic resources' more accurately characterizes the *intra*-active scenographic space of *Imagining Autism* that moves beyond binary, linear, reciprocal exchanges between inner and outer worlds into an active, vibrant and implicating ecology. 'The challenge is to create the conditions for the piece to work in an *ecology* of relation [my emphasis] that does not privilege the interactive, but seeks to open the way for the activation of the *more-than* [italics in the original] that the work has to offer' (Manning 2011: 48). The practitioners and the children are as much part of the 'transformative mixes' as the objects and materiality encountered.

I have chosen here to concentrate on the Forest environment. This environment was always our first session. The children enter straight into the main space of it without a journey (in Outer Space for example, they travel to the moon in a space ship). In the Forest they are led straight into the dappled lit space by a Forest Ranger they meet outside, they crunch fragrant leaves under foot and throw them in the air, meet the Woodpecker who lives in an opening in the tree, help Mole (a Bunraku type puppet) plant her garden, lie in the hammock, warm themselves at the campfire, 'freeze' as they listen to hissing snakes (the mild 'crisis') and 'fall asleep' until morning (often several times for the pleasure of all the lights going down and then up, waking the Forest Ranger for the umpteenth time!).

The Forest arguably gave opportunities for the more able and verbally skilled autistic children[16] to learn the norms that guide social action, norms which Ingar Brinck describes as 'dynamic, situated and heterogeneous' (2014: 737). 'Fundamentally', Brinck declares, everyday interaction is 'sensory motor and contextual' (which describes actions in the Forest) and 'people attune effortlessly to the meaningful perception of each other's emotion, attention, and intention in real time' (Brinck 2014: 749). Clearly 'effortlessly' does not apply to autistic children who lack neurotypical empathy and social imagination ('theory of mind') – the ability to put yourself in another's shoes. The play in Imagining Autism demonstrated the children's difficulties in these areas.

Brinck examination of children's play distinguishes carefully between 'constitutive' rules that govern a game,[17] violations of which very young children can recognize (2014: 739), and normative rules of social behaviour that emerge from intersubjective encounters, for example and importantly, in play. The social norms that are much more fluid and unpredictable than constitutive rules of games take much longer for children to adopt successfully (2014: 741). These normative rules are culturally and situation-dependent. Brinck traces how these social norms (clearly not the same as the constitutive rules of a game) develop primarily from intersubjective experience and 'practical engagement' (2014: 751); game and play situations in childhood provide these essential opportunities to learn. 'Foxy in the Forest', for example, prompted some unusual behaviours between the children. On one occasion, a rare example of changing the 'constitutive' rules of a game[18] ('What's the Time Mr Wolf?') in favour of normative behaviour (adapting to others) emerged (see Brinck 2014: 742–743). Children spontaneously began a game of 'What's the Time Mr Wolf?' with Foxy. They engaged in sustained peer play, probably remembering the game from a pre-project 'getting to know you' session. In the Forest, playing on their own, the constituent rules were spontaneously bent to accommodate the less able children so they could all continue to play. This is precisely what Brinck describes as happening amongst (neuro-typical) children when adults are not there to enforce the rules (2014: 743). 'Normativity', Brinck says, is 'intersubjective' (2014) and negotiable, a practical skill that depends on participatory engagement. Less able children in *Imagining Autism* also began to negotiate 'compliance' with social norms, albeit at a more rudimentary level. Jimmy, for example, encouraged by his peer Kim, was obsessed with prisons and they both insisted on entering and re-entering the Woodpecker's 'house' (prison) behind the tree. Children were never prevented from such actions (the back of the tree was not intended to be entered) unless health and safety was an issue; so Jimmy and Kim spent some time in and out of this space but gradually accepting that it was the Woodpecker's home, as he refused to move out; and they stopped 'playing' in it as a prison responding to it as his home.

Brinck further breaks down the actual means of learning social norms. Registering emotion, that is recognizing feelings as both positively and negatively charged, is according to Brinck important for learning: for example, experiencing pleasure or joy while sharing something, or sorrow at losing something because intersubjective cooperation has failed. Lizzie, for example, engaged emotionally with the Woodpecker hand puppet who was desperately and incompetently guarding the nest and eggs from Foxy's thieving (expressing sorrow for the Woodpecker's situation and showing joy in helping). Moreover the Woodpecker seemed to provoke positive emotions in the children provoking pleasurable engagements across the spectrum of ability, even if the child did not engage specifically with his fears for the eggs. Brinck identifies non-verbal agreement as a further learning tool. Non-verbal agreement might consist of, for example, a shared look in play that leads to a shared engagement producing similar pleasurable emotion: Lizzie 'shushed' her peers, and used body language to draw them in, beckoning them to share with her in taking the eggs and hiding them in various places from Foxy's greed. Finally Brinck identifies conversation as reinforcing understanding of social norms. This might be something as specific as sharing a reading book with a child, commenting upon emotions in the characters: similar to this, practitioners indeed often commented aloud on characters in the environment and what they were feeling. Conversation might also simply be verbalization during play, and Lizzie engaged in conversation not only with the Woodpecker (reassuring him) but with her peers and the practitioners discussing the situation. We cannot know exactly how much Lizzie herself was helped in her learning by these specific encounters or how much she helped her peers who were less verbal and empathic than herself, develop emotional engagement and social norms; but the positive results identified by the psychologists indicate that the more able children made the most positive gains in both these areas.[19]

As an example of the 'spectacularly transformative mixes of organismic and extra organismic resources' identified above (Stephan et al. 2014: 69), Eleanor, who was a silent and introverted child outside the pod and often hung back from engaging within it, transformed herself into the character Foxy. She found the Foxy mask (practitioners' costumes were typical loose elements), tried it on, took it off and was clearly about to abandon the attempt. Practitioner Gemma Williams who played Foxy was alerted to Eleanor's actions by a colleague.[20] Gemma, in costume, at once turned to Eleanor, took off her heavy Foxy coat and helped Eleanor into it, followed by the tall Fox mask that sits above the head. Fully costumed, Eleanor made an impulse forward towards the snoozing Forest Ranger she can see in the tent. Gemma working only through the body not words, put a hand on Eleanor's arm to pause her; and then showed her the 'Fox' stance and movement. At this point, costume becomes 'actant' in Latour's sense (Latour 1996, 2005). Actant theory derives from the new materialist recognition that objects have agency, in the sense that they have and are dynamic energy forces that we need to respect, sense and work with. The material world is not dead matter. Costume as 'actant' here actively transforms our normal quotidian body image which we carry with us, in that its weight and padding around the hips changes the wearer – the hips feel larger, pushing body weight forward. The height and weight of the head mask further physically extend our body image upwards (we feel taller) and it acts like a heavy crown. In everyday life the sense of our head is very strong and consequently our face feels 'larger' than any other body part we are presenting to others. Wearing something heavy on the head enhances this, and somehow sharpens our sense of direction, self-importance, focus and energy. Imitating Gemma exactly, Eleanor now stood still and rippled her 'paws', focussing on her 'goal': the 'sleeping' and 'unsuspecting' Forest Ranger in the tent. Somatic experience of an object (costume) here translated into cognitive affect. She felt empowered to move forward alone as Foxy, into the tent, silently, and surprise the 'sleeping' Ranger, practitioner Robin Hatcher. He, despite his *apparently* having no idea Eleanor was about to wake him up, instantly jumped up in response, shooing Foxy out of his tent and telling her off. In fact the DVD footage shows Eleanor laughing delightedly and scrabbling her paws again in defiance, even making a gleeful Foxy noise as the Ranger shoos her playfully out of his tent. The practitioner's alertness to the actions around him and instant response reveals the Forest as a space of extended cognition where practitioners and children are thinking together through the material environment. The space is itself 'acted' as much as it is acted *in*: the thought is only possible because of the dynamic, changing environment. Gemma at once seized hold of another furry mask (a loose element in the pod) and pretended to be a baby fox.

Technician/practitioner Mel Woods drew attention to Eleanor as Foxy 'mother' by exclaiming: 'Oh she's a *lady* Fox!' Fellow classmate Ronnie heard this, pausing in his noisy parachuting game, peered over the hammock's edge and smiling broadly said to Eleanor: 'You're my friend Foxy'. For the first two sessions Ronnie had been deeply cynical about the pod, loudly telling us that it was all a pretence and he wasn't fooled for a moment.[21] Eleanor's transformation as Ronnie's 'Foxy' friend is complete and the emotional delight and sense of well-being in both children through play is visible.

The Forest is a 'space of action' (Gray Read 2013) which, to use Gray Read's expression, we did not 'architect' (2013: 7) in advance. Its agency was released in practice, and this in turn subtly changed those releasing it. It was also a space of extended cognition whose elements were both part of the thinking and developed the *very means to think*. The gestalt model of action and progress where change in one part changes the whole is a useful paradigm to understand emergent meanings from this particular episode and from the constant iterations of practice in the pod. The gestalt pattern is a structure but a dynamic one, that has movement and change built in to it. When a new part is taken in to a whole, it is not just the whole that changes but all its constituent parts change as well: in other words change is not just linear (a model of addition or subtraction) but 'more ecological interactive' (Manning 2011: 48), moving 'beyond the linear model of a localized interactivity' (2011: 47) into work that is implicated and transforming.[22] Similarly an emergent system in chaos theory is volatile and complex but not without structure, but the structure has to be understood differently as constantly in motion. Emergent systems 'move with a superficially chaotic randomness that is underlain by patterns of complex organization, which in turn function as foci for further reorganization and development ... there is a continuous refining and reassembling of key elements that results in systems' capacities to evolve into new and unexpected forms' (Coole and Frost 2010: 14). Emergence permeates the Foxy encounter in the Forest on several levels.

Firstly there is, fairly obviously, evidence of Eleanor and the practitioner(s') thinking with and through each other. The sequence can be described as 'a mercurial stabilization of dynamic processes' (2010: 13). In describing, analysing and sharing Eleanor embodying the Fox in front of our eyes in this scene, I want to focus on (in Malafouris's words) 'how a material sign means, and not on what it means' (Malafouris 2003: 39). Unlike the way scenography has been typically discussed, the scene does not 'represent' anything: it simply is. Materiality here is 'not an external stimulus' but 'a constituent part of the mechanism itself' (2003: 37). This is of course extended cognition as defined by Andy Clark and Robert Wilson: 'Natural extended cognitive systems are those cognitive systems containing natural resources from the cognizer's environment that have been functionally integrated into the cognitive repertoire of that cognizer' (Wilson and Clark 2009: 62). In the words of Coole and Frost there is 'no longer a quantitative relationship between cause and effect' (2010: 14) but a far more fluid process. Consider the silent bodily communication between Eleanor and Gemma. Mental 'ideas' (working it out and then acting it out) played no part in their exchange in the sense that:

> Corporeal space is lived spatiality, orientated to a situation wherein the lived/living/lively body embarks on an architectural dance that actively spatializes (and temporalizes) through its movements activities, and gestures. The body introduces patterns, intervals, duration and affects into Cartesian or Euclidean space from within it, and it continually reconfigures its own corporeal schema in responding to and recomposing its milieu (Umwelt). (Coole 2010: 102)

Eleanor is here involved in an 'architectural dance' and reconfigures her own corporeal schema as she responds to and recomposes the scenographic space of which she is a part. As Diana Coole says of the great phenomenologist of embodiment Maurice Merleau-Ponty, his aim is 'to explain a generative, self-transformative, and creative materiality without relying on any metaphysical invocation of mysterious, immaterial forces or agencies' (Coole 2010: 93). The process of knowing (which implicates everyone in the Forest) is deeply physical, practical, wordless, and we recognize that the physical world is 'a mercurial stabilization of dynamic processes' (Coole and Frost 2010: 13). We should perhaps 'consider anew the location and nature of capacities for agency' (2010: 9) since their material agentic bodies and 'actant' objects were integral parts of cognitive learning.

Experience in the pod gradually changed practitioners' 'knowing' of scenographic space. Proof of this is how much better the project ended than it began. In the end the children led the action rather than the practitioners. In early sessions practitioners had tended to speak far too much and to impose their play upon the children seeking a 'result'. Moreover there were necessary early adjustments in the team learning to work sensitively together, as not everyone was able to abandon more linear models and adopt a process of patient waiting, openness, listening and (often) silence. Performance in the Forest was a way not just of 'knowing' but, in the words of Werry, it is a way of knowing 'how one might come to know' (Werry 2010: 225). We came to understand that the means of this knowing are through a particular kind of material engagement, neither mechanistic nor mystical, and we (and the children) gradually get better at it. Practitioners in this episode can be said to be using scenographic 'tools' with a high degree of skill.

In his article 'Walking the Plank: Meditations on a Process of Skill', Tim Ingold explores the 'processional quality of tool use', the 'synergy of practitioner, tool and material' and the 'coupling of perception and action' illustrated by cutting a plank of wood with a saw (Ingold 2011: 53). The process of this entirely practical act of sawing ('setting out', 'carrying on with repetition and rhythm but no duplication', 'putting things away' as a preparation for the next encounter – that is, the 'end' is really a new beginning) – can be mapped with uncanny precision upon *Imagining Autism* as a whole, and upon many particular action sequences within the pod, as here.

'New' scenography refuses the humanist tradition that asserts the superiority of the individual mind that feels it is 'in charge' of material matter and can communicate ideas (perhaps in the form of a stage set) in a linear fashion to audiences. We acknowledge the power of complex cognitive *affect* via the 'sensory motor and contextual' interactions of scenography, in other words, affect is the unpredictable and ever changing cognitive *effect* of intersubjective encounters. The key is absolute openness to the situation, the experience, the material world, temporarily abandoning linear models of progress that attempt to reach a goal. At the beginning I contrasted skills-based approaches in autism, which adopt linear models of progress, with more embodied approaches. What *Imagining Autism* offers, to use Manning's words is a more 'ecological' than 'interactive' experience (2011). 'Meaning', says Malefouris, 'is not a quality which [is] "added on" to the physical existence of a thing' (Buchli in Malefouris 2003). Meaning is emergent, and to quote Manning, goes beyond the 'linear model of a localized interactivity' (Manning 2011: 45); the individual is not a 'bounded, semi-autonomous entity' (Heft 2013: 18).

Karen Barad develops her notion of intra-action discussed earlier into 'diffraction', her term for the way that the instrument of measurement changes the object you are measuring: intra-action becomes not a matter of 'interference but entanglement' (Barad 2012: 52). There is no 'knowing from a distance'. Barad couches this entanglement eloquently in terms of the complexities of quantum physics, but in essence it relates to basic phenomenology, the rejection of Cartesian dualism, that is, the separation of mind and matter, and it asserts (as does situated cognition) that the mind as inextricably entangled in the external world, including the reciprocity of other bodies and other living beings. The scenographic space of the pod is a space of change: but as Henri Bergson claimed, change does not imply moving from one immobile state to another but a 'perpetual becoming' (Bergson 1946: 179). 'There do not exist things made, but only things in the making, not states that remain fixed, but only states in the process of change' (1946: 188). Barad like Bergson makes hugely exciting, intoxicating claims about the motility of all matter and its potential to release energy; moreover, she and other new materialists (Coole and Frost 2010: 24–36) challenge the dominant paradigm of world politics through a deep ecological sensibility. This same sensibility is empowering within the educational context I have outlined: fluid scenographic space connects us to a powerful material world of agency and change. As a result, there is an ethical dimension in this type of work, and we carry personal responsibility in engaging with it. It demands we try to understand and move closer to the autistic participants' perceptual experience.

Earlier I described the scenographic space of *Imagining Autism* as potentially 'explosive': and this is why.

New materialists describe 'active processes of materialization of which embodied humans are an integral part, rather than the monotonous repetitions of dead matter from which human subjects are a part' (Coole and Frost 2010: 8). Autists, it would seem, especially though not exclusively those on the severer end of the spectrum, also tend not to inhabit a region of 'dead matter'. Autist Donna Williams in her autobiography *Nobody Nowhere* describes how as a child, among other things, she saw minute detail, 'tiny spots which I called stars'. She says, 'They are actually air particles but my vision was so hypersensitive that they often became a hypnotic foreground with the rest of "the world" fading away. By looking through the stars and not at them, I could see them' (Williams 1992: 9). When she was very young she 'discovered the air was full of spots. If you looked into nothingness, there were spots...'. She was soothed by being 'lost in the spots' (1992: 3). Autists often have the ability to see the material world differently, even to the extent I would claim of realizing 'a materiality that materializes, evincing immanent modes of self-transformation' (Coole and Frost 2010: 9) . For example, in *The Reason I Jump* Naoke Higashida, an autistic child, describes many facets of his world including his perception of material form:

> Really, our vision of the world can be incredible, just incredible ... you may be looking at the exact same things as us, but how we perceive them appears to be different. When you see an object, it seems that you see it as an entire thing first, and only afterwards do its details follow on. But for people with autism, the details jump straight out at us first of all, and then only gradually, detail by detail, does the whole image sort of float up into focus ... our hearts kind of drown in it, and we can't concentrate on anything else. (Higashida 2013: Question 32)

It would be easy to become sentimental over such a creative vision which clearly causes Naoke as much pain and discomfort as it does pleasure but by comprehending their potentially transformative sensory modes, we can empathize and move alongside them in mutual trust rather than blundering in with insistent demands that they share our vision of the world.

Within the pod there are numerous instances of children showing extreme visual or haptic sensitivity to the scenography around them. Children crumble materials such as the polystyrene lumps of 'moon rock' or tear the ultra violet cardboard fish into tiny pieces and watch the specs float down in the light of the projector against the screen. Elsewhere, a child stands in ecstasy, wrapped up in a hanging curtain of translucent white fabric through which he can see coloured lights and shapes. Another child twirls ceaselessly a cheap see-through plastic umbrella trimmed with coloured fairy lights, lost in pleasure; in the Arctic this same child skates on the foil 'ice' and lies on her back making 'snow' angels in the torn up paper. Children frequently hide within play tubes and even lidded dustbins, or insistently crawl under the cloths of many textures and colours, enjoying the sensation, the dark and the silence. Such simple sensory pleasures are normally closed to us as we grow older, and practitioners learnt to accompany the children in these experiences, silently waiting, as preludes to more complex sequences of action and communication. Understanding the children's 'new conceptions' of matter (Coole and Frost 2010: 11) reminds us that the material world only appears to us as it does because of our habitual perception we are used to, and enables us to move closer their world in order that they might move closer to ours. One episode that demonstrated to us the power of the tool we had was a child, Jay, in the first school who became too distressed to enter the pod. He had been happy in weeks one and two (Forest and Outer Space) but he became very upset at being taken into the Arctic (a bright white environment) and terrified the following week of the darkness of Under Water. Although the practitioners were confused and disappointed by his negative response, especially after a successful first two weeks, Jay was of course allowed to remain outside the pod on these two occasions and he then left the project all together. The positive that emerged from this was a much greater understanding of Jay's hidden difficulties by his teachers, which may have resulted in some long term benefit to him.[23] It seems likely that Jay is one of the children Olga Bogdashina (2003) describes whose sensory difficulties vary from day to day, week to week. He had a visual impairment of which the school had been unaware but his reactions to the Arctic and Under Water made his visual difficulties clear;[24] he could be hypersensitive to light and dark but not consistently. In addition Jay was intermittently hypo-haptic (i.e. under-sensitive to touch) and unable to 'ground' himself in the space, so he chewed his jumper, sand and anything he could get into his mouth and was often much calmer when staff strapped him firmly into his chair. Despite the 'positive' of identifying Jay's hitherto unrecognized visual impairment, it was distressing to realize that we had unwittingly and momentarily combined his hypo-haptic sense with a sense of pitch blackness or blinding whiteness. Such is the ethical responsibility theatre practitioners have, to watch, listen, respond or hold back completely. 'Vibrant and explosive' space can also be risky.

The rich and sensory 'expanded' scenography of *Imagining Autism* is capable of bringing about 'transformative mixes' of materiality and mind to those who participate in it. The pod structure is an architecture, a 'frame and foil' to its motile interior elements, action and dynamics (Feuerstein and Read 2013: 178), architecture which is 'ongoing action' rather than 'object' (Gray Read 2013: 7). As Gray Read says, the ideal architect focusses on 'making things happen rather than making things' (2013: 5). In the scenographic space of *Imagining Autism*, the 'process of design emerges as interaction, improvisation and negotiation' (2013: 7). Margaret Werry, an anthropologist faced with understanding 'new' embodiments of the world in Polynesian Oceanic culture that she felt were alien to her experience, pleaded for a research method that 'must become a slow, plural, vulnerable, experimental, curious, concrete, messy, modest process of engaging with different realities' (Werry 2010: 228). Slow, vulnerable and modest: paradoxically, I could ask for no better description of our method, as we moved cautiously and learned slowly within the affective, dynamic and explosive ecologies of *Imagining Autism*.

Notes

1   *Imagining Autism: Drama, Performance and Intermediality and Interventions for Autistic Spectrum Conditions* was an Arts and Humanities Research Council funded project based at the University of Kent (October 2011–March 2014). Investigators were Professor Nicola Shaughnessy (Drama), Dr Melissa Trimingham (Drama), Dr Julie Beadle-Brown (Tizard Centre) and Dr David Wilkinson (Psychology). Participating Schools were St Nicholas School Canterbury (Spring Term 2012), Laleham Gap, Broadstairs (Summer Term 2012) and Helen Allison School, Meopham (Autumn Term 2012). The schools covered a wide spectrum of ability. The project worked with 6–8 participants in each school, aged 8–11, with a diagnosis of autism. The intervention involved participants in weekly forty-five-minute sessions in a portable installation (the 'pod'). These pioneering interdisciplinary methods of intervention and evaluation have generated evidence that drama can impact positively upon the symptoms of autism. The research has also challenged many of the myths surrounding the condition, offering new insights into the imagination in autism. For further information on the project, visit http://www.imaginingautism.org. A documentary film of the project *Imagining Autism: Now I See the World* is available through the Routledge Performance Archive http://www.routledgeperformancearchive.com/search/video/1554.

2 This triad formed the basis of the previous diagnostic criteria which have now been replaced by the controversial new diagnostic criteria for autism in 'DSM V' which does not recognize Asperger's Syndrome as a separate condition within high functioning autism.

3 One of the most accessible texts that covers possible biomedical approaches to autism is Temple Grandin and Richard Panes's *The Autistic Brain: Exploring the Strength of a Different Kind of Mind* (2014), which explores among other aspects of autism the structure of the autistic brain, which is in most instances totally indistinguishable visually from the neurotypical brain.

4 I use the word therapy (and therapeutic) cautiously as a short hand here ('arts therapy') as it will be broadly understood. However, many of the approaches recently developed within the arts including *Imagining Autism* do not take a traditional therapeutic approach (broadly, these tend to be based in psychoanalytic approaches) but develop phenomenological and embodied methods. Phenomenological and holistic approaches also refuse to see skills as 'bolt on' extras to compensate for deficits.

5 For example, the work of Prof. Tim Ingold at Aberdeen University, 'Knowing from the Inside: Anthropology, Art, Architecture and Design' http://www.abdn.ac.uk/research/kfi/ and the recent AHRC (Arts and Humanities Research Council) project 'Material Witness: the interrogation of Material objects for Humanities Researchers' http://www.kent.ac.uk/mems/news/?view=246. Material Witness is funded by the AHRC's Collaborative Skills Development scheme, and run by the University of Kent and its partners within *CHASE* (Consortium of Humanities and Arts South East)

6 This 'the scenographic turn' as identified by Joslin McKinney (2015: 79).

7 It is worth acknowledging that *Imagining Autism*'s scenography has many synergies with the work of other companies working with autists and PMLD children and adults, such as Horse and Bamboo Theatre (where the author worked throughout the 1980s including many multi-sensory special needs projects), Oily Cart, Bamboozle and Innersense, and much of what emerges from this study will I hope throw light on other work.

8 The project's efficacy in addressing autistic symptoms was evaluated by the psychologists and gathered sufficient evidence for a larger planned research project.

9 This is reminiscent of McConachie's 'container' schema where by the community event (*Imagining Autism*) is held within the larger community 'container' of the school: 'the spatial relations concept of "containment" is fundamental to the work of any community based theater' (McConachie 2012: 112). He talks of 'mingling' in a space and how the spatial dynamic of the container has 'helped to build communities for centuries' (e.g. in carnival).

10 *Imagining Autism* evolved out of a Kent Innovation and Enterprise funded an 'Ideas Factory' joint proposal 'Play and Autism' (Nicola Shaughnessy) and 'Puppetry and Autism' (Melissa Trimingham), working in St Nicholas School in Canterbury, Kent. It won Kent University Innovative Project of the Year, 2010–2011.

11 See Heft (2013: 16–17), critiquing Bronfenbrenner's interactionist model of socio-cultural influences.

12 See also Heft (2013: 17) and Werry (2010: 225).

13 The writer discusses Sinha in 'Touched by Meaning: Haptic Effect in Autism' (Trimingham 2012).

14 Rodriguez and Moro (2008) critique the lack of notice taken in child development of objects in the development of infant intersubjectivity and understanding social realities.

15 Andy Clark's essay 'Embodied, Embedded and Extended Cognition' is an isolated voice in *The Cambridge Handbook of Cognitive Science* (2012).

16 The children at Laleham Gap School, Broadstairs, were verbally fluent and at the able end of the spectrum. They had however all received a diagnosis of autism rather than Asperger's Syndrome, a distinction that still then applied under the diagnostic criteria for autism (DSM IV).

17 For example, in 'What's the Time Mr Wolf' which the children spontaneously played in the Forest, the 'constituent' rules are that the Wolf, standing with his back to the slowly advancing line of children, replies to the children's chanted question (What's the time Mr Wolf?') with random times ('1 o'clock', '6 o'clock') until he suddenly answers 'Dinner time!' and chases the children, trying to catch them.

18 See previous note.

19 In the quantitative and qualitative testing by *Imagining Autism* psychologists, it was the more able children who made the greatest advances in reciprocal social interaction and emotion recognition and the most significant reduction in the severity of autistic symptoms as rated by parents and teaching staff.

20 This was the Principal Investigator, Nicola Shaughnessy, whose role developed into that of roving director/dramaturge who alerted practitioners into action like this, or signalled to the technician changes in the environment (e.g. night falling) when she felt the moment was right.

21 In Outer Space we had decided to take Ronnie in before the others in the schedule and to show him round on his own, which he had relished; and in Arctic, we had assigned him a special role of going in first and being found utterly 'frozen' in the snow, by the rest of the group. He sustained this role until his peers had worked out a way of waking him up.

22 This is in fact the Dynamic Systems Theory model (DST) explained straightforwardly by John Lutterbie (2013: 104–105).

23 Jay took part in the psychologists' tests and showed improvements in a number of areas long term; he was however excluded from the results as his contact with the pod had been so curtailed.

24 The psychologists had specifically asked children with visual impairments to be excluded from the project.

References

Adebayo, Mojisola. (2015), 'Revolutionary Beauty Out of Homophobic Hate: A Reflection on the Performance I Stand Corrected', in Gareth White (ed.), *Applied Theatre Aesthetics*, 123–155, London: Bloomsbury.

Adolfson, John and Thomas Berhage. (1974), *Perception and Performance Under Water*, New York: Wiley.

Adorno, Theodor W. (1997), *Aesthetic Theory*, trans. Robert Hullot-Kentor, Minneapolis, MN: University of Minnesota Press.

Al-Issa, Ihsan and Michel Tousignant, eds (1997), *Ethnicity, Immigration and Psychopathology*, New York: Plenum Press.

Ambrozy, Lee, ed. (2011), *Ai Weiwei's Blog: Writings, Interviews, and Digital Rants 2006–2009*, trans. Lee Ambrozy, Cambridge, MA: MIT Press. Available online: https://mitpress.mit.edu/books/ai-weiweis-blog (accessed 31 July 2015).

Anderson, Benedict. (2013), 'Out of Space: The Rise of Vagrancy in Scenography', *Performance Research*, 18 (3): 109–118.

Appadurai, Arjun. (1997), *Modernity at Large: Cultural Dimensions of Globalization*, New Delhi: Oxford University Press.

Aranguiz, P. (2004), 'Santiago de Chile, Nueva Arquitectura y Espacio Público. Arquitecturas de Fin de Crisis. Plaza Civica', *Revista de Urbanismo*, 11: 54–75.

Aronowitz, Stanley. (1988), *Science as Power: Discourse and Ideology in Modern Society*, Minneapolis, MN: University of Minnesota Press.

Aristotle. *Poetics*, trans. S.H. Butcher, MIT Classics. Available online: http://classics.mit.edu/Aristotle/poetics.1.1.html (accessed 18 May 2016).

Aronson, Arnold. (1981), *The History and Theory of Environmental Scenography*, Ann Arbor, MI: University of Michigan Press.

Aronson, Arnold. (2005), *Looking into the Abyss: Essays on Scenography*, Ann Arbor, MI: University of Michigan Press.

Aronson, Arnold. (2008), 'The Power of Space in a Virtual World', in D. Hannah and O. Harsløf (eds), *Performance Design*, 23–38, Copenhagen: Museum Tusculanum Press.

Aronson, Arnold. (2010), 'Postmodern Design', in J. Collins and A. Nisbet (eds), *Theatre and Performance Design: A Reader in Scenography*, New York: Routledge.

Aronson, Arnold. (2012), 'The Dematerialization of the Stage', in A. Aronson (ed.), *The Disappearing Stage: Reflections on the 2011 Prague Quadrennial*, 86–95, Prague: Theatre Institute.

Artists Without Walls. (2004), 'The Divide', Available online: http://w3.osaarchivum.org/galeria/the_divide/chapter19.html (accessed 20 November 2015).

Arzobispado de Santiago Fundacion Documentacion y Archivo de la Vicaria de la solidaridad (2014), 'Sala Virtual Vicaria de la Solidaridad', *Vicaria de la Solidaridad*, 14 July, Available online: http://www.archivovicaria.cl/historia_02htm (accessed 14 July 2014).

Augé, Marc. (1995), *Non-Places: Introduction to an Anthropology of Supermodernity*, London: Verso.

Balsamo, Anne. (2011), *Designing Culture. The Technological Imagination at Work*, Durham and London: Duke University Press.

Banham, Simon. (2015), 'Intro: Weather', *PQ 2015*, Available online: http://www.pq.cz/en/program /intro/weather (accessed 25 July 2015).

Barad, Karen. (1998), 'Getting Real: Technoscientific Practices and the Materialization of Reality', *Differences*, 10 (2): 87–128.

Barad, Karen. (2003), 'Posthumanist Performativity: Toward an Understanding of How Matter Comes to Matter', *Signs*, 28 (3): 801–831.

Barad, Karen. (2007), *Meeting the Universe Halfway: Quantum Physics and the Entanglement of Matter and Meaning*, Durham, NC: Duke University Press.

Barad, Karen. (2012), 'Matter Feels, Converses, Suffers, Desires, Yearns and Remembers', Interview with Karen Barad in Rick Dolphijn and Iris van der Tuin (eds), *New Materialisms: Interviews and Cartographies*, Open Humanities Press, MPublishing, Available online: http://hdl.handle.net/2027 /spo.11515701.0001.001 (accessed 16 April 2016).

Baugh, Christopher. (1994), 'Brecht and Stage Design: The Bühnenbildner and the Bühnenbauer', in Peter Thomson and Glendyr Sacks (eds), *The Cambridge Companion to Brecht*, 235–253, Cambridge: Cambridge University Press.

Baugh, Christopher. (2005), *Theatre, Performance and Technology: The Development of Scenography in the Twentieth Century*, Hampshire: Palgrave Macmillan.

Baugh, Christopher. (2012), 'Baroque to Romantic', in Christine Dymkowski and David Wiles (eds), *The Cambridge Companion to Theatre History*, 33–54, Cambridge: Cambridge University Press.

Baugh, Christopher. (2013), *Theatre, Performance and Technology: The Development and Transformation of Scenography*, 2nd edn, Basingstoke: Palgrave Macmillan.

Bay-Cheng, Sarah, Chiel Kattenbelt, Andy Lavender and Robin Nelson. (2010), 'Portal: Digital Culture and Posthumanism', in Sarah Bay-Cheng, Chiel Kattenbelt, Andy Lavender and Robin Nelson (eds), *Mapping Intermediality in Performance*, 123–124, Amsterdam: Amsterdam University Press.

Beacham, Richard. (1999), *Spectacle Entertainments of Early Imperial Rome*, New Haven: Yale University Press.

Beckwith, Tobias. (2014), *Beyond Deception, Volume 2*, Richmond, CA: Triple Muse Publications.

Beer, Tanja. (2016), 'Ecomaterialism in Scenography', *Theatre and Performance Design*, 2 (1–2): 161.

Benjamin, Walter. (1992), *Illuminations*, trans. Harry Zohn, London: Fontana/Collins.

Bennett, Jane. (2010), *Vibrant Matter*. London: Duke University Press.

Bennett, Jill. (2005), *Empathic Vision: Affect, Trauma, and Contemporary Art*, Stanford, CA: Stanford University Press.

Bennett, Susan. (1997), *Theatre Audiences: A Theory of Production and Reception*, London: Routledge.

Bergson, Henri. (1946), *The Creative Mind: An introduction to Metaphysics*, trans. Mabelle Louise Andison, New York: Philosophical Library.

Bernstein, Robin M. (2009), 'Dances with Things: Material Culture and the Performance of Race', *Social Text*, 27 (4): 67–94.

Berthoz, Alain. (2000), *The Brain's Sense of Movement*, Cambridge, MA: Harvard University Press.

Bhabha, Homi K. (1983), 'The Other Question … Homi K. Bhabha Reconsiders the Stereotype and Colonial Discourse', *Screen*, 24 (6): 23–25.

Bharucha, Rustom. (2000), *The Politics of Cultural Practice: Thinking Through Theatre in an Age of Globalization*, Hanover and London: Wesleyan UP.

Birch, Anna and Joanne Tompkins. (2012), *Performing Site-specific Theatre: Politics, Place, Practice*. Basingstoke: Palgrave Macmillan.

Bishop, Claire. (2004), 'Antagonism and Relational Aesthetics', *October*, 110 (Fall): 51–79.

Bishop, Claire. (2012), *Artificial Hells*, London: Verso.

Blanning, T. C. W. (2002), *The Culture of Power and the Power of Culture*, Oxford: Oxford University Press

Bleeker, Maaike. (2008), *Visuality in the Theatre*, London: Routledge.

Boal, Augusto. (1979), *Theatre of the Oppressed*, London: Pluto Press.

Bogdashina, Olga. (2003), *Sensory Perceptual Issues in Autism and Asperger Syndrome: Different Perceptual Worlds*, London: Jessica Kingsley.

Böhme, Gernot. (2013), 'The Art of the Stage Set as a Paradigm for an Aesthetics of Atmospheres', *Ambiances,* Available online: http://ambiances.revues.org/315 (accessed 30 August 2016).

Bohne, Julian. (2013), 'Lampedusa Asylum-Seekers Bed Down in Hamburg Protestant Church', *DW Akademie*, 23 October, Available online: http://www.dw.com/en/lampedusa-asylum-seekers-bed-down-in-hamburg-protestant-church/a-17179429 (accessed 4 July 2015).

Bouissac, Paul. (2010), *Semiotics at the Circus*, Berlin: Walter de Gruyter.

Bourriaud, Nicolas. (2002), *Relational Aesthetics*, trans. Simon Pleasance and Fronza Woods with Matthieu Copeland, Dijon, France: Les presses du réel.

Bowen, Hugh M. (1968), 'Diver Performance and the Effect of Cold', *Human Factors*, 10 (5): 445.

Bradwell, Mike. (2010), 'Theatre Blog', *The Guardian*, 28 June, Available online: https://www.theguardian.com/stage/theatreblog/2010/jun/28/theatre-outside-box-corporate-sponsorship (accessed 2 August 2015).

Brejzek, Thea. (2010), 'From Social Network to Urban Intervention: On the Scenographies of Flash Mobs and Urban Swarms', *International Journal of Performance Arts and Digital Media*, 6 (1): 111–124.

Brejzek, Thea, ed. (2011), *Expanding Scenography: On the Authoring of Space*, Prague: Arts and Theatre Institute.

Brejzek, Thea. (2015), 'The Scenographic (re-)turn: Figures of Surface, Space and Spectator in Theatre and Architecture Theory 1680–1980', *Theatre and Performance Design*, 1 (1–2): 17–30.

Brejzek, Thea. (2017), 'Scenery', in Arnold Aronson (ed.), *Routledge Companion to Scenography*, London: Routledge.

Brejzek, Thea, Wolfgang Greisenegger and Lawrence Wallen, eds (2009), 'Introduction', in *Space and Truth: Monitoring Scenography 02*, 5–8, Zurich, Switzerland: HDK University of the Arts.

Brinck, Ingar. (2014), 'Developing an Understanding of Social Norms and Games: Emotional Engagement, Nonverbal Agreement, and Conversation', *Theory & Psychology*, 24 (6): 737–754.

Brockett, Oscar, Margaret Mitchell and Linda Hardberger (2010), *Making the Scene: A History of Stage Design and Technology in Europe and the United States*, San Antonio, TX: Tobin Theatre Arts Fund.

Brook, Peter. (2008), *The Empty Space*, London: Penguin.

Brown, Joe. (2008), 'Le Rêve Creates Unique Environment', *Las Vegas Sun*, 4 April, Available online: http://lasvegassun.com/news/2008/apr/04/le-reve-creates-unique-environment/ (accessed 8 September 2015).

Brown, Ross. (2010a), 'Sound Design; The Scenography of Engagement and Distraction', in Jane Collins and Andrew Nisbet (eds), *Theatre and Performance Design: A Reader in Scenography*, 340–347, London and New York: Routledge.

Brown, Ross. (2010b), *Sound: A Reader in Theatre Practice*, Basingstoke: Palgrave Macmillan.

Brown, Ross. (2011), 'Towards Theatre Noise' in L. Kendrick and D. Roesner (eds), *Theatre Noise: The Sound of Performance*, 1–13, Newcastle-upon-Tyne: Cambridge Scholars Publishing.

Burian, Jarka. (1971), *The Scenography of Josef Svoboda*, Middletown, CT: Wesleyan University Press.

Butler, Judith. (1993), *Bodies That Matter. On the Discursive Limits of 'Sex'*, New York and London: Routledge.

Butler, Judith. (2006), *Gender Trouble*, Tenth Anniversary Edn, New York: Routledge.

Carlson, Marvin. (1989), *Places of Performance: The Semiotics of Theatre Architecture*, Ithaca and London: Cornell University Press.

Carlson, Marvin. (1993), 'The City as Theatre', in M. Carlson (ed.), *Places of Performance: The Semiotics of Theatre Architecture*, Ithaca, NY: Cornell University Press.

Carlson, Marvin. (1996), *Performance: A Critical Introduction*, London and New York: Routledge.

Cassius, Dion. (1867), *Histoire Romaine.* Tome neuvième: livre LXI: 9, Paris: Librairie de Firmin Didot frères.

Chabris, Christopher F. and Daniel J. Simons (2010), *The Invisible Gorilla: And Other Ways Our Intuitions Deceive Us*, New York: Crown.

Chabris, Christopher F. and Daniel J. Simons (2011), 'Selective Attention Test', Available online: http://www.youtube.com/watch?v=vJG698U2Mvo (accessed 7 May 2016).

Chekhov, Anton. ([1895] 1951), *Plays*, trans. Elisaveta Fen, London: Penguin Group.

Cixous, Hélène. (1995), 'The Place of Crime, The Place of Pardon', in R. Drain (ed.), *Twentieth-Century Theatre Reader*, 340–344, London and New York: Routledge.

Clark, Andy. (2008), *Supersizing the Mind: Embodiment, Action, and Cognitive Extension*, Oxford: Oxford University Press.

Clark, Andy. (2012), 'Embodied, Embedded and Extended Cognition', in Keith Frankish and William M. Ramsey (eds), *The Cambridge Handbook of Cognitive Science*, 275–291, Cambridge: Cambridge University Press.

Cohen-Cruz, Jan, ed. (1998), *Radical Street Performance: An International Anthology*, London: Routledge.

Collins, Jane. (2009), 'Review of *Performance Design*', *Blue Pages*, Society of British Theatre Designers.

Collins, Jane and Arnold Aronson (2015), 'Editors' Introduction', *Theatre and Performance Design*, 1 (1–2): 1–6.

Colness-Himes, Linda. (1999), 'Developing Art Critical Agency in an Undergraduate Art Education Writing Course: A Case Study', *Marilyn Zurmuehlen Working Papers in Art Education*, 15 (1): 53–61.

Conan, Michel. (2007), *Performance and Appropriation: Profane Rituals in Gardens and Landscapes*, Cambridge, MA: Harvard University Press.

Coole, Diana. (2010), 'The Inertia of Matter and the Generativity of Flesh', in Diana Coole and Samatha Frost (eds), *New Materialisms Ontology, Agency, and Politics*, 92–115, Durham and London: Duke University Press.

Coole, Diana and Samantha Frost (2010), 'Introducing the New Materialisms', in Diana Coole and Samantha Frost (eds), *New Materialisms Ontology, Agency, and Politics*, 1–49, Durham and London: Duke University Press.

COOP Himmelblau. (1980), *Architektur muss brennen* [Architecture must burn], Graz, Austria: Technical University.

COOP Himmelblau. (1983), *Architecture Is Now*, New York: Rizzoli.

Coyne, Richard. (2010), *The Tuning of Place: Sociable Spaces and Pervasive Digital Media*, Cambridge, MA: The MIT Press.

Crary, Jonathan. (2001), *Suspensions of Perception; Attention, Spectacle and Modern Culture*, London: MIT Press.

Davis, Mike. (2005), 'The Great Wall of Capital', in Michael Sorkin (ed.), *Against the Wall; Israel's Barrier to Peace*, 88–99, New York: New Press.

Debord, Guy. (1983), *The Society of the Spectacle*, trans. Fredy Perlman, Detroit, MI: Black & Red.

Deleuze, Gilles. (1993), *The Fold: Leibniz and the Baroque*, trans. Tom Conley, Minneapolis, MN: University of Minnesota Press.

Deleuze, Gilles and Félix Guattari. (1994), *What Is Philosophy?* trans. Hugh Tomlinson and Graham Burchell, New York: Columbia University Press.

den Oudsten, Frank. (2011), *Space. Time. Narrative: The Exhibition as Post-Spectacular Stage*, Farnham: Ashgate Publishing.

Derrida, Jacques. (1982), *Margins of Philosophy*, trans. Alan Bass, Chicago: University of Chicago Press.

Derrida, Jacques. (1992), *Given Time: I. Counterfeit Money*, Chicago: University of Chicago Press.

Desplazamiento del Palacio de la Moneda (minga). Directed by Roger Bernat. Performed by Representative of Comité de refugiados Peruanos. Street Performance (Puente), Santiago. 14 January 2014.

Dewey, John. (1980), *Art as Experience*, New York: Perigee Books.

Di Benedetto, Stephen. (2003), 'Sensing Bodies: A Phenomenological Approach to the Performance Sensorium,' *Performance Research*, 8 (2): 100–108.

Di Stefano, Jon. (2008), 'You Are Here: Moving Image + Documentary Paradigm + Performativity', in D. Hannah and O. Harsløf (eds), *Performance Design*, 253–266, Copenhagen: Museum Tusculanum Press.

Diamond, Elin. (1996), *Performance and Cultural Politics*, London and New York: Routledge Press, 1996.

Dolphijn, Rick and Iris van der Tuin, eds (2012), *New Materialisms: Interviews and Cartographies*, Open Humanities Press, MPublishing, Available online: http://hdl.handle.net/2027/spo.11515701.0001.001 (accessed 16 April 2016).

Donald, Minty. (2014), 'Entided, Enwatered, Enwinded: Human/More-than-Human Agencies in Site-specific Performance', in M. Schweitzer and J. Zerdy (eds), *Performing Objects and Theatrical Things*, 118–131, Basingstoke: Palgrave Macmillan.

Donald, Minty. (2016), 'The Performance "Apparatus": Performance and Its Documentation as Ecological Practice', *Green Letters: Studies in Ecocriticism*, 20 (3): 251–269. Available online http://dx.doi.org/10.1080/14688417.2016.1191998 (accessed 22 August 2016).

Doona, Liam. (2002), 'Hope, Hopelessness/Presence, Absence: Scenographic Innovation and the Poetic Spaces of Jo Mielziner, Tennessee Williams and Arthur Miller', in Malcolm Griffiths (ed.), *Exploring Scenography*, 55–64, London: The Society of British Theatre Designers in association with Nottingham Trent University.

Duffy, Stella. (2013), 'Celebrating Joan Littlewood: It's Time to Build Her Fun Palaces', *The Guardian*, 9 September, Available online: https://www.theguardian.com/stage/theatreblog/2013/sep/18/theatre-joan-littlewood-culture-fun-palaces (accessed 18 September 2015).

Edinborough, Campbell. (2011), 'Developing Decision-Making Skills for Performance Through the Practice of Mindfulness in Somatic Training', *Theatre, Dance and Performance Training*, 2 (1): 18–33.

Edwards, Elizabeth and Janice Hart (2004), *Photographs Objects Histories: On the Materiality of Images*, London: Routledge.

Egyptians Act 1530 (22 Henry VIII, c. 10), London: HMSO.

Eisenman, Peter. (2007), *Written into the Void: Selected Writings 1990–2004*, New Haven and London: Yale University Press.

EXYZT. (2015), 'Manifesto', Available online: www.exyzt.org (accessed 18 September 2015).

Fenemore, Anna. (2001), 'The Pigeon Project: A Study of the Potential for Embodied Praxis in Performance Spectating', unpublished thesis (Doctor of Philosophy), Manchester Metropolitan University.

Feuerstein, Marcia and Gray Read, eds (2013), *Architecture as a Performing Art*, London and New York: Routledge.

Filingeri, Davide, Damien Fournet, Simon Hodder and George Havenith. (2014), 'Why Wet Feels Wet? A Neurophysiological Model of Human Cutaneous Wetness Sensitivity', *Journal of Neurophysiology*, 112 (6): 1457–1469, 15 September 2014, Available online: http://jn.physiology.org/content/112/6/1457 (accessed 8 September 2015).

Fischer-Lichte, Erika. (2008), *The Transformative Power of Performance*, London: Routledge.

Fischer-Lichte, Erika. (2009), 'Culture as Performance', *Modern Austrian Literature*, 42 (3): 1–10.

Fool Us/Penn & Teller: Fool Us in Vegas (2011 onwards), [TV series] UK/USA: 1/17 Productions and September Films.

Foucault, Michel. ([1967] 1984), 'Of Other Spaces. Utopias and Heterotopias', trans. Jay Miskowiec, *Architecture/Mouvement/Continuité*, 5 (October 1984): 46–49.

Freshwater, Helen. (2009), *Theatre & Audience*, Basingstoke: Palgrave Macmillan.

Fuchs, Elinor. (1996), *The Death of Character. Perspectives on Theatre After Modernism*, Bloomington, IN: Indiana University Press.

Fundación Teatro a Mil (FITAM). (2015), '"Remote Santiago", Del cementerio general al Barrio Mapocho', *FITAM Youtube Chanel*, 8 February, Available online: https://www.youtube.com/watch?v=o255-5ehyvl (accessed 10 August 2015).

Gardner, Lyn. (2009), *The Roman Tragedies*, Review in *The Guardian*, 21 November, Available online: http://www.theguardian.com/stage/2009/nov/21/roman-tragedies-lyn-gardner-review (accessed 20 November 2015).

Gilbert, Helen and Joanne Tompkins. (1996), *Post-Colonial Drama, Theory, Practice, Politics*, London: Routledge.

Grandin, Temple and Richard Panek (2014), *The Autistic Brain: Exploring the Strength of a Different Kind of Mind*, London: Ebury Publishing, Random House Group.

Greenfield, Rebecca. (2012), 'The 19th Century Technology Behind Coachella's Tupac Hologram', *Atlantic Wire*, 17 April, Available online: http://www.theatlanticwire.com/technology/2012/04/19th-century-technology-behind-coachellas-tupac-hologram/51229/ (accessed 7 May 2016).

Gröndahl, Laura. (2012a), 'Space–Event–Agency–Experience', in Riku Roihankorpi and Teemu Paavolainen (eds), *Open Access E–Publication of the DREX Project Centre for Practise as Research in Theatre*, University of Tampere, Available online: http://t7.uta.fi/drex/DREX/11_TextsAndPublicationsEn_files/1_Grondahl.pdf (accessed 8 August 2015).

Gröndahl, Laura. (2012b), 'Redefining Scenographic Strategies', Conference paper presentation at *Inter-disciplinary.net* 3rd Global Conference, Salzburg, Austria, 13–15 November 2012, Available online: http://www.inter-disciplinary.net/critical-issues/wp-content/uploads/2012/10/lauraperpaper.pdf (accessed 1 July 2016).

Groys, Boris. (2007), *The Idiot* by Foyodor Dostoevsky, Available online: https://www.volksbuehne-berlin.de/praxis/der_idiot/ (accessed 18 September 2015).

Guha, Sankha. (2010), 'They're Ready for Their Close-Up in the Capital of Estonia', *The Independent*, 12 August, Available online: http://www.independent.co.uk/travel/europe/theyre-ready-for-their-closeup-in-the-capital-of-estonia-2164137.html (accessed 12 August 2015).

Hancock, Ian. (2002), *We Are the Romani People*, Hatfield: University of Hertfordshire Press.

Hannah, Dorita. (2011), 'Building Babel', in Thea Brejzek, Wolfgang Greisenegger and Lawrence Wallen (eds), *Space and Desire, Scenographic Strategies in Theatre, Art and Media: Monitoring Scenography 03*, 58–67, Zurich, Switzerland: Zurich University of the Arts.

Hannah, Dorita. (2014), Dorita Hannah website, Available online: http://www.doritahannah.com/#!commercial/ctzx (accessed 25 July 2015).

Hannah, Dorita. (2015), 'Constructing Barricades and Creating Borderline Events', *Theatre and Performance Design*, 1 (1–2): 126–143.

Hannah, Dorita and Olav Harsløf. (2008), *Performance Design*, Copenhagen: Museum Tusculanum Press.

Haraway, Donna. (1991), *Simians, Cyborgs and Women: The Reinvention of Nature*, New York: Routledge Press.

Hardt, Michael and Antonio Negri. (2004), *Multitude: War and Democracy in the Age of Empire*, New York: Penguin Books.

Harvie, Jen. (2005), *Staging the UK*, Manchester: Manchester University Press.

Harvie, Jen. (2013), *Fair Play: Art, Performance and Neoliberalism*, Basingstoke: Palgrave Macmillan.

Hawthorn, Christopher. (2013), 'The Politics of Spanish Architect Andres Jaque', in *Architect Magazine*, 18 November, Available online: http://www.architectmagazine.com/design/the-politics-of-spanish-architect-andres-jaque_o (accessed 15 September 2015).

Heddon, Dee. (2008), *Autobiography and Performance*, Basingstoke: Palgrave Macmillan.

Heft, Harry. (2013), 'Environment, Cognition and Culture: Reconsidering the Cognitive Map', *Journal of Environmental Psychology*, 33: 14–25.

Heidegger, Martin. (1977), *Question Concerning Technology, and Other Essays*, trans. William Lovitt, New York: Harper & Row.

Herzog, Jacques and Pierre de Meuron. (2006), '274 Tristan and Isolde Stage Design', *Herzog and De Meuron*, n.d., Available online: http://www.herzogdemeuron.com/index/projects/complete-works/251-275/274-tristan-and-isolde-stage-design.html (accessed 15 September 2015).

Higashida, Naoki. (2013), *The Reason I Jump*, trans. Keiko Yoshida and David Mitchell, London: Hodder and Stoughton.

Higher Education Funding Council for England. (September 2009), *Second Consultation on the Assessment and Funding of Research*.

Hobson, R. Peter and Jessica A. Hobson. (2008), 'Engaging, Sharing, Knowing: Some Lessons from Research in Autism', in Jordan Zlatev, Timothy P. Racine, Chris Sinha and Esa Itkonen (eds), *The Shared Mind: Perspectives on Intersubjectivity*, 67–88, Amsterdam and Philadelphia: John Benjamins Publishing Company.

Holmberg, Arthur. (1996). *The Theater of Robert Wilson*, Cambridge: Cambridge University Press.

Hopkins, Albert A., ed. (1901), *Magic: Stage Illusions and Scientific Diversions, Including Trick Photography*, New York: Munn & Company.

Howard, Pamela. (2002), *What Is Scenography?* Abingdon and Oxon: Routledge.

Howes, David. (1991), *The Varieties of Sensory Experience: A Sourcebook in the Anthropology of the Senses*, Toronto, ON: University of Toronto Press.

Human Body Parts. Performed by Snuff Puppets Company. Street Performance (Plaza de Armas), Santiago. Santiago a Mil, 2013, Available online: http://www.jhc.cl/santiagoamil/?p=13129&lang=en (accessed 14 July 2014).

Hutchins, Edward. (2012), 'Material Anchors for Conceptual Blends', *Journal of Pragmatics*, 37: 1555–1577.

Ingold, Tim. (2000), *The Perception of the Environment: Essays on Livelihood, Dwelling and Skill*, London: Routledge.

Ingold, Tim. (2005), 'The Eye of the Storm: Visual Perception and the Weather', *Visual Studies*, 20 (2): 97–104.

Ingold, Tim. (2010a), 'Bringing Things to Life: Creative Entanglements in a World of Materials', ESRC National Centre for Research Methods NCRM Working Paper Series (5: 2010), Available online: http://eprints.ncrm.ac.uk/1306/1/0510_creative_entanglements.pdf (accessed 7 May 2016).

Ingold, Tim. (2010b), 'The Textility of Making', *Cambridge Journal of Economics*, 34 (1): 91–102.

Ingold, Tim. (2011), *Being Alive: Essays on Movement, Knowledge and Description*, London: Routledge.

Ingold, Tim. (2012), 'Toward an Ecology of Materials', *Annual Review of Anthropology*, 41: 427–442.

Ingold, Tim. (2014), 'Overcoming the Distinction Between "practical" and "intellectual" Craft', Seminar workshop 5 March 2014, *Centre for Practice-Led Research in the Arts*, University of Leeds.

Inostroza, Nicolás. (2014), 'Roger Bernat invita a desplazar el Palacio de la Moneda en una Minga', Fundación Teatro a Mil FITAM, 13 February, Available online: http://www.jhc.cl/santiagoamil/?p=21450 (accessed 15 July 2015).

Invisible Flock. (2012), *Bring the Happy*. (Performances 2012-ongoing), Available online: http://invisibleflock.com/portfolio/bringthehappy/.

Irwin, Kathleen. (2007), *The Ambit of Performativity. How Site Makes Meaning in Site-Specific Performance*. Helsinki: University of Arts and Design. Available online: http://dx.doi.org/10.7592/methis.v2i3.498 (accessed 30 August 2016).

Jackson, Shannon. (2011), *Social Works: Performing Art, Supporting Publics*, London: Routledge.

Kattenbelt, Chiel. (2008), 'Intermediality in Theatre and Performance: Definitions, Perceptions and Medial Relationships', *Culture, Language and Representation: Cultural Studies Journal of Universitat Jaume I*, VI: 19–29.

Kaye, Nick. (2000), *Site-Specific Art: Performance, Place and Documentation*, London: Routledge.

Kaye, Nick. (2007), *Multi-media: Video, Installation, Performance*. London: Routledge.

Kennedy, Dennis. (1993), *Looking at Shakespeare: A Visual History of Twentieth Century Performance*, Cambridge: Cambridge University Press.

Kerkhoven, Marianne and Anouk Nuyens, eds (2012), *Listen to the Bloody Machine. Creating Kris Verdonck's* End, Utrecht and Amsterdam: Utrecht School of the Arts and International Theatre & Film Books Publishers.

Kershaw, Baz. (1999), *The Radical in Performance: Between Brecht and Baudrillard*, London and New York: Routledge.

Khan, Omar. (2008), 'SEEN: Fruits of Our Labour', in Dorita Hannah and Olav Harsløf (eds), *Performance Design*, 282–292, Copenhagen: Museum Tusculanum Press.

Kiesler, Friedrich. (1924), 'Internationale Ausstellung neuer Theatertechnik', Exhibition Catalogue, Vienna Kunsthandlung Wuerthle and Sohn, Available online: http://www.kiesler.org/cms/index.php?lang=3&idcat=18 (accessed 15 September 2015).

Kiesler, Friedrich. (1939), 'On Correalism and Biotechnique. Definition and Test of a New Approach to Building Design', *Architectural Record*, 86 (3): 60–75.

Kleinman, Adam. (2012), 'Intra-Actions: Interview of Karen Barad by Adam Kleinman', *Mousse*, 34: 76–81, Available online: https://www.academia.edu/1857617/_Intra-actions_Interview_of_Karen_Barad_by_Adam_Kleinmann_ (accessed 1 August 2015).

Klich, Rosemary and Edward Scheer. (2012), *Multimedia Performance*, Basingstoke: Palgrave Macmillan.

Kolarevic, Branko and Ali Malkawi, eds (2004), *Performative Architecture: Beyond Instrumentality*, New York and London: Spon Press.

Krak, Nikolaj. (2014), 'When Bombs Receive Applause', *Kristeligt Dagblad,* 11 July, Available online: http://www.kristeligt-dagblad.dk/2014-07-11/when-bombs-receive-applause (accessed 22 November 2015).

Krauss, Rosalind. (1979), 'Sculpture in the Expanded Field', *October*, 8 (Spring 1979): 30–44.

Kuhn, Gustav and Michael F. Land. (2006), 'There's More to Magic than Meets the Eye', *Current Biology*, 16 (22): 950–951.

Kwon, Miwon. (2002), *One Place After Another: Site-Specific Art and Locational Identity*, Cambridge and London: MIT Press.

Kwon, Miwon. (2014), 'The Wrong Place', *Art Journal*, 59 (1): 32–43.

Langer, Ellen J. (1989), *Mindfulness*, Reading, MA: Addison-Wesley Pub. Co.

Latour, Bruno. (1996), 'On Actor Network Theory', *Soziale Welt*, 47 (4): 369–381.

Latour, Bruno. (2005), *Reassembling the Social: An Introduction to Actor-Network Theory*, Oxford: Oxford University Press.

Lazar, Julie. ([1983] 2015), '*Available Light* Interviews: Frank Gehry, Lucinda Childs, and John Adams', *KCET Los Angeles*, 5 June, Available online: http://www.kcet.org/arts/artbound/counties/los-angeles/available-light-moca-lucinda-childs-frank-gehry-john-adams.html (accessed 15 September 2015).

Leder, Drew. (1990), *The Absent Body*, London: University of Chicago Press.

Lefebvre, Henri. (1991), *The Production of Space*, trans. Donald Nicholson-Smith, Oxford: Blackwell Publishers Ltd.

Lehmann, Hans-Thies. (2006), *Postdramatic Theatre*, trans. Karen Jürs-Munby, London: Routledge.

Libeskind, Daniel. (1985), 'The Space of Encounter', in *Three Lessons in Architecture: The Machines*, Bloomfield Hills, MI: Cranbrook Academy of Art, Available online: http://libeskind.com/work/cranbrook-machines/ (accessed 18 September 2015).

Libeskind, Daniel. (2000), *The Space of Encounter*, New York: Universe Publishing.

Libeskind, Daniel. (2002), 'Saint Francis of Assisi', trans. B. Schneider, in *City Up*, Available online: http://www.cityup.org/case/zone/20090115/44188.shtml (accessed 15 September 2015).

Lippard, Lucy. (1998), *Lure of the Local: Senses of Place in a Multicentered Society*, New York: The New English Press.

Liu, Jonathan. (2011), 'Are Architects Performance Artists? A Conference Addresses "Performativity"', *The Observer*, 7 December, Available online: http://observer.com/2011/07/are-architects-performance-artists-a-conferenaddresses-performativity (accessed 10 December 2015).

Lorimer, Hayden. (2005). 'Cultural Geography: The Busyness of Being "More-Than-Representational"', *Progress in Human Geography*, 29: 1, 83–94.

Lotker, Sodja. (2015), Intro to the PQ 2015, Available online: http://www.pq.cz/en/program/intro/ (accessed 25 July 2015).

Lotker, Sodja and Richard Gough. (2013), 'On Scenography: Editorial', *Performance Research*, 18 (3): 3–6.

Lucht, Nicole. (2014), 'Diving the Dream in *Le Rêve* at Wynn Las Vegas', 10 March, Available online: http://blog.vegas.com/las-vegas-shows/diving-the-dream-in-le-reve-at-wynn-las-vegas-44119/ (accessed 17 December 2014).

Lutterbie, John. (2013), 'Wayfaring in Everyday Life: The Unravelling of Intricacy', in Nicola Shaughnessy (ed.), *Affective Performance and Cognitive Science: Body, Brain and Being*, 103–115, London: Bloomsbury.

MacCannell, Dean. (2005), 'Primitive Separations', in M. Sorkin (ed.), *Against the Wall: Israel's Barrier to Peace*, New York: New Press.

Machon, Josephine. (2009), *(Syn)aesthetics: Redefining Visceral Performance*. Basingstoke: Palgrave Macmillan.

Machon, Josephine. (2013), *Immersive Theatres: Intimacy and Immediacy in Contemporary Performance*, London: Palgrave Macmillan.

Mackenzie, Ruth. (2015), 'Curatorial Statement for the Holland Festival', Available online: http://www.hollandfestival.nl/en/about-hf/about-hf/ (accessed 25 July 2015).

Macknik, Stephen L., Susana Martinez-Conde and Sandra Blakeslee. (2010), *Sleights of Mind: What the Neuroscience of Magic Reveals About Our Everyday Deceptions*, New York: Henry Holt and Co.

Malafouris, Lambros. (2003), 'The Cognitive Basis of Material Engagement: Where Brain, Body and Culture Conflate', in Elizabeth De Marrais, Chris Gosden and Colin Renfrew (eds), *Rethinking Materiality, the Engagement of Mind with the Material World*, 37–46, Cambridge: McDonald Institute for Archeological Research.

Manning, Erin. (2011), 'Fiery Luminous, Scary', *SubStance*, 40 (3) (Issue 126): 41–48.

Marranca, Bonnie. (1996), *The Theatre of Images*, Baltimore and London: John Hopkins University Press.

Martinez Lemoine, René. (2003), 'The Classical Model of the Spanish-American Colonial City', *The Journal of Architecture*, 8 (3): 355–368.

Massey, Doreen. (1994), *Space, Place, and Gender*, Minneapolis: University of Minnesota Press.

McAuley, Gay. (2000), *Space in Performance: Making Meaning in the Theatre*. Ann Arbor, MI: University of Michigan Press.

McConachie, Bruce. (2012), 'Using Cognitive Science to Understand Spatiality and Community in the Theatre', *Contemporary Theatre Review*, 12 (3): 97–114.

McKenzie, Jon. (2001), *Perform or Else: From Discipline to Performance*, London: Routledge Press.

McKenzie, Jon. (2008), 'Global Feeling', in Dorita Hannah and Olav Harsløf (eds), *Performance Design*, 113–128, Copenhagen: Museum Tusculanum Press.

McKinney, Joslin. (2013), 'Scenography, Spectacle and the Body of the Spectator', *Performance Research*, 18 (3): 63–74.

McKinney, Joslin. (2015), 'Vibrant Material: The Agency of Things in the Context of Scenography', in Maaike Bleeker, Jon Foley Sherman and Eirini Nedelkopoulou (eds), *Performance and Phenomenology: Traditions and Transformations*, 121–139, London: Routledge.

McKinney, Joslin and Kara McKechnie. (2016), Interview with Katrin Brack, *Theatre and Performance Design*, 2: 1–2, 127–135.

McKinney, Joslin and Philip Butterworth. (2009), *The Cambridge Introduction to Scenography*, Cambridge: Cambridge University Press.

Merleau-Ponty, Maurice. (1962), *Phenomenology of Perception*, New York: Humanities Press.

Merleau-Ponty, Maurice. (2002), *Phenomenology of Perception*, trans. Colin Smith, London: Routledge.

Merx, Sigrid. (2013), 'The Politics of Scenography: Disrupting the Stage', *Performance Research*, 18 (3): 54–58.

MoMa. (2012), *IKEA Disobedients* [architectural performance by Andrés Jaque Arquitectos], Available online: http://www.moma.org/explore/multimedia/videos/235/1158 (accessed 15 September 2015).

Moran, Dermot. (2000), *Introduction to Phenomenology*, London: Routledge.

Moynet, Jean-Pierre. (2016), *L'Envers du Théâtre: machines et decorations* (1873), trans. Christopher Baugh, Dacre Hall: Theatreshire Books.

Mroué, Rabih. (2014), *The Pixelated Revolution* (cited in 'The Pixelated Revolution: Rabih Mroué on the Syrian Revolution' by Sophie Tarnowska, *Printemps Numérique*, 13 June, Available online: http://printempsnumerique.info/en/the-pixelated-revolution/ (accessed 20 November 2015).

Müller, Bernd. (2014), 'Siemens Takes to the Stage', *Siemens: Pictures of the Future*, 22 December, Available online: http://www.siemens.com/innovation/en/home/pictures-of-the-future /infrastructure-and-finance/livable-and-sustainable-cities-han-show-theater.html.

Mulvey, Marianne. (2012), 'What Does Performance Have to Do with Architecture? How Can a Building Perform, and How Can We Perform a Building?', *Tate blog*, 29 November, Available online: http://www.tate.org.uk/context-comment/blogs/what-does-performance-have-do -architecture-how-can-building-perform-and-how (accessed 10 December 2015).

Nagler, Alois Maria. (1964), *Theatre Festivals of the Medici, 1539–1637*, New Haven and London: Yale University Press.

Negroponte, Nicholas. (1975), *Soft Architecture Machines*, Cambridge, MA: MIT Press.

Nelson, Robin. (2006), 'New Small Screen Spaces: A Performative Phenomenon?', in Freda Chapple and Chiel Kattenbelt (eds), *Intermediality in Theatre and Performance*, 137–150, Amsterdam and New York: IFTR/FIRT.

Neumann, Bert. (2001), 'Imitation of Life', Interviewed by Anja Nioduschewski in *Theater der Zeit*, October.

Newton, William, ed. (1863), *The London Journal of Arts and Sciences (and Repertory of Patent Inventions)*, XVIII, London: Newton and Son.

Noë, Alva. (2004), *Action in Perception*, Cambridge, MA: MIT Press.

Obrist, Hans-Ulrich. (2010), 'Manifestos for the Future', *e-flux*, Available online: http://www.e-flux.com /journal/manifestos-for-the-future/ (accessed 1 October 2015).

O'Dwyer, Néill. (2015), 'The Scenographic Turn: The Pharmacology of the Digitization of Scenography', *Theatre and Performance Design*, 1 (1–2): 48–63.

OMA. (2012), 'Syracuse Greek Theatre Scenography', Available online: http://www.oma.eu /projects/2012/syracuse-scenography/ (accessed 15 September 2015).

O'Sullivan, Simon. (2005), *Art Encounters Deleuze and Guattari: Thought Beyond Representation*, Basingstoke: Palgrave Macmillan.

Paavolainen, Teemu. (2012), *Theatre/Ecology/Cognition Theorizing Performer-Object Interaction in Grotowski, Kantor and Meyerhold*, New York: Palgrave Macmillan.

Palmer, Scott. (2013), *Light: Readings in Theatre Practice*, Basingstoke: Palgrave Macmillan.

Palmer, Scott. (2015), 'A "chorèographie" of Light and Space: Adolphe Appia and the First Scenographic Turn', *Theatre and Performance Design*, 1 (1–2): 31–47.

Parker, Ellie. (1996), 'Talking About Theatre Design', *Studies in Theatre Production*, 13 (1): 72–82.

Pastier, John. (2012), 'Build Maestro, Frank Gehry Designs Sets for LA Philharmonic's Don Giovanni', *The Architects Newspaper*, 21 June, Available online: http://archpaper.com/news/articles .asp?id=6126#.VfEnDmSqpBc (accessed 15 September 2015).

Paterson, Mark. (2007), *The Senses of Touch: Haptics, Affects and Technologies*, Oxford: Berg Publishers.

Peace Camp. (2012) [Performance] Deborah Warner/Artichoke. Available online: http://www.artichoke .uk.com/events/peace_camp/ (accessed 20 December 2016)

Peacock, John. (1995), *The Stage Designs of Inigo Jones: The European Context*, Cambridge: Cambridge University Press.

Pearson, Mike. (2010), *Site-Specific Performance*, Basingstoke: Palgrave Macmillan.

Pees, Matthias. (1999), *Daemonen.* [Theatre performance] Details, Available online: http://www .volksbuehne-berlin.de/praxis/daemonen/?langtext=1 (accessed 18 September 2015).

Pollack, Gerald H. (2014), *Wasser – Viel mehr als H2O*. Kirchzarten bei Freiburg: VAK Verlags GmbH.

Prague Quadrennial archive [web resource], Available online: http://services.pq.cz/en/archive (accessed 1 July 2016).

Prague Quadrennial of Performance Design and Space 2015 (2015), [catalogue], Prague: Arts and Theatre Institute.

Príhodová, Barbora, Joslin McKinney and Sodja Lotker. (2016), 'Editorial: The Prague Quadrennial of Performance Design and Space 2015', *Theatre and Performance Design*, 2 (1–2): 5–16.

Prosser, Catherine and Anna Robb. (2014), 'The Backstage World of "The House of Dancing Water"', *StageBiz*, 8 May, Available online: http://stagebitz.com/2014/05/backstage-house-of-dancing -water/ (accessed 17 December 2014).

Ramaer, Joost. (2014), 'Jelinek and Stemann Give Voice to Illegal Immigrants', *Theatrekrant*, 10 June, Available online: http://www.theaterkrant.nl/recensie/die-schutzbefohlenen/ (assessed 15 July 2015).

Ramszy, A. (2015), 'Activist Artist Regains Passport After Years of Uncertainty', *Globe and Mail*, 23 July.

Rancière, Jacques. (2007), 'The Emancipated Spectator', *Artforum International*, 45 (7): 270–281.

Rancière, Jacques. (2009), *The Emancipated Spectator*, New York: Penguin Random House.

Rancière, Jacques. (2011), *The Emancipated Spectator*, trans. G. Elliott, London: Verso Books.

Randi, James. (1992), *Conjuring*, New York: St. Martin's Press.

Read, Alan. (2013), *Theatre in the Expanded Field: Seven Approaches to Performance*, London: Bloomsbury Methuen Drama.

Read, Gray. (2013), 'Introduction: The Play's the Thing', in Marcia Feuerstein and Gray Reid (eds), *Architecture as a Performing Art*, 1–13, London and New York: Routledge.

Rebellato, Dan. (2009), *Theatre & Globalization*, Basingstoke: Palgrave Macmillan.

Rewa, Natalie. (2004), *Scenography in Canada: Selected Designers*, Toronto, ON, Canada: University of Toronto Press.

Reysenbach de Haan, F. W. (1957), 'Hearing in Whales', *Acta Otolaryngol* (Suppl. 134): 1–114.

Rimini, Protokoll. (2014a), *Situation Rooms – A Multiplayer Video Piece.*, Available online: http://www .rimini-protokoll.de/website/en/project_6009.html (accessed 20 November 2015).

Rimini, Protokoll. (2014b), *Situation Rooms (Radio)*, Available online: http://www.rimini-protokoll.de /website/en/project_6314.html (accessed 20 November 2015).

Rimmele, Claudio. (2013), 'Interviewing Stefan Kaegi: Discovering the City Through Theatre', *Bettery magazine*, 18 November, Available online: http://www.rimini-protokoll.de/website/en /article_6295.html (accessed 7 July 2015).

Robins, Apollo. (2011), '"Brain Games": How Easily Our Brains Are Fooled', [TV news broadcast], Fox News, 8 October, Available online: http://video.foxnews.com/v/1208338780001/brain-games-how -easily-our-brains-are-fooled/ (accessed 7 May 2016).

Robinson, Aileen. (2014), '"All Transparent": Pepper's Ghost, Plate Glass, and Theatrical Transformation', in Schweitzer Marlis and Joanne Zerdy (eds), *Performing Objects and Theatrical Things*, 135–148, Basingstoke: Palgrave Macmillan.

Rodriguez, Cintia and Christiane Moro. (2008), 'Coming to Agreement: Object Use by Infants and Adults', in Jordan Zlatev, Timothy P. Racine, Chris Sinha and Esa Itkonen (eds), *The Shared Mind: Perspectives on Intersubjectivity*, 89–114, Amsterdam and Philadelphia: John Benjamins Publishing Company.

Roselt, Jens. (2013), 'Change Through Rapprochement: Spatial Practices in Contemporary Performances', in Erika Fischer-Lichte and Benjamin Whistutz (eds), *Performance and the Politics of Space*, New York: Taylor and Francis.

Rossi, Bastiano. (1589), *Descrizione dell'apparato e degli'intermedi fatti per la commedia rappresentata in Firenze nelle nozze de' Serenissimi Don Fernando Medici e Madonna Cristina di Lorene, Garn Duchi di Toscana*, Florence: Padovani.

Rousseau, Bryant. (2007), 'The ArchRecord Interview: Vito Acconci', *The Architectural Record*, June, Available online: http://archrecord.construction.com/features/interviews/0718acconci/0718acconci-1.asp (accessed 15 September 2015).

Rufford, Juliet. (2015), *Theatre & Architecture*, London: Macmillan Publishers.

Ruskin, John. (1849), *Seven Lamps of Architecture*, Boston: Dana Estes and Company Publishers.

Said, Edward. (1979), *Orientalism*, New York: Vintage.

Salter, Chris. (2010), *Entangled, Technology and the Transformation of Performance*, Cambridge, MA: MIT Press.

Santiago (en) Vivo (2017), Dir. Marcela Oteíza, Chile/USA: Wesleyan University and FITAM.

Saslow, James M. (1996), *The Medici Wedding of 1589*, New Haven and London: Yale University Press.

Schechner, Richard. (1994), *Environmental Theater*, New York: Applause.

Schwarte, Ludger. (n.d.), 'Performative Architecture – Setting a Stage for Political Action', trans. Robert Bryce and Ann-Cathrin Drews, *Pavilion. Journal for Politics and Culture*, Available online: http://pavilionmagazine.org/ludger-schwarte-performative-architecture-setting-a-stage-for-political-action (accessed 18 September 2015).

Schweder, Alex. (2014), *Alex Schweder* [website], Available online: http://www.alexschweder.com (accessed 12 September 2015).

Sell, Mike. (2007), 'Bohemianism, the Cultural Turn of the Avantgarde, and Forgetting the Roma', *TDR: The Drama Review*, 51 (2) (T194): 41–59, Available online: http://muse.jhu.edu/issue/11584.

Shaughnessy, Nicola, ed. (2013a), *Affective Performance and Cognitive Science*. London: Bloomsbury Methuen Drama.

Shaughnessy, Nicola. (2013b), 'Perceiving Differently: The Neuro-Divergent Aesthetic and Contemporary Performance', *Interdisciplinary Science Reviews*, 38 (4): 321–334.

Shearing, David. (2015), 'Audience Immersion and the Experience of Scenography', PhD thesis, University of Leeds, Available online: http://etheses.whiterose.ac.uk/9467/.

Simons, Daniel J. and Daniel T. Levin. (1998) *The 'Door' Study* [video film], Champaign, IL: Viscog productions, Available online: http://www.youtube.com/watch?v=FWSxSQsspiQ&feature=related (accessed 7 May 2016).

Sinha, Chris. (2005), 'Blending Out the Background: Play, Props and Staging in the Material World', *Journal of Pragmatics*, 37: 1537–1554.

Sinha, Chris. (2009), 'Objects in a Storied World: Materiality, Normativity, Narrativity', *Journal of Consciousness Studies: Controversy in Science and the Humanities*, 16 (6–8): 167–190.

Small, Jocelyn P. (2013), 'Skenographia in Brief', in G. W. M. Harrison and V. Liapis (eds), *Performance in Greek and Roman Theatre*, 111–128, Leiden: Brill.

Sofer, Andrew. (2012), 'Spectral Readings', *Theatre Journal*, 64: 323–336.

Sørensen, Allan (@allensorensen72 9 July 2014) Available online: https://twitter.com/allansorensen72/status/486954506517639170/photo/1?ref_src=twsrc%5Etfw (accessed 22 November 2015).

Sørensen, Allan (@allensorensen72: 11 July 2014) Available online: https://twitter.com/allansorensen72/status/486954506517639170/photo/1?ref_src=twsrc%5Etfw (accessed 22 November 2015).

Spivey, Michael. (2007), *The Continuity of Mind*, Oxford: Oxford University Press.

Spruijt, Rob. (2013), 'Identifying and Interacting: Notes on the Architecture of the Visual Brain', in Brunella Antomarini and Adam Berg (eds), *Aesthetics in Present Future: The Arts and the Technological Horizon*, Lanham, MD: Lexington Books.

Starn, Randolf and Loren Partridge. (1992), *Arts of Power: Three Halls of State in Italy, 1300–1600*, Berkeley: University of California Press.

Steinmeyer, Jim. (2003), *Hiding the Elephant: How Magicians Invented the Impossible and Learned to Disappear*, New York: Carroll & Graf Publishers.

Steinmeyer, Jim. (2006), *Art & Artifice and Other Essays on Illusion: Concerning the Inventors, Traditions, Evolution & Rediscovery of Stage Magic: With Twenty-Three Diagrams*, New York: Carroll & Graf Publishers.

Stephan, Achim, Sven Walter and Wendy Wilutzky (2014), 'Emotions Beyond Brain and Body', *Philosophical Psychology*, 27 (1): 65–81.

Strong, Roy. (1973), *Splendor at Court: Renaissance Spectacle and the Theatre of Power*, Boston: Houghton Mifflin.

Strong, Roy. (1984), *Art and Power: Renaissance Festivals, 1450–1650*, Berkeley: University of California Press.

Tabački, Nebojša. (2015), 'Diving into the Abyss', *Theatre and Performance Design*, 1 (1–2): 64–78.

Taylor, Lou. (2002), *The Study of Dress History*, Manchester: Manchester University Press.

Taylor, Mark C. (1990), *Tears*, Albany, NY: State University of New York Press.

Teichmann, Michael. (2002), 'Nomadic and Sedentary', *Rombase: Didactically Edited Information on Roma*, Available online: http://rombase.uni-graz.at/cd/data/ethn/topics/data/nomadic.en.pdf (accessed 1 October 2015).

The Drowned Man: A Hollywood Fable (2013–2014), [Performance] Punchdrunk/National Theatre, London.

The Weather Machine (2015) [Performance] David Shearing Company, stage@leeds, Leeds, Excerpt and documentation, Available online: http://www.davidshearing.com/works/the-weather-machine/ (accessed 1 July 2016).

Thompson, Evan, ed. (2001), *Between Ourselves: Second Person Issues in the Study of Consciousness*. Thorverton, Devon, UK: Imprint Academic, Published simultaneously as a special triple issue of the *Journal of Consciousness Studies*, 8 (5–7).

Thompson, James. (2009), *Performance Affects: Applied Theatre and the End of Effect*, Basingstoke: Palgrave Macmillan.

Thompson, Benjamin, Bruce C. Hansen, Robert F. Hess and Nikolaus F. Troje (2007), 'Peripheral Vision: Good for Biological Motion, Bad for Signal Noise Segregation?' *Journal of Vision*, 7 (10): 1–7.

Thrift, Nigel. (2007), *Non-Representational Theory: Space, Politics, Affect*, London: Routledge.

To the Memory of H.P. Lovecraft ([1999], 2008) [mixed media artwork] Mike Nelson, in *Psycho Buildings*, The Hayward Gallery, London.

Tribble, Evelyn. (2011), *Cognition in the Globe: Attention and Memory in Shakespeare's Theatre*, Basingstoke: Palgrave Macmillan.

Trimingham, Melissa. (2011), 'How to Think a Puppet', *Forum Modernes Theater*, 26 (1): 121–136.

Trimingham, Melissa. (2012), 'Touched by Meaning: Haptic Effect in Autism', in Nicola Shaughnessy (ed.), *Affective Performance and Cognitive Science: Body, Brain and Being*, 229–240, London: Bloomsbury.

Trussler, Simon. (1994), *The Cambridge Illustrated History of British Theatre*, Cambridge and New York: Cambridge University Press.

Turner, Cathy. (2010), 'Mis-Guidance and Spatial Planning: Dramaturgies of Public Space', *Contemporary Theatre Review*, 20 (2): 149–161.

Turner, Cathy. (2015), *Dramaturgy and Architecture: Theatre, Utopia and the Built Environment*, Basingstoke: Palgrave Macmillan.

Twaalfhoven, Merlijn. (2008), *Carried by the Wind*. Excerpt, Available online: www.merlijntwaalfhoven.com/en/muziekprojecten-in-conflictgebieden/carried-by-the-wind/ (accessed 13 August 2015).

Vaarik, Daniel. (n.d.), 'NO 75 Unified Estonia Assembly', Available online: http://www.no99.ee /productions/no75-unified-estonia-assembly (accessed 7 August 2015).

Varela, Francisco, Evan Thompson and Eleanor Rosch. (1991), *The Embodied Mind: Cognitive Science and Human Experience*, Cambridge, MA and London: MIT Press.

Veltruský, Jiří. (1964), 'Man and Object in the Theater', in Paul L. Garvin (ed. and trans.), *A Prague School Reader*, Washington, DC: Georgetown University Press.

Verdensteatret. (2004), *The Telling Orchestra*, Available online: http://verdensteatret.com/the-telling -orchestra/ (accessed 29 August 2016).

Vergara, Carlos. (2012), 'Chile-Vuelve la Protesta Estudiantil', *La Nacion*, 20 April, Available online: http://www.lanacion.com.ar/1466526-chile-vuelve-la-protesta-estudiantil (accessed 14 July 2014).

Verhoeven, Dries. (2006), *The Big Movement*, Available online: http://driesverhoeven.com/en/project /de-grote-beweging/ (accessed 25 August 2016).

Versweyveld, Jan. (2014), telephone interview with Dorita Hannah, 25 March.

Viebrock, Anna and Jacques Herzog. (2011), 'Stage Design and Architecture', interview by Hubertus Adam, *SAM Swiss Architecture Museum*, No 9.

Vitruvius, Marcus Pollio. (1960), *Ten Books of Architecture*, trans. M. H. Morgan, New York: Dover Publications.

von Arx, Serge. (2016), 'Unfolding the Public Space: Performing Space or Ephemeral Section of Architecture, PQ 2015', *Theatre and Performance Design*, 2 (1–2): 82–94.

Welton, Martin. (2012), *Feeling Theatre*, Hampshire: Palgrave Macmillan.

Werry, Margaret. (2010), 'Interdisciplinary Objects, Oceanic Lights: Performance and the New Materialism', in Henry Bial and Scott Magelssen (eds), *Theatre Historiography: Critical Interventions*, 221–234, Ann Arbor, MI: University of Michigan Press.

White, Gareth. (2012), 'On Immersive Theatre', *Theatre Research International*, 37 (03): 221–235.

Wikipedia. (2016) *Karen Barad*. [Online]. Available online: https://en.wikipedia.org/wiki/Karen_Barad (accessed 26 April 2016).

Wiles, David. (2003), *A Short History of Western Performance Space*, Cambridge: Cambridge University Press.

Wilkie, Fiona. (2004), *Out of Place: The Negotiation of Space in Site-Specific Performance*, University of Surrey, Available online http://epubs.surrey.ac.uk/823/1/fulltext.pdf.

Wilkie, Fiona. (2012), 'Site-Specific Performance and the Mobility Turn', *Contemporary Theatre Review*, 22 (2): 203–212.

Willett, John. (1986), *Caspar Neher: Brecht's Designer*, London: Methuen.

Williams, Donna. (1992), *Nobody, Nowhere; the Remarkable Autobiography of an Autistic Girl*, London: Doubleday.

Wilmeth, Don B. and Christopher Bigsby (1998), *The Cambridge History of American Theatre 1*, Cambridge: Cambridge University Press.

Wilson, Mick. (2010), 'Fundamental Questions of Vision: Higher Arts Public Education, Research and Citizenship', in Kieran Corcoran and Carla Delos (eds), *ArtFutures: Current Issues in Higher Arts Education*, 20–29, Amsterdam: ELIA, Available online: http://www.elia-artschools.org/userfiles /Image/customimages/products/58/ArtFutures.pdf (accessed 31 July 2015).

Wilson, Robert A. and Andy Clark (2009), 'How to Situate Cognition, Letting Nature Take Its Course', in Philip Robbins and Murat Aydede (eds), *The Cambridge Handbook of Situated Cognition*, 55–77, Cambridge: Cambridge University Press.

Wintroub, Michael. (1998), 'Civilizing the Savage and Making a King: The Royal Entry Festival of Henri II (Rouen, 1550)', *The Sixteenth Century Journal*, 29 (2): 465–494.

Wise, Michael Z. (2003), 'Inside Job', *Los Angeles Times*, 13 August, Available online: http://articles .latimes.com/2003/aug/17/entertainment/ca-wise17 (accessed 15 September 2015).

Yan, Hairong. (2007), 'Position Without Identity: Interview with Gayatri Chakravorty Spivak', *positions: East Asia Cultures Critique*, 15 (2) (Fall 2007): 429–448, Available online: doi: 10.1215/10679847 -2006-036 (accessed 1 October 2015).

Zhang, Haimei. (2011), *Building Materials in Civil Engineering*, Philadelphia, PA: Woodhead.

Žižek, Slavoj. (2002), *Welcome to the Desert of the Real!: Five Essays on September 11th and Related Dates*, London and New York: Verso.

Zlatev, Jordan, Timothy P. Racine, Chris Sinha and Esa Itkonen (2008), 'Intersubjectivity: What Makes Us Human?' in Jordan Zlatev, Timothy P. Racine, Chris Sinha and Esa Itkonen (eds), *The Shared Mind: Perspectives on Intersubjectivity*, 1–16, Amsterdam and Philadelphia: John Benjamins Publishing Company.

Zupanc Lotker, Sodja. (2015), 'Expanding Scenography: Notes on the Curational Developments of the Prague Quadrennial', *Theatre and Performance Design*, 1 (1/2): 7–16.

Index

Note: Productions are listed under the performer, director or theatre company. An italicised lower case 'n' in a reference denotes a footnote, e.g. 180n11 refers to footnote 11 on page 180. The letter 'f' following locators refers to figures, e.g. 56f refers to a figure on page 56.